Rocky Mountain National Park: A History

ROCKY MOUNTAIN NATIONAL PARK

A HISTORY

BY C. W. BUCHHOLTZ

UNIVERSITY PRESS OF COLORADO

The University Press of Colorado is a cooperative publishing enterprise supported,
in part, by Adams State College, Colorado State University, Fort Lewis College, Mesa
State College, Metropolitan State College of Denver, University of Colorado, University
of Northern Colorado, University of Southern Colorado, and Western State College of
Colorado.

Published by the University Press of Colorado
P.O Box 849
Niwot, Colorado 80544
ISBN 0-87081-146-0 (paper)
Library of Congress Catalog Card Number 83-071197
Printed in the United States of America

For four extraordinary people,

Rocky Mountain Ranger Robert Frauson
Ranger-Naturalist Dr. D. Ferrel Atkins
My parents, Edward and Meryl Buchholtz

CONTENTS

ACKNOWLEDGMENTS

The idea of *Rocky Mountain National Park: A History* was first generated in 1976. Much of the credit for insuring the publication of this volume should go to Glen Kaye, Rocky Mountain National Park's Chief Naturalist. Mr. Kaye's enthusiasm for the project made the research proceed smoothly and his advice and assistance were always helpful. In addition, numerous people associated with Rocky Mountain National Park offered their time and knowledge, especially Superintendent Chester L. Brooks, Edgar Menning, James Wilson, Dr. Ferrel Atkins, Michael Smithson, Teresa Vazquez, Marji Dunmire, Connie Neal, Jody Magnuson, Kris Johnson, and Jean Menning. Devoting hours to the painstaking task of photographic reproduction were Walter Richards, Bill Chase, and Skip Betts.

National Park Service officials at the Rocky Mountain Regional Office in Denver frequently and freely provided information and assistance. James Randall, James Olson, Dr. Michael Schene, Jim Harpster, Mary Culpin, Dr. Adrienne Anderson, Dr. Ann Johnson, and Dr. Kenneth Hornbeck were particularly generous with their knowledge. Ruth Larison at the Rocky Mountain Regional Office library was especially considerate in her assistance.

The efforts of Joe Barker at the Federal Records Center in Denver, of Lee Carr of the United States Forest Service, and Richard Crawford at the National Archives in Washington, D.C. expedited many research problems. Mel Busch, curator of the Estes Park Area Historical Museum, rendered special help with photographs.

Over the years, ideas and details supplied by Bob Frauson, William Colony, Robert Haraden, Doug Erskine, Gary Bunney, Frank Betts, and Jerry Hammond proved to be especially beneficial to this study.

The assistance of Ellen Leuthauser, Jean Deahn, and Karen Sackett of the Arapahoe Community College Library is appreciated as are the efforts of Mrs. Lennie Bemiss of the Estes Park Public Library. Staff members of the Edwin A. Bemis Library in Littleton, the Estes Park Public Library, the Colorado State Historical

Society, Norlin Library of the University of Colorado, and the Western History Department of the Denver Public Library also provided help. Of special importance were my colleagues, Carroll Williams, Richard L. Morgan, Sally Kurtzman, Jenni Caldwell, Claire Rogers, and Jackie Wilcox, who frequently assisted in clarifying some of the finer points in history and in writing as well as adding their encouragement to this effort.

The Rocky Mountain Nature Association generously granted research funds for this project, enabling the author to initiate this study, and for that award he is particularly grateful. Living with a task as absorbing as this book has not been easy, and the author wishes to thank his wife Marcy and his sons Brett, Austin, and Jesse for their consideration and understanding.

FOREWORD

Rocky Mountain National Park: A History is more than just the story of Rocky Mountain in its brief tenure as a national park. Its scope includes the earliest traces of human activity in the region and outlines the major events of exploration, settlement, and exploitation. Origins of the national park idea are followed into the recent decades of the Park's overwhelming popularity. It is a story of change, of mountains reflecting the tenor of the times. From being a hunting ground to becoming ranchland, from being a region of resorts to becoming a national park, this small segment of the Rocky Mountains displays a record of human activities that helps explain the present and may guide us toward the future.

As a professional park historian, planner and manager I have been ever aware of the dilemma the Congress created when it charged the National Park Service with both "conserving the scenery . . . and providing for the public enjoyment . . ." It is a challenge I have enjoyed, because it has reminded me that as a manager I must balance these two concepts, emphasizing preservation if need be, or public use if the needs of visitors were not receiving due consideration. Like the scale of old, an emphasis of the moment would tilt the scale so that it was never in perfect balance. Curt Buchholtz has related this fluctuating pattern in the Park's history in an interesting and accurate manner.

During the early years of the Park's existence the emphasis was on publicizing the area to attract more and more visitors. At times the publicity exceeded the bounds of good taste as park personnel encouraged the "freest possible use" as the language in the Park's Establishment Act encouraged.

The growth in auto touring influenced use of the Park throughout its history, with the result that the recent accelerating growth of the Front Range communities in Colorado has caused a revolutionary change in the Park's management. From the early pre-auto days when visitors spent two or three weeks at a private lodge within the Park, to the post-World War II fast-moving visitor who tries to visit several parks during a two-week vacation and thus spends two or three days at the most in or near the Park, the Park has become a day-use area where more and more visitors spend part of a day in the Park motoring, hiking, and then moving on. Rocky Mountain National Park is taking on the trappings of a suburban national park. However, designating over 90% of the Park as wilderness will help preserve this area for today's and tomorrow's visitors.

Curt Buchholtz's view of this process will help provide the visitor and management with a better idea of where we've been, where we are and where we may be going. The reader will be better informed to weigh the problems and opportunities the Park faces and to assist in directing not only this park but all national parks in maintaining that ever-delicate and critical balance between preservation and use.

Chester L. Brooks
Superintendent
Rocky Mountain National Park
1983

AN INTRODUCTORY NOTE

It was a rainy September day in 1982 when I hiked to the ruins of Rocky Mountain National Park's largest ghost town, Lulu City. As a disintegrating monument to the mining era, a few crumbling log walls testified to the town's existence a hundred years before. A rustic National Park Service sign tersely recounted the futile search for quick wealth that occurred on the surrounding slopes. The rainy weather enhanced a somber feeling of failure that pervaded that site. And an aura of mystery hung in the air, filled with ghosts and ruined dreams. But at the same time there was a lively aspect to that setting. Lightning from a rain storm danced off nearby ridges; thunder echoed through the valley; and pellets of rain bounced into the infant Colorado River that tumbled nearby. All around the old townsite nature appeared busy reclaiming that spot, rebuilding the meadowland on either side of the well-worn hiking trail. There, at Lulu City, history hardly seemed distant; it was something anyone could touch, smell, feel, and almost hear. Any historian would like to take a reader on a jaunt such as that, a hike into history.

Our search for the past is a little like kicking around in an old ghost town. It is delightful to imagine how those oldtimers lived, to try to guess what problems they encountered, to become envious of their successes, to feel haughty when viewing their failures. Ghost towns, like history itself, encourage us to believe that we, too, might stumble upon a nugget or two, but of wisdom rather than wealth. It does not seem to matter that others have kicked the same tin cans, for it is the search alone that enchants us. Our curiosity moves us to try to understand the past.

Located astride the Continental Divide in north-central Colorado, Rocky Mountain National Park encompasses 417 square miles of the rugged Front Range and Mummy Range of the Rockies. With its high country predominating, elevations in the Park climb from 7,800 feet above sea level along the eastern slope to a height of 14,255 at the Longs Peak summit. The sweep in elevation pro-

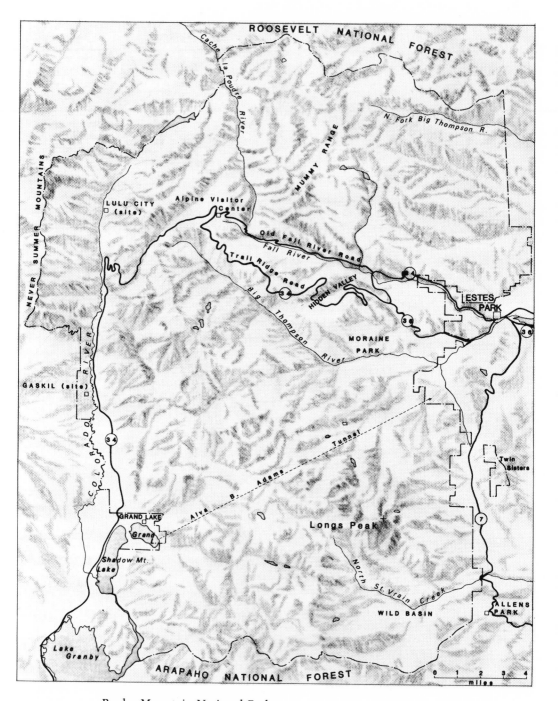

Rocky Mountain National Park

duces the scenic grandeur of the area and it also creates three distinct life zones. In the lower regions is the montane zone, noted for its meadows and Ponderosa pine as well as a mix of Douglas fir, lodgepole pine, and aspen. Farther above lies the subalpine zone with its Englemann spruce, alpine fir, and limber pine. And beyond the tree line, above 10,500 feet in elevation, lies the alpine zone, remarkable for its barren-looking tundra which constitutes nearly a third of the Park's terrain. Geographically, the Park's eastern slope forms the headwaters of the St. Vrain, Big Thompson, Fall, and Cache La Poudre rivers while western slope streams form and feed the Colorado River. The villages of Grand Lake on the western slope and Estes Park on the eastern side act as gateways for travelers entering the Park, with more distant towns such as Granby, Loveland, Lyons, or Longmont also offering access. The predominent roadway in the region is Trail Ridge Road, which bisects the Park. Crossing the crest of the Rockies, it climbs to an elevation of 12,183 feet and strides Fall River and Milner passes as it angles over the mountains. Rocky Mountain National Park retains a wild interior, dotted with lakes and ribboned with streams. With its rugged backbone of jagged mountains, the Park displays wilderness and wildlife, spectacular scenery and ecological treasures, a popularity and a past, all of which enhance its reputation as The Heart of the Rockies.

Over the years the pull of the Rockies has produced a steady stream of people coming to investigate these wonders. Most people came and left without telling us what they saw or experienced. Only dimly can we trace any native American presence here. With a bit more clarity we can discover a few tracks left by adventuresome trappers and hunters and by Joel Estes, one of the region's earlier pioneers. Somewhat more literate travelers followed, however, bringing such writers as William N. Byers in the 1860s, Isabella Bird in the 1870s, and Frederick Chapin in the 1880s. With these accounts our historical knowledge of the region grows. Quite a number of other happy pleasure-seekers, hunters, and homesteaders came to these mountains as well, with such men as the Earl of Dunraven attempting to gain personal possession of the whole area. Rudimentary in its earliest forms, publicity detailing the beauties and charm of the region started in conversations, letters, newspaper articles, and a book or two. Gradually, that publicity attracted those seeking amusement in fishing, hunting, or a hundred other pastimes. Prospectors searching for gold and silver also arrived, along with a handful of ranchers. The ranchers, in turn, developed an infant resort business, discovering that recreation produced a gold of its own.

Meanwhile, a growing demand for water—one of the Rockies' main resources—stimulated the building of diversion projects, canals, and reservoirs. Wide use of water prompted demands for conservation, resulting in protection for the area as a national forest. Also from conservationist ideology came thoughts of preservation. Those ideals, combined with the developing resort interests and with recreation, resulted in the establishment of Rocky Mountain National Park in 1915. The creation of this national park publicized the region even more. Over the years, National Park Service officials cultivated a national playground idea in Rocky Mountain National Park while also protecting this preserve from exploitation. Each year saw the Park grow busier, especially as scenic highways made the region more accessible and acceptable to modern travelers. A boom in park tourism resulted. Eventually, more elaborate steps had to be initiated to protect the Park against this onrush of people. Too much popularity meant renewed efforts toward preservation.

At every stage of this story, from the earliest trapper to the most

However they traveled, whether they came to visit or to stay, people quickly discovered that this stretch of the Rocky Mountains was well worth the trip. (Rocky Mountain National Park Historical Collection, hereinafter cited RMNPHC)

recent tourists, scenery and adventure compelled people to record their observations and experiences. Many writers merely described the mountain panorama in superlatives that beggar literary economy; far fewer recorded events of historical significance. Only a handful of writers ever attempted to chronicle the march of mankind into these mountains and place the events of the past into perspective.

It is into this historical gap that this volume attempts to venture. Naturally, brevity mandates that not every pioneer's name can grace the pages that follow. Not every event can be fully described. History, after all, is partly the process of selection: every subject offered here has been chosen from a dozen left unmentioned, selected for significance, and offered as an example of a mentality or way of life that characterized an era in the Park's history. Many gaps will still remain. Based on research and seasoned judgement,

Like the beckoning notes scribbled by vacationers, dozens of documents allow historians to journey through time, to sample the pleasures of the past. (RMNPHC)

however, an historical panorama will unfold, for the history of Rocky Mountain National Park is more than just a series of dates or the sentences from people's post cards. It is more than floods and fires, and more than old newspaper articles and dusty accounts. It is the story of mankind encountering mountains: of trappers and travelers, ranchers and resort operators, prospectors and water project developers, conservationists and crusaders, preservationists and park rangers, as well as millions of vacationing visitors. The people of Rocky Mountain National Park's past provide a tale that deserves to be told.

I
TALES, TRAILS, AND TRIBES

"In the beginning of time there were no mountains, no streams, no hunting grounds and no forests. In those days there were no red men roaming the plains, no bison, no antelope and no living things. Even there was no earth, but only the blue sky and the clouds and the sunshine and the rain."
from a Ute legend of Creation[1]

WHEN HISTORY is not written, humans speculate about the past. It takes quite an imagination to envision the first human visitors tramping into the vast mountain chains of the American West. And so far no one has discovered the names of the first people who walked into a small segment of these mountains later to be named Rocky Mountain National Park. One might wonder what these early travelers looked like. Were they properly attired for their outing? What was their purpose in exploring such a rugged region? Were they wandering around in a search for good hunting or fishing? Did they appreciate the scenery? Did they stay long? Or did they travel through quickly, merely taking an adventurous break from otherwise humdrum lives? Written historical accounts offer few answers.

Questions about these unnamed travelers continue to tax the minds of today's scholars. Geologists have examined the mountains and have provided timetables that cover thousands of years, allowing for the construction of nature's wonders, detailing the movements of glaciers, discovering when lakes, streams, and valleys were formed. Listening and recording, ethnologists asked elderly Indians to recall their youthful travels and, as a result, some thoughtful memories and legends were gathered for our consideration. Meanwhile, exacting historians, expecting to find written documents or eyewitness accounts for evidence, could only offer names of nineteenth century travelers and settlers who claimed to be the region's first visitors. But now all those pioneers are recognized as relative newcomers in the history of this area. For when it comes to identifying Rocky's first hikers, fishermen, and hunters, facts are scarce.

A nineteenth century photographer portrayed this typical Ute encampment, then common within Colorado but rarely seen in Rocky Mountain National Park. (Colorado Historical Society)

Those who paint the most believable portraits of this vague and early segment of our historical profile are members of the most recent generation of archeologists. Painstakingly reconstructing the past, archeologists examine artifacts ranging from stone projectile points and knife blades to ill-formed granite chips. Results of their studies now make it certain that man has been entering these mountainous regions for thousands of years.

The first studies were of native Americans who ranged throughout Colorado during the nineteenth century, principally the Utes and the Arapahos. Early settlers spotted these tribes in the neighborhood, and at one time the federal government recognized their claims to this territory. No one doubted that they frequented Estes Park, Grand Lake, or the mountains in between, for they left some well-worn trails, a few pine pole wickiups, bits of pottery, and some lost or discarded hunting equipment and tools. The Ute and Arapaho tribes also left some intriguing stories about events occurring here, either factual or fancied, recalled from memory and legend. Building on that information and inspired by significant archeological discoveries on the nearby Great Plains during the 1920s and 30s, both amateur and professional archeologists started recognizing artifacts that could be dated much farther back into the dim past. While scholars may never validate an Indian tale regarding an act of creation, they have enabled our examination of Rocky Mountain National Park's human past to begin some ten to fifteen thousand years ago.

It is now understood that migrating people arrived on the Great Plains of North America after crossing from Asia during the final stages of the Pleistocene or Ice Age. Only when the great continental ice caps began melting were nomadic hunters able to work their way southeastward from Alaska. Archeologists now assume that aboriginal entry into North America became possible by movement through an ice free corridor located between the massive ice cap and the glacier-filled Rocky Mountain ranges anytime between thirty thousand and ten thousand years ago. This early era of human activity has been termed the Lithic stage, referring to the use of stone as a primary source for tools and weapons.

Gradually these people moved southward, perhaps taking decades to migrate. Their lives depended upon hunting, particularly in stalking herds of the now extinct mammoth. Out on the plains, only thirty-five miles due east of the Park at the Dent archeological site, twelve of these mammoth remains have been discovered. Crafted stone Clovis projectile points, clearly in association with those skeletons, allowed scientists to refer to these early inhabitants as "the elephant hunters of the West."[2] Using radiocarbon dating procedures, archeologists found this kill site to be eleven to twelve thousand years old. Called Paleo-Indians or Early Man, these people co-existed with now extinct megafauna or large mammals. As the earliest ancestors of tribes known to history, they undoubtedly hunted within this general region as the great continental ice sheets continued to recede northward.

At least four carefully crafted Clovis and Folsom projectile points located in Rocky Mountain National Park correspond with this earliest arrival of hunters. Finding some of this evidence on Trail Ridge, one archeologist argued that even these few clues gave proof of people crossing the mountains sometime between ten thousand and fifteen thousand years ago. He did concede that later Indians might have transported these early points into the Park, but patination, or weathered "varnish" upon these stone points helped testify to their longevity at their alpine resting spots. Such scanty evidence, however, led the researcher to conclude "that this environment held little interest for peoples adapted to hunting the mammoth and the bison."[3] Nevertheless, discovery of these ancient projectile points, as well as dozens of a more recent age, showed Trail Ridge to be a usable east-west route for crossing the mountains soon after hunters inhabited the plains nearby.

While wandering mammoth and bison hunters may have strayed

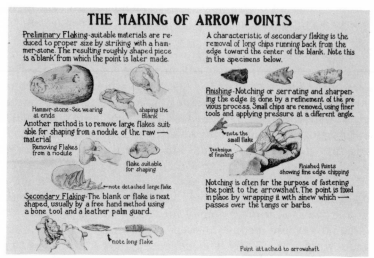

With no diaries, chronicles, or other written records to study, scholars have had to examine the remains of ancient tools — such as stone scrapers, blades, and projectile points — as well as pottery sherds and chipping debris in order to reconstruct the lifestyle of ancient hunters. It now appears certain that prehistoric hunters visited this region starting some 10,000 to 25,000 years ago.

across the mountains, no evidence suggests that they stayed. Periodic trips through the Park, while heading for better hunting grounds, may have been the rule for hundreds of years. Gradually, perhaps as a result of a warming, drier climate, the mammoths disappeared from the Great Plains and became extinct. Whether hunted into extinction by the Paleo-Indians (as some scientists believe) or merely unable to adapt to a drier, warmer climate, no one knows for sure. But Early Man, meanwhile, adapted to that loss. Those people merely changed their appetites and targets, now selecting the superbison as their primary quarry.

Only forty miles northeast of Rocky Mountain National Park archeologists have located the famous Lindenmeier site, an ancient Folsom camping spot used repeatedly some eleven thousand years ago. The bison *Antiquus*, now also extinct, was hunted there. It was larger than the modern bison by twenty percent and had horns at least twice as large. Depending upon that animal as a primary food supply, bands of Paleo-Indians followed the herds, camping in such spots as Lindenmeier Valley, possibly exploiting seasonal fruits, nuts, and grass seeds to supplement their diets. They probably moved their camps from fifty to a hundred times each year. Without question these hunters were skilled at survival and

Living a nomadic lifestyle, hunting for buffalo, and raiding for horses kept the Ute and Arapaho tribes busy invading each other's territory and attacking each other's camps during the first half of the nineteenth century. At times, the Rocky Mountains acted as a barrier between enemies. (From *A Lady's Life in the Rocky Mountains*, by Isabella L. Bird. Copyright 1960 by the University of Oklahoma Press)

understood well how best to exploit the natural resources around them. They also devised new hunting techniques, perfecting group or communal drives or attacks as they surrounded their hoofed meals. It also seems likely that these hunters developed a great familiarity with the land over which they roamed, becoming aware of every usable animal or plant. Hunting for unusual animals in unfamiliar territory could leave a person quite hungry. Certainly these people could predict the behavior of animals they hunted and knew when and where wild crops were ready for harvest.

The basic lifestyle of these nomadic hunters probably changed very little over several thousand years. Their shelters were merely animal hide tents, brush huts, or rock shelters; clothing was made from the skins of animals they butchered; dogs were their only domesticated animal. Over time they changed and refined styles in the manufacture of their stone knife blades, spear points, scrapers, and other equipment. And while making their implements and tools of stone and bone was artistically creative, their art remained primarily utilitarian. Most of the items made were quite disposable, easily refashioned in the trained hands of a Paleo-Indian craftsman. Hundreds of bits of their cast-off equipment became mementos of their ancient presence.

Around eight thousand years ago, prehistoric Indians in this region of North America began to display traits of a new lifestyle. They became more exploitive of nature generally, decreasing their dependence upon herds of giant bison. This era, lasting in many ways into the period of written history, has been termed the Archaic stage. Hunting continued, of course, with the smaller modern bison as the key menu item for plains inhabitants. But hunters also became more active in exploiting regions beyond the Great Plains for a greater variety of foodstuffs and other materials. And so the Rocky Mountains began experiencing more visits from this time forward. Even so, use of Rocky Mountain National Park's resources may have been confined to its trails and passes as hunters left the plains and headed for Middle Park. From projectile points located at Forest Canyon Pass, on a slope above Chapin Pass, at Fall River Pass, on Flattop Mountain, near Oldman Mountain, as well as on numerous ridgetops, in valleys, and on mountain saddles, one archeologist concluded: "Evidence indicates intermittent occupation of the Park rather than continuous occupation. Travel back and forth across the Continental Divide was the primary reason why Indians entered the mountains. Small camps indicate seasonal hunting in the valleys and on the mountains."[4]

Seasonal hunting, then, attracted Archaic man, just as it would later attract the nineteenth century "discoverer" Joel Estes. But mountain sheep and elk might not have been the only reasons Archaic hunters came to the high country. Significant fluctuations in the climate began to produce a much hotter and drier weather out on the plains. This period, known as the Altithermal, may have lasted for 2,500 years, from 5500 B.C. to 3000 B.C. Some scholars believe that ancient inhabitants left the plains entirely during this period, and may have vacated the Front Range of the Rockies as well. But other studies give evidence of continued use of these moister, cooler mountains as refuges from a harsher climate. Evidently man used this area more heavily at this time period. Plants and animals necessary for their survival could be found here in abundance. More than just seasonal refugees, the people adapted.

Recent discoveries at alpine sites south of the Park have demonstrated that some camp sites and large game drive systems date between 3850 and 3400 B.C. Even these well-used sites, however, are believed to have been temporary, seasonal camps, with Indians migrating to milder spots during winter. It is suspected that groups of people, primarily extended families, migrated each year from the lower elevations of the foothills up to the high country as seasonal conditions permitted and as wild plants ripened and animals became active.

The most intriguing archeological remains from this era are the

In addition to using mountain passes for routes of travel, prehistoric people also hunted in the high country. They constructed rock walls to enhance the natural contour of the slopes, creating "game drive systems." Once thought to be Indian "forts" used to defend territory, it is now recognized that these walls allowed concealment in open country and helped guide sheep, deer, or elk toward awaiting hunters. More than forty such U-shaped and funnel-shaped drive systems have been identified along the crest of the Front Range. (RMNPHC)

large stone structures of the game drive systems. Scholars have identified forty-two of these low-walled rock structures at locations along the Front Range crest. They are dry laid stone walls or closely built rock cairns, producing a slight barrier along the natural slopes. Some of these walls may stretch for hundreds of feet in length. One of these structures, for example, lies close to today's Trail Ridge Road. At one time pioneers speculated that these walls were fortifications, used by one tribe to defend its territory against an invader. Today, evidence points toward their use in hunting animals in country devoid of cover. Commonly used in other arctic or tundra environments, these slight walls served as devices that permitted hunters to direct or herd game animals toward men waiting with weapons. Quite a variety of walls were constructed, depending upon the lay of the land. Normally they were built by piling rocks in long rows, forming a perceptible barrier or wall. Sometimes the walls formed a U or V shape or had parallel rows; some also had pits nearby to help conceal an ambushing hunter. It is clear that building these rock-walled drive lines took considerable amounts of time and labor, but it is also assumed that these helpful structures were used repeatedly for centuries.

It is probable that twenty to twenty-five people were needed to conduct an animal hunt of this type, with some Indians driving the mountain sheep or elk toward awaiting hunters poised to kill. Spears tipped with razor sharp stone points, or darts thrown with an atlatl or spear thrower may have been used to kill the animals. Mule deer, mountain sheep, elk, and bison became the primary animals hunted. Black and grizzly bears, pronghorn, and mountain lions might also have been killed on occasion. Smaller animals, hunted at lower elevations near the seasonal camping spots and in other lower valleys, also augmented the ancient diet. These animals may have included wolves, coyote, beaver, porcupine, foxes, marmots, skunks, racoons, rabbits, squirrels, and other small birds and game.

Hunting smaller mountain animals did mean that the hunters' quarry yielded far less meat than a typical superbison or even the modern bison. That meant that more animals had to be killed to provide the same amount of meat. So eating a wider variety of smaller game and also locating numerous edible plants and berries became a way of life. Indians harvested blueberries, raspberries, creeping wintergreen berries, Colorado currants, and many others. Their potherbs included fern-leafed lovage, fireweed, marsh marigold, and alpine sorrel. Roots dug, cooked, and eaten included American bistort and alpine spring beauty. In addition, dozens of other plants and animals found at different elevations from the foothills to the alpine regions were probably a part of their ancient menu.

By the time the Altithermal ended and mankind repopulated the plains, these people could no longer be classified as merely hunters; rather, they had become foragers. Upon their return to the prairie, bison hunting regained its importance in their lives, as one could expect, considering that a thousand pounds of meat would be available to a hunter from killing just one of these animals. Middle Park and the Great Plains once again returned to the center of ancient hunting activities. And those regions would remain primary hunting grounds into our historic era. Though now more flexible in their diets, these ancestors of the historic tribes depended upon bison; yet they could also return seasonally to hunt in the mountains as well. An abundance of archeological material, ranging from fire pits to grinding stones to tools to bits of burned bone, as well as hundreds of stone chips left from tool-making, gives ample proof of recurrent visitation to this region from 2500 B.C. onward.

Between A.D. 400 and 650, the technological innovation of the bow and arrow was introduced. Perhaps brought into the region by Woodland Culture moving in from the east and the Colorado plains, remains of that equipment in the form of small, serrated,

Europeans introduced horses to America, enabling tribes such as the Ute and Arapaho to extend their travels and hunting range. One of their main quarry, the bison or buffalo, provided the raw materials for tepee covers, blankets, moccasins, sinew for thread and bowstrings, in addition to supplying food in abundance. (RMNPHC)

and corner-notched arrowpoints are found in considerable numbers throughout the Park. In addition, the first traces of pottery sherds can be dated from this era. It is possible that tribes known to history, Shoshoni or Ute, may have finally laid claim to these mountains and to the hunting grounds on either side. And for a while at least, between A.D. 650 and 1000, game-drive systems continued to be used.

Abner Sprague, one of the original settlers of the 1870s, remarked: "That the Indians made Estes Park a summer resort there is no question, as evidence of their summer camps were everywhere throughout the Park when the White pioneer came." Whether those old camps were Shoshoni or Ute, Arapaho or Apache, Sprague did not clarify and perhaps could not tell. But he did add: "There was no sign of permanent camp, such as a winter stopping place would have to be for them to live in comfort at these altitudes. . . ."[5] Judging from the observations of men such as Sprague as well as earlier explorers, such tribes as the Ute and Shoshoni probably laid the longest and strongest claims to these mountains through their occasional summer visits.

Exactly when the Utes came into Colorado, along with their allies the Shoshonis and the Comanches, continues to be an issue debated among ethnologists, anthropologists, and historians. Even where these Native Americans originated is in doubt. Perhaps they had migrated from the Great Basin or further southwest or from Mexico. Some scholars suggest that these tribes are simply the

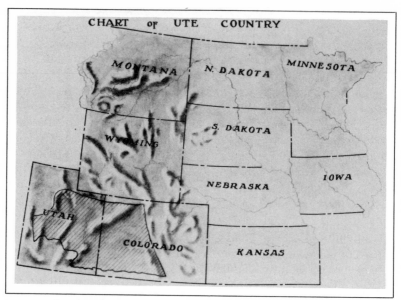

Pressure from gold seekers forced the Ute to negotiate treaties during the 1860s and 1870s, steadily reducing their claims upon the Rocky Mountains and western Colorado. (RMNPHC)

descendents of the earlier Paleo-Indian and Archaic peoples of the region. They may have emerged from the hunting-gathering Desert Culture identified farther west. The language of the Utes and their allies was similar, based in Shoshonean. Whatever their origins, it is now suspected that these people gradually invaded and dominated Colorado's three large western slope parks—South, Middle, and North—as well as its mountains sometime about a thousand years ago.

The Utes have been termed "central based wanderers" since they did not rely upon agriculture and had to travel to hunt or gather their food. Winter might find several families camped together, but springtime would start small bands on familiar trails toward hunting grounds, berry patches, or the like. Small family units hunted together, living off land that could not support large populations. They stalked deer or antelope or snared jackrabbits. They also dug roots and picked berries when those items became available. Their shelters consisted of both bison-hide tipis and brush-covered wickiups. Permanent dwellings were unnecessary since these people were nomadic. Their quest for food tended to separate the Utes into several bands during most of the year. Many families also separated from the bands to hunt or forage on their own. While food was not abundant, studies indicate that these people were

Considered to be friendly by early trappers and pioneers, the Utes were rapidly dispossessed once prospectors demanded "The Utes Must Go!" (RMNPHC)

probably not preoccupied by an endless task of food acquisition. Scholars do believe, however, that all bands of Utes knew times of great hunger.

There is some evidence that springtime brought an assembly of all the Ute bands for a tribal Bear Dance. The Utes, like other tribes in the mountain West, respected and honored those ursine competitors for the annual berry crop. The Bear Dance also provided some social contact for a people forced to forage alone and in relative isolation. Within this social and economic context, spots like Middle Park and Estes Park, similar to other valleys in the Colorado Rockies, may have served families of Ute, Shoshoni, or Comanche hunters for season after season over hundreds of years.

The Utes, in particular, entered the pages of recorded history when they finally met the Spanish. By the early 1600s, Spanish explorers had pushed their way out of Mexico toward Colorado; prospectors and missionaries followed in their wake, working gradually northward. Eventually they encountered the Ute people. Although Spanish documents do not refer to the "Yutas" until 1680, it is probable that trade started prior to that date. The Utes began exchanging meat and hides for agricultural produce. They also began buying horses. High prices for such valued animals proved to be no deterrent to trade whatsoever and it was reported that they "started trading their children for horses."[6]

Horses revolutionized the Ute lifestyle, just as they had that of Ute neighbors the Shoshoni and Comanche. Mobility was the key to change. By the early 1700s, combined forces of mounted Ute and Comanche warriors came raiding out of the mountains, attacking the homes of plains-dwelling Apaches who were then living in eastern Colorado. Raids also began against Spanish settlements in New Mexico and continued sporadically until a treaty was finally negotiated with Spanish officials in 1789. But horses not only brought mobility and aggressive attacks; they also transformed the Utes into skillful bison hunters. Hunting trips onto the eastern plains meant that the buffalo soon became the Utes' "chief economic resource, providing tepee covers, blankets, sinew thread, bowstrings, horn glue, skin bags, moccasins, and meat in greater quantities than the Utes had ever known."[7] Bison meat could also be dried, reducing its weight by ten times, and then easily transported and stored for months. About one-half pound of this highly concentrated dried meat could serve as an adequate daily ration for an adult. Anthropologist George Frison clarified: "The flesh from two full-grown adult bison or twenty antelope would dry into about 100 pounds. This quantity has the potential to sustain a family group of six persons for about a month, which would tide the family over critical times during most winters."[8]

Eventually the Utes and their Comanche comrades had a falling out. In 1748 a fight developed between these two aggressive tribes. It is supposed that the alliance between them was not very strong to begin with, and was certainly further aggravated when the Comanches obtained firearms from French traders who had entered the plains by this time. By 1755 the Utes had been forced to retreat back to the western slope of the Rockies. And there they remained, reasonably well protected throughout the next century. They did return to hunt on the Great Plains once or twice each year, but they tended to remain within the protective shadow of the Rockies. It was during this era of war-making and hunting that the Utes

Through the years Ute dominions waxed and waned. Horses permitted a wave of aggression, extending across the Colorado plains. But Ute territories dwindled steadily during the nineteenth century. (Colorado Historical Society)

probably traveled across Rocky Mountain National Park's east-west trails. Trail Ridge, Flattop Mountain, and the Fall River routes were probably used, with Forest Canyon and its Pass an obvious pathway. Certainly the Ute tribe and other Indians were not confined just to these trails; many other passes, saddles, and canyons could have been used to cross the Front Range, and several were far more popular than those in Rocky Mountain National Park.

So within a few decades horse power had transformed Ute society. Of course certain aspects of their older way of life endured. Food gathering, for example, continued as usual and their diets remained diverse. Ute women continued to seek chokecherries, sunflower seeds, and various other edible roots and grass seeds. They also constructed willow weirs and caught fish, adding variety to their meals. The men continued to hunt mule deer and antelope, even though the bison was preferred.

Any changes in their food supply were small when compared with the transformation of the Ute political and social structure. The horse allowed war-making to play a major role in their lives. Larger bands took the place of single families as the primary living unit, especially since numbers insured protection when enemies made retaliatory raids. When proceeding onto the plains for a bison hunt, several hundred Utes might join together for the expedition. War leaders also became far more important. Their influence also extended into other matters within Ute society, creating the basis of a political framework. Eventually seven major divisions or bands among the Ute evolved. Those living in the southern part of Colorado were the Weeminuche, the Mouache, and the Capote. Living in the west-central region were the Tabeguache or Uncompahgre. And three groups comprised the Northern Utes, namely the Grand River, the Yampa, and the Uinta bands. Estimates of their total population vary anywhere from 2,500 to 10,000 people. In 1875 the Commission of Indian Affairs listed 40 bands of Ute with a total of 9,625 persons. Whatever their number, the 1700s saw them at the height of their power. Historian Wilson Rockwell concluded that the eighteenth century "marked the zenith of Ute strength and glory."[9]

Their century of glory and aggression was quickly tempered by the arrival of the Arapahos around 1790. Migrating from the Red River and Manitoba country far to the northeast, the Arapaho people were probably pressured into moving late in the seventeenth century due to constant attacks from the Assiniboin and Cree. Within a few generations, they had adapted to using horses, hunting bison, and gaining all the general characteristics of a Plains Indian culture. Eventually they moved across the Missouri River, entered the Black Hills region, and used the hunting territory of

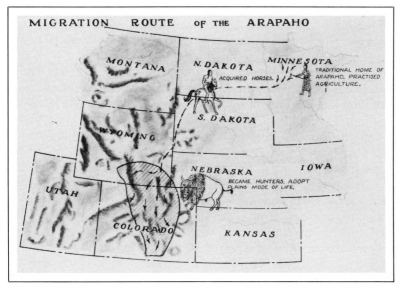

"The Arrapahoes reside south of the Snakes," an early western traveler observed. "They are said to be a brave, fearless, thrifty, ingenious, and hospitable people. They own large numbers of horses, mules, dogs, and sheep. The dogs they fatten and eat. Hence the name Arrapahoes—dog eaters." (RMNPHC)

the upper Great Plains. Only a few decades later, however, during the 1780s, the Arapaho were attacked by the expansionist Sioux who came from the east. That pressure forced the Arapahos and their allies the Kiowa and Cheyenne to move farther south, eventually into the South Platte country adjacent to the Front Range of the Colorado Rockies. There, for a reason unknown to us, they began a continuous war with the Utes.

These Arapaho invaders were given a variety of names. The Shoshoni and Comanches called them "Saretika" or Dog Eaters as a comment upon one of their prized menu items. They were also called the Bison Path People, the Tattooed Breasts, and the Big Nose People, depending upon which characteristic caught the eye of the name-givers. The Pawnee called them "larapihu" or "tirapihu," meaning buyer or trader. Thus derived from their skill at trading, the name Arapaho—variously spelled—seemed to stick. The Arapaho called themselves "Inunaina," or simply "Our People."[10]

Not long after entering the Great Plains the Arapaho separated into two major divisions, the Arapaho proper and the Gros Ventre. The Gros Ventre split off, migrated northward, and roamed the northern side of the Missouri River in Montana. The remaining

Arapaho began traveling south and west. The Arapaho were sub-divided into four bands, sometimes named the Long Leg or Antelope, the Greasy Face, the Quick-to-Anger, and the Beaver. Band names, like those of individuals, changed frequently. Each band had a chief and a council of the four chiefs made major decisions in concert and consensus. The Arapaho were not numerous, with their population probably never exceeding 2,500 persons. But their impact upon the Colorado region was greater than their numbers might indicate. Although they considered eastern Colorado their heartland, they were nomads and roamed a vast region of the plains and mountains. They hunted and raided nearly every square mile from the Wind River Mountains of Wyoming clear down to the Arkansas River valley in southern Colorado. Their movement and aggressiveness found them fighting the Crow Indians to the north, the Pawnees to the east, and the Utes and Shoshonis across the mountains to the west.

Living on the Great Plains over the period of several generations, the Arapaho became the apex of mobile, nomadic hunters. They excelled at horse riding; they were skilled at hunting bison, using the technique of driving herds off sharp-edged cliffs. These "buffalo jumps" allowed the Arapaho to turn a mass slaughter into a vast butchering site. Working upon the slain animals, the Arapaho could obtain hides for their tepees, bone for their tools, sinew for their thread, leather for their clothing, and food for their stomachs. Arapaho life centered around the hunt. And, at the beginning of the nineteenth century, the plains and mountains of Colorado supplied an abundance of their quarry. But it is probably their invasion of hunting grounds traditionally used by the Utes that brought them into a conflict with those older residents.

Historian Virginia Trenholm reported an Arapaho belief that the "Man-Above created the Rockies as a barrier to separate them from the Shoshonis and Utes."[11] Clashes between those tribes were numerous and sparked the stuff of legend. Memories of this continual tribal conflict are a part of Rocky Mountain National Park's heritage. The very thought of Indian fighting Indian, of bloody battlegrounds, seemed to enchant early settlers who watched Indians become relegated to reservations. Yet tangible evidence and reliable accounts of most of those battles do not exist.

Some of the tales are nevertheless intriguing. A story often repeated tells of a band of Utes peacefully camping at Grand Lake. Some Arapaho warriors with their Cheyenne allies crossed Willow Creek (Forest Canyon) Pass with an eye toward mischief. Ute scouts failed to spot the invaders and a surprise attack resulted. During the raging battle that followed, an effort was made to pro-

The bow and arrow proved effective in hunting and warfare for centuries, but firearms introduced by traders soon made those old weapons obsolete. (Colorado Historical Society)

tect women and children by putting them upon a makeshift raft and sending it out upon the lake. As the fighting continued no one seemed to notice that a strong wind began blowing, ripping the raft apart, and drowning all of the women and children. The Utes won their battle, drove the attackers away, but then realized that they had lost their families. From that point forward, it was said, the Utes avoided Grand Lake because it was haunted by the spirits of those who had died there. There could be important elements of truth in this tale, but it might also be mere wishful thinking on the part of settlers who hoped the Utes would not return. They preferred the legend over the reality of worrying about being attacked.

East of the Divide, early settler Abner Sprague commented that "it is well established that conflicts between tribes took place in the (Estes) Park." He did not explain whether artifacts, bones, or hearsay provided a basis for that "fact." But he did clarify the location: "One battle ground being located without question, Beaver Park and the Moraine between there and Moraine Park. There is the ruins of a fortified mound at the west end of Beaver Park, where the weaker party made their last stand."[12] Were these "ruins" really an Indian fort, or in reality a game drive system? The truth may never be known.

One of the few eyewitness accounts regarding an actual fight came from Charles S. Strobie. In 1865 he was twenty years old and had just traveled across the plains from Chicago, forced to fight Indians along the way. He reported crossing "the Snowy Range by way of Berthoud Pass" in 1866 and living with Nevava's band of Utes "who were hostile to the plains Indians." Then he recalled: "I was the only white man with the Ute 'war party' when we had a fight with the Arapahoe and Cheyennes in Middle Park, near Grand Lake. We repulsed them and took seven scalps. Others were killed or wounded, but they were thrown across the ponies' backs and carried off." The victorious Utes, with Strobie tagging along, returned to their main camp near Hot Sulphur Springs where "we had scalp dances and parades every forenoon and night for two weeks."[13]

Using Rocky Mountain National Park's passes and trails to catch enemies by surprise or to find better hunting grounds gave both the Utes and the Arapahos cause to enter this region. Other activities occurring in these mountains were probably less dramatic. One lesser known attraction, that of trapping eagles, may have drawn solitary Indians toward these peaks. It was common for Indians to seek high country locations, conceal themselves in a brush covered pit, and lure eagles toward a hunk of meat placed as bait upon the brush. Ethnologist Alfred Kroeber explained: "Only certain men could hunt the eagle. For four days they abstained from food and water. They put medicine on their hands. In four days they might get fifty or a hundred eagles. A stuffed coyote-skin was sometimes set near the bait."[14] Whether the summit of Longs Peak was actually used as an eagle trap, as later Arapaho informants claimed, cannot be verified. The first recorded climbers found no evidence of any pit or other traces of human activity when they arrived at the top of Longs Peak in 1868. Yet other mountains or high country ridges might well have been used for snaring eagles, creatures considered so valuable because of their decorative feathers.

Tales of trapping eagles on Longs Peak may sound improbable, but may not be as fanciful as a few other reported exploits. One example, told by an Arapaho, Gun Griswold, about his father Old Man Gun, detailed a bear hunting technique. Griswold recalled: "He used to daub himself all over with mud and lie down in the bear trail. A bear would come along and not know what to make of him, turn him over with his paw, feel his heart and his mouth. All at once Gun would spring up and give a terrible yell. The bear would jump back so quickly that he would break his back."[15] Today's fishermen who enjoy telling tall tales about "the one that got away" may find a nodding kinship with that remarkable hunter.

A chief of the Yampa band of Utes, Colorow was typical of Indian leaders of his generation, virtually powerless to prevent his people's removal to reservations. (Colorado Historical Society)

In July of 1914 a belated effort was made to consult with Arapaho Indians regarding their memories of these mountains. Gun Griswold and Sherman Sage, with Tom Crispin acting as interpreter, were guided on a pack trip by Shep Husted. Oliver Toll recorded their observations and produced a book entitled *Arapaho Names and Trails*. That tour also led to the use of many Indian place names in the area. (RMNPHC)

All the Indian claims upon these mountains, fought over for decades, were doomed to be quickly extinguished. The discovery of gold in Colorado brought thousands of prospectors and miners flooding into the territory after 1858. Most promises made to either the Ute or the Arapaho regarding their rights to this land underwent speedy revisions as the white population increased. According to the Fort Laramie Treaty of 1851, territory of the Arapaho stretched between the North Platte and Arkansas Rivers, from the Continental Divide of the Rockies eastward onto the plains of Nebraska and Kansas. Only a decade later, through the Fort Wise Treaty of 1861, the federal government hoped to confine these wanderers to the much smaller Sand Creek Reservation located along the Arkansas River. In 1865 another reservation was chosen in southern Kansas and northern Oklahoma. And by 1878, the Arapaho had finally been removed from Colorado entirely, some living on the Wind River Reservation in Wyoming while others lived upon the Cheyenne and Arapaho Reservation in Oklahoma.

The Utes lost their claims a little later, although just as rapidly. For a while they seemed to be protected by the mountains and were slightly more tolerant of settlers and prospectors. Their presence was not regarded as bothersome to the new invaders until later in the 1870s. Historian Robert Black noted that "often they were overlooked, which was the supreme insult." He added that "the average prospector or pioneer rancher had few objections to aboriginal comings and goings, but when certain Utes began to treat [Middle Park] as their own, slaughtering game, violating fences, and terrorizing housewives, there were vigorous complaints."[16] Earlier in the 1860s, treaties had granted the Ute people rights to the western one third of Colorado. But when gold was discovered in the San Juan Mountains Indians were forced to cede that region in 1873. Escalating violent clashes late in the decade led to growing public hatred toward the Indians. Demands for reprisals sealed the Utes' fate; the popular cry became "The Utes must go!"[17] And their fate meant removal from most of Colorado during the 1880s. Only a small strip of land in the southwestern corner of the state and a reservation in Utah would remain within their possession. So, within a generation, any Indian claims upon the area later to become Rocky Mountain National Park were negotiated away. The Indians' influence in the region remained safely in memories and legends.

As the Indians left, settlers of the Grand Lake and Estes Park region expressed a feeling of relief. As with most of Colorado's early pioneers, they preferred to have the Indians carefully confined. A Denver newspaper reflected a popular sentiment: "The great

menace to the advancement and development of this grand southwestern country is no more. Eastern people can now come to this
section in the most perfect security."[18] Reverend Elkanah Lamb,
settler at the base of Longs Peak in the 1870s, expressed an attitude
common to the frontier. "The Indians of the plains at that time,"
he wrote in his memoirs, "were an intolerable nuisance, always
visiting our camps to buy, steal, and annoy."[19] His conclusions
about "the Red devils" left little room for sympathy: "Seemingly
the red man . . . [has] not the capacity or the necessary will-power
for the improvement or possible development of nature's grand and
prolific resources that are comprised of soils, forests, and mineral
fields, and, therefore, it appears to be destined for the white man."[20]

When rendered harmless, Indians became a curiosity, if not a
source of pride. In 1914, as detailed mapping necessitated more
names for mountain peaks and other features, members of the
Colorado Mountain Club invited some elderly members of the
Arapaho to return to the Estes Park-Grand Lake region. During a
two week camping trip through the mountains, Oliver Toll duti-
fully recorded the words, place-names, stories, and observations
of Gun Griswold, age 73, and Sherman Sage, age 63. As a result
of their visit, dozens of Indian names were assigned to these mountains. Although half a century had elapsed since these men used
the trails, their observations were prized as one last contribution
from another culture.

Commenting on this "rash of Indian names" suddenly dotting
the landscape, Louisa W. Arps and Elinor E. Kingery, nomenclature authorities, stated that "the Rocky Mountain National Park
area includes 36 Indian names, not counting names in translation
like Gianttrack and Lumpy Ridge and Never Summer. This is one
of the greatest concentrations of Indian names in one small area
on the face of the U.S.A."[21]

Even though the Indians themselves disappeared from the area
quickly, mementos of their presence remained. If only in place-
names such as Neota Creek, the Ute Trail, or Niwot Ridge, their
centuries of traveling through and hunting in this region would
be remembered. The bitterness between settlers and Indians over
the ownership of this particular stretch of mountains disappeared
with time. Some would argue that Indian ties to this region were
transitory and shallow anyway; their homes were elsewhere. But
perhaps the Indians were simply overwhelmed and became fatalis-
tic; they had little choice but to leave and accept reservations and
a new way of life. Some ancient tools and stone structures, some
tracks and trails, and some legends stayed to mark their prior use
of the land.

Brush lodges, probably serving as temporary camps for seasonal hunters, remained as one of the few signs of Indian activity spotted by early pioneers. (RMNPHC)

A Ute interpretation of the afterlife explains their concept of a final settlement. "Heaven with them is in three great strata," author Hamlin Garland recorded. "In the highest is the Ute spirit land, and all the Utes have wings. In the second are the buffalo and all the game and beautiful forests and meadows. In the lowest strata are the white men."[22]

2

INTO THE DOMAINS OF SILENCE AND LONELINESS

"We stood on the mountain looking down at the headwaters of Little Thompson Creek, where the Park spread out before us. No words can describe our surprise, wonder and joy at beholding such an unexpected sight."

Milton Estes on the discovery of Estes Park, October 15, 1859[1]

IT IS hard for historians who dwell on the heroic to admit that almost none of the famous explorers of the West ever set foot in the land that would become Rocky Mountain National Park. Other hidden spots and easier routes caught their attention. In the past, attempts have been made to link such famous individuals as Kit Carson and John Charles Fremont to this stretch of mountains. Sadly, those claims are quite unreliable. For even though explorers and travelers appeared in the general region during some two hundred and fifty years, it was not until 1859 that someone would approach these mountains close enough to claim discovery. More isolated peaks, lakes, and valleys lingered in obscurity even longer. The same mountains that draw visitors today acted to deter people of an earlier era because of the rigorous barriers they posed to travel.

The earliest European explorations into Colorado's mountains and plains approached from the south. Between 1540 and 1600, Spanish expeditions marched out of Mexico, probing the Great Plains and examining much of today's American Southwest. Around 1600, the Spanish began colonization efforts near Taos and Santa Fe. By mid-century, an expedition under Juan de Archuleta penetrated Colorado, becoming the first recorded adventurers to do so. Archuleta, with a troop of soldiers, moved northward after some rebellious pueblo Indians. Fifty years later, in 1706, Juan de Ulibarri marched into Colorado with forty soldiers and one hundred Indian allies, once again hunting Indians who had fled their benevolent dictatorship. Both of these Spanish units probably confined their visits to a military purpose and to the Arkansas River Valley.

While entering sections of today's Colorado, the Spanish discovered that other Europeans had been visiting the Great Plains. Indians told of French traders coming from the East, and they produced firearms as evidence of growing commerce. In 1719, another military force marched northward hoping to chastise the Utes and Comanches for their New Mexican raids. In 1720, an expedition proceeded all the way to the Platte River in today's Nebraska to determine the extent of French influence. Under the leadership of Don Pedro de Villasur, this force of one hundred men traveled along the South Platte River, which they called the Rio Jesus Maria, and probably spotted Colorado's famous Front Range. An attack by unfriendly Pawnees left eighty-eight Spaniards dead and twelve remaining troopers dashing for the safety of Santa Fe. Needless to say, Spanish interest in their northern frontier dwindled.

Official Spanish expeditions seemed to center on military necessity. How many private citizens ventured northward into Colorado's mountains, searching for treasures of silver and gold, is unknown. One intriguing hint about those adventurous souls came in 1859 from a prospector named Samuel Stone. Exploring a region "near the headwaters of Big Thompson Creek, close to the base of Long's Peak," Stone reportedly came upon "what appeared to be the site of an old mining camp." Aside from shafts, excavations, and cabins, Stone reported finding that much of the timber in the area had been cut and even "a portable outfit for distilling" including "a kettle-like copper vessel and a small copper 'worm' of several coils." Denver's frontier editor William N. Byers suggested that this was a "Spanish digging" and inquired about mining activity among some old-timers in Santa Fe. There he discovered a local tradition about some "Portugese adventurers" who passed through that town on a mining expedition to the north. In Santa Fe folklore, however, the Portuguese simply disappeared, presumably meeting their doom among the Indians.[2]

If the record of Spaniards spotting these mountains seems sketchy, it is probably because the major interests in their lives centered closer to Santa Fe. They believed that Colorado's mountains offered far less potential for wealth than the mines of Mexico or the genteel encomiendas of New Mexico. Even their French competitors of the eighteenth century failed to develop any serious interest in exploring the heart of the Rockies. That failure is most surprising because the French *voyageurs* penetrated so many other isolated regions. As early as 1720, according to some reports, the French in Illinois "heard rumors of Spanish mining in what would seem to have been the mountain-parts of Colorado."[3] Apparently, French gold seekers never investigated those rumors. But French traders, active even after France lost its North American claims

Artist Frederick Remington portrayed a dauntless mountain man. (Author's Collection)

A timid rodent, the beaver was among the first of the West's resources to be exploited. Trappers and traders roamed a wide area for two generations seeking beaver pelts in the early nineteenth century. (RMNPHC)

in 1763, did explore the river systems of the Great Plains. Those unnamed fur seekers gave familiar sights some memorable names. Longs Peak and its lofty companion Mount Meeker, for example, became known as "Les deux Oreilles" (The Two Ears) among the early French trappers who eyed those landmarks from out on the plains.[4]

Obscure Frenchmen had far less to do with national claims or domination than did European leaders. By 1801, Napoleon Bonaparte had cleverly regained French ownership over the vast Louisiana region. Spanish holdings once again faded southward. But Napoleon quickly became disenchanted with his dream for a giant North American empire and sold this stretch of ill-defined real estate to the United States for $15 million. The miffed Spanish now looked northward to face a restless new neighbor, an ambitious nation intending to assert its claims clear to the crest of the Continental Divide — and beyond.

American ownership was advanced by both official explorers and frontier traders. In 1806, Lieutenant Zebulon Pike made a foray for the U.S. Army into southeastern Colorado and South Park, only to be arrested and sent home by the Spanish. Americans were still regarded as trespassers. But at the same time, free trappers such as James Pursley began exploring Colorado, testing its potential in beaver. His keen eyes also spotted flakes of gold as early as 1805. Groups of Missouri traders, led by such men as A. P. Chouteau and Julius De Munn, followed in hopes of commercial ventures. They found Indians willing to parley, and plenty of valuable beaver. They worked along the Colorado Front Range between 1811 and 1817, only to have the protective Spanish authorities confiscate their wealth of collected pelts. Other trappers such as Ezekial Williams would follow in their wake, sometimes able to elude both the Spanish military patrols and hostile Indians while extracting a few precious beaver pelts from the Rockies. Dangers aside, the growing profits from the fur trade insured a continuing march toward the Rocky Mountains over the next three decades.

But fur traders and trappers were not known for their literary talents. Little about their explorations is known; accounts of their journeys are typically vague. Although many of them probably penetrated today's Rocky Mountain National Park, their tracks and tales have long since vanished.

Official explorers, on the other hand, were expected to provide long and detailed reports. It is through their eyes that we catch early glimpses of the region. Following American victory in the War of 1812, Congress decided to promote trade and commerce in the West. A major thrust was intended toward the upper Missouri River. The so-called Yellowstone Expedition of 1819 planned to establish forts, make treaties with Indians, collect data on the area, and generally assert American ownership, while also evicting British traders. One of the leaders of this highly organized effort was Major Stephen Harriman Long. He had joined the topographical engineers in 1817 and now was designated as leader of the scientific phase of this highly touted effort. But the Yellowstone Expedition proved to be a fiasco. It spent far too much money and proceeded up river so slowly that it had made its way only as far as Council Bluffs by the end of the 1819 season. While members built a winter camp and leisurely studied the Omaha Indians, Congress voted to withhold further financial support. Partly to make a final stab at some accomplishment, two minor expeditions were organized. One group headed toward Minnesota while Major Long took a contingent westward toward the mountains.

He headed a party of twenty-two men as they followed the course of the Platte River, a stream that Frenchmen earlier had named for its flat appearance. Long's task was to make observations of the animal life, the geological and biological features, and perhaps study some Indians as well. By late June of 1820 they approached the mouth of the South Fork of the Platte, moved up along that stream, and entered the present state of Colorado.

On Friday, June 30th, the official expedition journalist, Captain John R. Bell, noted that at eight in the morning "we discovered a blue strip, close in with the horizon to the west—which was by some pronounced to be no more than a cloud—by others, to be the Rocky Mountains." Not since the Pike expedition fourteen years earlier had anyone "official" laid eyes on this range. Bell con-

Major Stephen H. Long led the 1820 expedition that crossed the Great Plains and scouted the base of the Rockies. (Colorado Historical Society)

tinued his euphoric description, stating that the day was slightly hazy but that eventually their view sharpened, "and we had a distant view of the summit of a range of mountains — which to our great satisfaction and heart felt joy, was declared by the commanding officer to be the range of the Rocky Mountains. . . ." He added that "a high Peake was plainly to be distinguished towering above all the others as far as the sight extended." Later it would be that mountain to which Major Long's name would be attached. Then, like so many travelers who came after, Captain Bell noted the contrast of their tedious prairie journey with the scene that now lay before them. "The whole range had a beautiful and sublime appearance to us," he observed, "after having been so long confined to the dull and uninteresting monotony of prairie country. . . ."[5]

According to Dr. Edwin James, the expedition's botanist and geologist, three French guides helped direct Long's party toward the base of the Rockies. These men were listed as Bijeau, Le Doux,

Members of the Long Expedition viewed Colorado's Front Range as they traveled along the South Platte River. Their exploration of the mountains was confined to a climb of Pikes Peak. (RMNPHC)

and Julien. Joseph Bijeau was singled out by Dr. James as being particularly helpful because "he had formerly been resident in these regions, in capacity of hunter and trapper, during the greater part of six years." It was from Bijeau that the Long Expedition learned about the Rocky Mountain interior. "The mountains are usually abrupt," Dr. James related, "often towering into inaccessible peaks, covered with perpetual snows." Bijeau told of Colorado's large western slope parks, allowing James to report that "the vallies within the Rocky Mountains are many of them extensive, being from ten to twenty or thirty miles in width, and are traversed by many large and beautiful streams." Whether Bijeau or his fellow trappers ever visited Middle or Estes parks remains unknown, but it appears likely. "His pursuits," Dr. James concluded, "often led him within the Rocky Mountains, where the beaver are particularly abundant."[6]

Major Long and his men traveled southward along the foothills of the Front Range. They paused briefly to allow members to climb "the Peake" later named for Zebulon Pike, and then they returned eastward. Only the names of Major Long, Dr. James, and Joseph Bijeau remained behind, staying attached to mountains and creeks as a memory of their brief tour. Within a year or two, when their reports and observations were published, their conclusions about the future of this region were pessimistic. Traveling here was "extremely disagreeable;" the Great Plains were too dry and desolate to ever support a population, Major Long argued: "it is almost wholly unfit for cultivation;" it was a fine place for "savage"

Indians, who lived within "the shades of barbarism."[7] Only a few itinerant hunters could be attracted to this realm of wilderness.

So during the three decades following Major Long's brief tour, only the mountain men and a few bands of Indians ruled the Rockies. The era of the fur trade brought a handful of crusty characters, hardened by life in the wilderness, searching mostly for beaver. Rarely did these hunters build shelters; they tended to wander and they usually wintered with the Indians. Their personal equipment consisted mainly of those items essential for survival in the wilderness, called their "possibles" or "fixens." Historian Hiram Chittenden noted that a mountain man's baggage was spare, consisting of a rifle and its accessories, his traps, some knives, hatchets, and a few culinary utensils, some tobacco, coffee, sugar, and salt, some bedding made of a buffalo robe, and a horse and pack stock to haul his furs.

These "lonely hermits of the mountains" fell into a "habit of seclusion," preferring the company of wilderness and solitude to that of civilization. Chittenden portrayed the mountain man as "ordinarily gaunt and spare, browned with exposure, his hair long and unkempt, while his general make up, with the queer dress

Trappers led a solitary and hazardous life. Little evidence exists to prove that mountain men trapped beaver in the streams of Rocky Mountain National Park. (RMNPHC)

which he wore, made it often difficult to distinguish him from an Indian." His personality was described as "taciturn and gloomy" since he had become "accustomed to scenes of violence and death and the problem of self-preservation."[8] His language was an illiterate mixture of English, Spanish, French, and Indian words, sprinkled with expressions only used on the frontier. George

Ruxton, a western traveler in the 1840s, reported numerous camp-fire conversations. In one statement, a trapper responded to a question about the presence of hostile Indians: "Enfant de Garce, me see bout honderd, when I pass Squirrel Creek, one dam war-party, parce-que, they no hosses, and have de lariats for steal des animaux. May be de Yutes in Bayou Salade."[9] What he said was that skulking Indians ready to steal horses put the trappers on guard, regardless if those Arapaho were heading into South Park to attack the Utes.

In 1846, historian Francis Parkman toured the West and sat at a campfire one evening with several "uncouth figures," among whom were "two or three of the half savage men who spend their reckless lives in trapping among the Rocky Mountains. . . ." Parkman found very little in their demeanor or appearance worthy of praise. "They were all of Canadian extraction," he wrote, "their hard, weather-beaten faces and bushy moustaches looked out from beneath the hoods of their white capotes with a bad and brutish expression, as if their owners might be the willing agents of any villainy. And such in fact is the character of many of these men."[10]

Exactly how many beaver pelts may have been extracted from the streams of Rocky Mountain National Park during this fur trading era is not known. Yet signs of a lucrative trade dotted the nearby region, allowing us to assume that trappers worked every likely drainage. By the 1830s, small trading posts began to appear along the South Platte River just to the east of today's Park. About 1835, Fort Vasquez was established near the mouth of Clear Creek and by 1838 reestablished near the present town of Platteville. In 1837 or 1838, Ceran St. Vrain and his partners William and Charles Bent (well known as prominent Santa Fe traders and founders of Bent's Fort on the southern prairie) established Fort St. Vrain about a mile and a half below the mouth of St. Vrain Creek. Also by 1836, Lieutenant Lancaster P. Lupton built a trading post called Fort Lancaster, located about a mile north of today's Fort Lupton. A year later competitors Peter Sarpy and Henry Fraeb built Fort Jackson about ten miles south of Fort St. Vrain. All these posts vied for trade with the Indians, sought buffalo hides as well as beaver pelts, and served as depots for the trappers. But just as these posts were built, men's fashions in hats changed. Beaver felt gave way to silk, demands for beaver pelts declined, and within a decade all four forts were deserted. Traveler Francis Parkman noted on his 1846 journey that Fort St. Vrain "was now abandoned and fast falling into ruin. The walls of unbaked bricks were cracked from top to bottom." He added that "our horses recoiled in terror from the neglected entrance where the heavy gates were torn from their hinges and flung down." "The area within," Parkman concluded,

Fur trappers and traders were few in number and the American West was vast, helping explain why a small section of the Rockies might be ignored. (RMNPHC)

"was overgrown with weeds, and the long ranges of apartments once occupied by the motley concourse of traders, Canadians, and squaws, were now miserably dilapidated."[11]

One of the few individuals who visited this region during its fur trading heyday — and bothered to write about it — was Rufus B. Sage. A native of Upper Middletown, Connecticut, Sage traveled throughout the West between 1841 and 1844. He journeyed to Fort Hall, Idaho via the famed immigrant trail; he met and hunted with mountaineers; he helped transport furs down the Platte and Missouri rivers; he spent weeks at Fort Lancaster observing life there. "The business transacted at this post is chiefly with the Cheyennes," he later recalled, "but the Arapahos, Mexicans, and Sioux also come in for a share and contribute to render it one of the most profitable trading establishments in the country."[12]

He joined a futile attack by a company of Texans upon New Mexico in the spring of 1843 and returned to Fort Lancaster nearly destitute. It was in September of 1843 that he acquired a horse and some gear and proceeded westward into the mountains on a hunting excursion "where, unattended by any one, I had a further opportunity of testing the varied sweets of solitude."[13]

His account for September 30th told of heading "for ten or twelve miles, through a broad opening between two mountain ridges, bearing a northwesterly direction, to a large valley skirting a tributary of Thompson's creek, where, finding an abundance of deer, I passed the interval till my return to the Fort."[14] Historian Leroy Hafen credits Sage as having entered Estes Park. And if Sage's account can be accepted, he became the first man to report about the wonders of this region.

"The locality of my encampment presented numerous and varied attractions," Sage wrote, sounding a bit like an advertising man. "It seemed, indeed, like a concentration of beautiful lateral valleys, intersected by meandering watercourses, ridged by lofty ledges of precipitous rock, and hemmed in upon the west by vast piles of mountains climbing beyond the clouds, and upon the north, south, and east, by sharp lines of hills that skirted the prairie. . . ." Few modern writers have duplicated his vision of these "far-spreading domains of silence and loneliness." Hunting brought Sage into the mountains and in Estes Park he found wildlife abundant. "It also affords every variety of game, while the lake is completely crowded with geese, brants, ducks, and gulls, to an extent seldom witnessed." Thoughts of successful hunting waned in his mind, however, as he waxed philosophic about the beauties of nature. "What a charming retreat for some one of the world-hating *literati*! He might here hold daily converse with himself, Nature, and his God, far removed from the annoyance of man."[15]

Here he hunted for a month. "I was quite successful with my rifle," he noted, "and, by degrees, became much attached to the versatile life of lordly independence consociate with the loneliness of my situation."[16] On October 29th he left Estes Park, traveled down St. Vrain Creek (which he called Soublet's creek), and arrived at Fort Lancaster on October 30th. Soon he returned to the East, married, settled down, wrote and published a book about his travels, and spent the rest of his life farming near his home town. His *Rocky Mountain Life; or, Startling Scenes and Perilous Adventures in the Far West during an Expedition of Three Years* appeared in August of 1846. In some ways, his observations marked the end of the fur trading era. The old trappers and traders were being replaced by a new breed of frontiersman.

But neither Sage's visit nor his book stimulated a real rush to the Rockies. The 1840s and 1850s did see a number of men like him, however, "exploring parties" crossing the Great Plains, heading for California, investigating the unsettled wilderness. Between

A native of Connecticut, Rufus B. Sage explored the Front Range in the Autumn of 1843, offering the first documented glimpse of the Estes Park region. (Colorado Historical Society)

1842 and 1848, for example, the "Pathfinder of the West" John Charles Fremont made five government-sponsored expeditions westward. Returning from California in June of 1844, his expedition passed through Middle Park. There they met 200 Arapaho and Sioux encamped and hunting. He and his men did not tarry, but moved rapidly toward South Park and then to the plains. Fremont could have chosen a more direct route toward the plains leading through Rocky Mountain National Park, but he did not. However, he was aware that trails along the Continental Divide were well-known before his 1844 arrival. The "mountain coves, called Parks" and the "heads of the rivers, the practicability of the mountains passes, and the locality of the Three Parks were all objects of interest," Fremont noted as he began finding paths in Colorado, "and although well known to the hunters and trappers, were unknown to science and history."[17]

Some writers have argued that one of Fremont's guides, Kit Carson, fully explored and trapped all the territory around Longs Peak and even built a cabin near its base. William F. Drannan, only seventeen years old in 1849, claimed to have traveled widely with Carson. He told of crossing the Rockies from the Plains to North Park via the upper Cache la Poudre on one of those trips. Recalling his visit, he remembered considerable Indian activity on the trails. "It was the custom of the Utes," Drannan noted, "to cross over the mountains in small squads every spring and kill all the trappers they could find and take their traps and furs."[18] It is possible that Kit Carson and his sidekicks did explore all the hidden valleys of Rocky Mountain National Park, but those claims might also be wishful thinking on the part of those who hoped to forge a link with a legend.

The late 1840s saw people moving West in increasing numbers. American victory in the Mexican War assured national expansion; the gold rush to California attracted thousands. Persecuted Mormons joined land-hungry immigrants on a western surge of settlement. And the flotsam of those migratory movements began scattering into every nook of vacant territory.

Even tourists began to roam the West. Francis Parkman made his journey along the Oregon Trail in 1846 and George Ruxton took his tour the following year. Many would follow, but few visitors ever duplicated the famous hunting excursion of Sir St. George Gore, an Irish Baronet. His hunting expedition, which lasted from 1854 to 1857, centered in Wyoming but brought him briefly into Middle Park. Not one to travel light, Gore's "grand hunting party" included forty men, two valets and a dog handler, more than one hundred horses, twenty yoke of oxen, fifty hunting hounds, twenty-eight vehicles, and famous mountain men Jim Bridger and Henry Chatillon acting as guides. Lord Gore's stay in Middle Park lasted only from July through September of 1854. Whether he hunted around Grand Lake is unknown, but his party did find plenty of buffalo, deer, and elk. By October Lord Gore and his hunters trouped back to Fort Laramie. He would spend the remainder of his American jaunt on escapades into the northern Great Plains. His impact upon Middle Park was negligible. But he does represent a developing awareness, even in Europe, that the American West could be considered a place of adventure. Again, the area of Rocky Mountain National Park could not boast of entertaining this eccentric nobleman, but in time it would receive its share.

The discovery of gold changed everything. Decades of hunting, trapping, and trading in Colorado seemed almost lackadaisical when compared to the onslaught of prospectors who thundered onto the scene after 1858. Traces of gold had been discovered

Following the 1848 discovery of gold in California, prospectors roamed the West. Colorado's boom began in 1858, bringing a rush of people to the Rockies. (Author's Collection)

earlier, in 1805, 1835, 1843, 1849, and in 1854, but none of those "strikes" produced a "rush." In June of 1858, a company of one hundred Georgians, Missourians, and Cherokee Indians led by William Green Russell traveled up the Arkansas Valley to prospect in the drainage of the South Platte River. All but thirteen of this party deserted after a month due to poor panning and constant Indian scares. But by the end of July, Russell and his diehards managed to extract small amounts of gold dust amounting to $800 from the gravels of the South Platte and its adjacent streams. News traveled fast. Newspapers in Kansas and Missouri started publishing wildly optimistic reports about these finds, probably hoping to stimulate local economies by outfitting men rushing west. On July 24th, the *Weekly Kansas Herald* stated: "On the headwaters of the South Fork of the Platte, near Longs Peak, gold mines have been discovered and 500 persons are now working there."[19] Hyperbole helped to produce excitement. By October 29th, the *Lawrence* (Kansas) *Republican* announced that parties were forming and departing from Kansas, Nebraska, Missouri, Iowa, Ohio, and even from as far away as Michigan.

But many who rushed to Colorado soon believed they had been conned. Some gold could be panned from the creeks all right, but amounts remained very small. A. A. Brookfield, writing from St. Vrain's Creek on January 26, 1859, attempted to set the record straight: "We have found the best quantity of gold that has been discovered, and cannot make one dollar per day." "My impression of the mines," Brookfield concluded, "is that they are a d--d humbug."[20]

Others agreed that Colorado's gold rush was a hoax and began returning to the East. Yet, in May of 1859, George A. Jackson made a strike on Chicago Creek at Idaho Springs and John H. Gregory found a deposit on the North Fork of Clear Creek between today's Black Hawk and Central City. Newspaperman William N. Byers reached Gregory's diggings on May 20th, 1859, and found twenty men working with two favorable quartz leads discovered. Two weeks later he estimated that three thousand men were combing the area; thirty leads had been prospected and several hundred claims had been made. Colorado's future was assured. Thousands trekked across the plains with golden visions filling their heads. Reviewing this excitement in 1867, Ovando Hollister noted: "As they came within sight of Long's Peak, lying like a smoky thunderhead in the far and indefinite horizon, a hundred miles distant, we can imagine their exaltation of feeling."[21]

Most of the details of Colorado's boom-time growth and development need not detain us here. It is enough to say that a dozen or

An artist's depiction of Joel Estes displays the face of a frontiersman. Estes came to Colorado during the gold rush, turning to cattle ranching almost immediately. (RMNPHC)

more Front Range towns such as Denver, Boulder, and Golden, mushroomed overnight. Mixed with the prospectors came land speculators, town builders, merchants, ranchers, various elements of low life, and as wide an assortment of people as America could produce. Some estimate that a hundred thousand people flooded into Colorado as "Fifty-niners."

One fellow bitten by the "gold fever" bug was Joel Estes. A type of foot-loose man common to our westering, the Kentucky-born Estes started his life as a frontier farmer in Andrew County, Missouri. There he and his wife Patsy raised thirteen children while depending upon Black slaves for labor in carving out an estate. Along with thousands of others in 1849, Estes and his eldest son Hardin hit the trail to California. There they staked a valuable claim, eventually selling it for $30,000. During the next decade, wanderlust took Estes into other corners of the West. In 1854 or 1855, for example, he went to Oregon and back to California searching for a new spot to homestead. When news of Rocky Mountain gold reached his ears, Estes, then 53 years old, packed up his wife, six of his children, five Black slaves, a few friends, and a herd of cattle, and joined the stampede to the gold fields.

Above: After climbing through the foothills, Joel Estes and his son Milton found Estes Park and soon became enchanted with the scene. (RMNPHC)

An abundance of elk, deer, and mountain sheep meant easy hunting for the Estes family, as well as for sportsmen and market hunters in the years to come. (RMNPHC)

Arriving in Denver on June 15th, 1859, Estes scouted the region for a likely place to stake a claim or settle. He saw plenty of panning and placer mining activity, but he decided that the California Mother Lode had been much richer. He and his group camped for a few months near today's Golden, Colorado, helping to create that new settlement. In late September he decided to move, locating twenty-two miles north of Denver at a spot then known as Fort Lupton Bottom, near the South Platte River. He felt this new ranch site would insure adequate forage for his herd of cattle. There they built crude cabins, harvested some wild grass for hay, and prepared to spend the winter.

In mid-October, Estes, along with his twelve-year-old son Milton and perhaps some other friends, embarked upon a hunting or prospecting trip into the mountains. Traveling north and west across the ridges and along the creeks, Estes finally stood looking into a valley he assumed to be North Park. In fact, his eyes gazed upon today's Estes Park. "No words can describe our surprise, wonder and joy at beholding such an unexpected sight," Milton Estes would write some forty years later. "It was a grand sight and a great surprise."[22]

After exploring this valley for a few days, Estes concluded that it was not North Park after all. They found "no signs that white men had ever been there before us." Even the Indians had left very little evidence of their visits. "There were signs that Indians had been there at some time," Milton Estes recalled, "for we found lodge poles in two different places. How long before, we could not determine."[23]

Many details about the Estes family claiming this valley for their ranch have been lost or are clouded by time and conflicting memories. Nevertheless, it is clear that Joel Estes decided that this newly found park would be ideally suited for a cattle range. So, sometime in 1860, Estes and his sons returned, built two log cabins at the eastern end of the park, and took possession using the frontier custom of merely squatting upon vacant land. "We were monarchs of all we surveyed," Milton Estes remembered, "mountains, valleys and streams. There was absolutely nothing to dispute our sway. We had a little world all to ourselves."[24] Later that year they drove a herd of about sixty cattle from their ranch near the Platte River up through the foothills into their newly found mountain pasture.

Estes apparently hired several men to assist in herding and in guarding his cattle during the following winter and during the winter of 1861–1862 as well. Years later, one of those helpers, Dunham Wright, referred to that experience as "two of the happiest winters of my long life . . . feasting and fattening on mountain sheep and elk."[25]

Joel Estes, like other frontiersmen, was a resourceful man. He knew how to exploit the wealth of nature to insure both survival and personal profit. And Estes Park provided an abundance of wildlife that attracted his attention. Cattle took time to graze and fatten; elk and deer could be harvested immediately and easily sold in Denver. Prospectors with gold on their minds were too busy digging or panning to take time to hunt for their supper. So Joel Estes took advantage of easy hunting and that nearby demand for meat. His son Milton noted: "One fall and winter the writer killed one hundred head of elk, besides other game, such as mountain sheep, deer and antelope."[26] They butchered the animals, using some of the meat themselves, and "dressed many skins for clothing which we made and wore." Not surprisingly, the Estes family used this region much like the Indians and the trappers who preceded them. But a bit more exploitively, they also marketed the game animals. Milton Estes reported: "By this time (1863) we had made a trail to Denver, where we sold many dressed skins and many hindquarters of deer, elk and sheep. Much of the gold was not made into coins, so they sometimes weighed out gold dust to us in exchange."[27]

The Civil War interfered with Joel Estes's plans for his newly found park. In 1861 Estes made one of several trips back to Missouri, where, as a slave owner, he encountered hostility. So, seeking a favorable political climate, he decided to move to Texas. A brief attempt at cattle ranching did not prove successful there and he soon returned to Missouri, freed his slaves, and in 1863 decided that Colorado offered the brightest future. Between 1863 and 1866, Joel Estes and his family attempted to make their new homestead in the mountains into a profitable venture. But life there was not easy.

They discovered that the winters could be "very hard and cold." They found it was necessary to store up hay for their cattle and that meant cutting native grasses by hand using a scythe. When their hay supply became exhausted, it was necessary to drive the cattle down toward the foothills or to dig through snow drifts, enabling the herd to forage. Hunting continued to earn the family its extra income, and they took a four-day trip to Denver once every two months in order to market their quarry. In the city they picked up their mail and other news from the outside world. Life for the Estes women was equally lonely and harsh. Milton Estes recalled how primitive conditions were confronted by these pioneer women: "The women of our families, my mother, sister and wife, cheerfully shared with us the rugged life of the pioneer. With dutch-ovens, iron kettles hanging over open fire places, they cooked food that could not be surpassed. No modern methods could equal the splendid meals of wild game, hot biscuits, berries, cream, etc., that they prepared."[28]

It is difficult to tell to what extent the Estes family roamed across today's Rocky Mountain National Park. It seems certain that hunting ventures took them almost everywhere, from the slopes of Longs Peak itself into every major drainage nearby. Tales of fabulous hunting filled Milton Estes's memory. He told of killing "a whole band of thirteen deer, at one time, with a muzzle load-ing rifle;" he recalled the excitement of shooting an intruding bear "as big as an ox" one thrilling night; he remembered how easy it was to bag bighorn sheep on a particular rocky outcrop where the Estes hunters used "a trained dog that we set on them, and they would strike straight for the Sheep Rock, and then we would get the whole flock."[29] Hunting filled their time and their stomachs and insured their survival.

Although credited as the region's discoverers, Joel Estes and his family were not totally alone. Across the range, near Grand Lake, for example, another Missourian named Philip Crawshaw built a log cabin sometime around 1857 or 1858. He ran a trap line along the North Fork of the Colorado and other trappers occasionally joined him in his enterprise. He stayed in the region until 1861, when he felt he had his fortune made after trading furs for gold dust in Denver. While returning home to Missouri, the unfortu-nate Mr. Crawshaw was attacked by William Quantrill's infamous Confederate raiders and robbed of all his earnings. Another resident in these mountains, Alonzo Allen, was an adventurous prospector searching for gold throughout much of the Rocky Mountain Front Range. In 1864 he built a cabin southeast of Longs Peak, about two miles east of today's Allenspark. Details about men like Crawshaw or Allen are slim. And other trappers or prospectors, remaining nameless upon the pages of history, certainly haunted these moun-tains during the early 1860s.

One professional wanderer, editor William N. Byers of the *Rocky Mountain News*, made a visit to this portion of the Rockies in August of 1864. His excursion shows that people interested in "adventure and amusement" were also attracted to the mountains soon after the Colorado gold rush began. Starting from Denver with three companions, a wagon, horses, and camping gear, Byers pro-ceeded toward Longs Peak following the rugged cattle trail etched by the Estes family. Their route (which roughly followed today's Highway 36 from Lyons to Estes Park) was primitive, "so difficult

An 1873 photograph of Grand Lake displays a solitary log cabin, probably not unlike the structure built by Philip Crawshaw in the late 1850s. (RMNPHC)

was it to get along that we left the wagon in disgust; packed a few necessary articles on our horses, cached the balance, and pushed ahead with more rapidity." Soon they spotted Estes Park, "a very gem of beauty." Byers was impressed: "The landscape struck us at first sight as one of the most lovely we ever beheld, and three or four days familiarity with it only increased that admiration."[30]

There they visited the "home of Mr. Estes, the pioneer and sole occupant of this sylvan paradise." Earlier they met Joel Estes and one of his sons along the trail, heading for Denver. At the homestead Byers met Patsy Estes, "a pleasant old lady of forty-five or fifty years," as well as Milton Estes and his sister. Byers found that "we were the first visitors they had seen this year and they seemed overjoyed to look upon a human face more than their own." He added that "they are getting tired of the solitude and we suspect would like a change." Editorially he noted, "The picturesque will do for a time but like everything else it grows monotonous."[31]

Patsy Estes joined in pioneering with her husband, willing to face isolation and some brutal weather. The Spring of 1866 saw the Estes family move toward better ranching country on the Great Plains. (RMNPHC)

Byers and his three companions came not to "discover" but to climb Longs Peak. Apparently others had preceded them in that attempt. Byers referred to "all who had started up it had gone from this point . . . and they had invariably returned unsuccessful, pronouncing the highest summit impossible." On August 19th, Byers's party set out to scale Longs Peak regardless of past failures. Yet that same day they were disappointingly unable to locate a useable route to the summit. However, on the morning of August 20th, they stood atop Mount Meeker, "as high as anyone has ever gone" and "added our names to the five registered before. . . ." Just then, a climb of Longs Peak seemed impossible. "We are quite sure that no living creature, unless it had wings to fly, was ever upon its summit," Byers wistfully noted, "and we believe we run no risk in predicting that no man ever will be, though it is barely possible that the ascent can be made."[32]

So they descended to the Estes ranch and then journeyed homeward. Although a conquest of Longs Peak eluded them, Byers wrote glowingly about the region. "Eventually this park will become a favorite pleasure resort," he prophesied.[33] Encouraging others to visit the area, he added that "The trip to Longs Peak and back can be made in five days, but it is better to take six, seven, or eight days for it. Our's occupied six and a half altogether."[34] The promotion of tourism had begun.

The winter of 1864–65 proved to be particularly severe in Estes Park. Soon after, the Estes family decided to move. "We needed a milder climate and a wider range for the cattle," Milton Estes explained, "for we wanted to engage in stockraising on a larger scale."[35] So Joel Estes sold the mountain valley he had tried to homestead, now named for him by William Byers. Two men were ready to purchase Estes's rights to the land, a Michael Hollenbeck and a fellow named "Buck." Supposedly, the valley exchanged ownership for a yoke of oxen. On April 15, 1866, Joel Estes and his family left their mountain homestead, moving to southern Colorado to start another ranch. In 1875, Joel Estes died at the age of sixty-nine in Farmington, New Mexico. As happened among other pioneer families, the Estes children scattered across several states, from New Mexico to Iowa. But none remained in Estes Park. Like some who came later, Joel Estes had found it difficult to wring success out of the "sylvan paradise." Scenery and good hunting were no match for rough winters and loneliness.

Within a few short years, between 1859 and 1866, Estes Park and Longs Peak started to gain wide recognition. Men seeking gold used Longs Peak as a landmark; many maps included its name; the growing population of Denver gazed upon its slopes as they went about their chores; the range of Rockies between Estes Park and Grand Lake drew hunters, prospectors, and subsistence ranchers such as Joel Estes; and, among others, William Byers simply came to take a closer look. From as far away as France, the famous novelist Jules Verne granted Longs Peak its discovery in the world of literature. In 1865, Verne wrote a science fiction tale entitled *From the Earth to the Moon*. The popular writer told a tale of sending a projectile with three men and two dogs to the moon. A huge astronomical observatory on earth was necessary

Located on the southern horizon of Estes Park, Longs Peak beckoned climbers from the 1860s on. (RMNPHC)

for this great fictional enterprise, so Verne chose the isolated Longs Peak "in the territory of Missouri" upon which to place his 280-foot-long telescope, with a "magnifying power of 48,000 times."[36] From its position as merely one of a thousand peaks in the Rocky Mountains only a few decades earlier, Longs Peak emerged as the fictional center of world astronomy. From those few, nameless French trappers calling Longs Peak and Mount Meeker *Les deux Oreilles* to a French novelist predicting the heart of the Rockies as a future scientific center, these mountains began to match men's minds. Through the efforts of Spaniards, Frenchmen, and Americans, who acted as government officials, trappers and traders, prospectors, hunters, and writers, Longs Peak and its mountainous surroundings were gradually discovered.

3

SEARCHING FOR THE
SONG OF THE WINDS

"It became evident that we were not to be left monarchs of all we surveyed. Folks were drifting in prospecting, fossicking, pre-empting, making claims; so we prepared for civilization."
The Earl of Dunraven in Past Times and Pastimes[1]

A VISIT to the Rockies always seems to inspire the writing of post cards or letters to those back home. Whether the scenery sparks creativity, or new adventures warrant chatter, or excitement needs to be shared, people have been writing about their experiences in these mountains for many years. But of all those card and letter writers, few ever achieved the level of lasting fame accorded the adventurous English traveler Isabella L. Bird.

No one would ever suggest that Isabella Bird changed the course of Rocky Mountain history. After all, her 1873 visit lasted less than three months. She bought no land; she built no cabins; she started no famous hotels; she did not propose the establishment of a park. She merely wrote about what she saw and experienced. And she never returned in the remaining three decades of her life. Nevertheless, her description of an adventuresome climb up Longs Peak remains a minor classic. Her romantic imagination and descriptive pen painted vivid portraits of the region's inhabitants and its natural features. But even more valuable to us, her letters to her sister provide us with a glimpse at the changes sweeping across this mountainous landscape in the decade after Joel Estes and his family sold and moved out. Those were the years when William Byers attempted another climb of Longs Peak, a time that brought official government explorers, more mountain climbers, more hunters, more subsistence ranchers and settlers. It was a time that saw a flurry of health seekers, promoters, and literate tourists like Isa-

At the same time pioneers and prospectors attempted to scratch a living out of the Rockies, curious and affluent vacationers invaded the region. (RMNPHC)

bella Bird herself. After entering the region, she wrote on September 28th, 1873: "I have just dropped into the very place I have been seeking, but in everything it exceeds all my dreams."[2]

By 1867, people newly settled in Colorado had discovered that their mountains held more than gold. Although obsessed with gaining mineral wealth, noted observer Ovando Hollister in his book *The Mines of Colorado*, Coloradans also found that "rambles in the Mountains, riding, hunting, bathing, fishing, berrying, camping out, living on *air*, puts new cheeks on old bones and paints them the richest brown." Wilderness would work its wonders. Even with dynamite, Hollister predicted, man could hardly ever alter these mountains. "Silence and solitude are the inheritance of these forest wilds," he wrote, "where even the loudest explosions rouse only a faint, short echo, and where the song of the winds is an eternal and subdued sigh."[3]

At the same time another enthusiastic traveler, Bayard Taylor, suggested that much of Colorado would soon become a perfect summer resort. In his book *Colorado: A Summer Trip*, published in 1867, Taylor noted dozens of reasons why "Colorado will soon be recognized as our Switzerland." Among Colorado's glories was its air, "more delicious to breathe," according to Taylor; yet "it is neither too sedative nor too exciting; but has that pure, sweet, flexible quality which seems to support all one's happiest and healthiest moods."[4] Clearly, a mere visit to these mountains would start a person on the path to health.

In the late 1860s a man seeking better health became Grand Lake's first permanent resident. Joseph Wescott suffered from crippling rheumatism and had come to find a cure in the waters of Hot Sulphur Springs in Middle Park. Hot Sulphur Springs was just then an infant resort hoping to become a major spa. Feeling sufficiently cured to fend for himself, Wescott moved to Grand Lake to hunt and fish and also build a cabin. But harsh weather and deep snows in the winter of 1867 almost killed him. Fishing and hunting were poor if not impossible and Wescott nearly starved to death. "In desperation," local historian Nell Pauly reported, "he cut the deer hide from the seat of his chair and boiled it to a glutinous mixture, adding, for seasoning, a few herbs he was able to dig from the ground under the snow." After supposedly eating his shoes in a similar manner, "he kept a spark of life in his starving body until he was rescued by a hunting party which stumbled upon his lonely cabin." There, "almost demented and delirious from undernourishment," Wescott was saved.[5] And at Grand Lake he would remain, earning pioneer status in that community after having survived his first winter. With Wescott's arrival, progress came quickly, for occasional trappers soon gave way to tourists who began arriving during the summer of 1868.

East of the Divide, claims to the land of Estes Park rapidly changed hands as the harsh realities of ranching in the mountains became known. Among those making an effort to subsist in Estes Park during the late 1860s was a Welshman named Griffith Evans. Like other pioneers, he was persistent. Evans was ranching on the old Estes property in 1873 when Isabella Bird made her visit. "The ranchman, who is half-hunter, half-stockman," Mrs. Bird wrote describing Evans, "and his wife are jovial, hearty Welsh people from Llanberis, who laugh with loud, cheery British laughs, sing in parts down to the youngest child, are free hearted and hospitable, and pile the pitch-pine logs half-way up the great rude chimney." Hunting, ranching, and catering to a few visitors allowed the Evans family a lean living in Estes Park. Basic items such as food and shelter took on greater significance here. "There has been fresh meat each day since I came," Isabella Bird chirped, "delicious bread baked daily, excellent potatoes, tea and coffee, and an abundant supply of milk like cream. I have a clean hay bed with six blankets, and there are neither bugs nor fleas." What more could any frontier traveler ask? "The scenery is the most glorious I have ever seen," she added, as if noting a bonus, "and it is above us, around us, at the very door."[6]

While the Evans family hoped to exploit the mountains and assist a few travelers, William N. Byers returned to fulfill his dream of conquering the famed Longs Peak. As the pioneering editor of *The Rocky Mountain News*, Byers acquired a habit of tramping through the gold fields, wandering throughout Colorado, and promoting this developing territory in print. His failure to reach the Longs Peak summit in 1864 must have gnawed away at his adventurous pride. As he went about his tasks in Denver, Longs Peak probably loomed like a failure on his horizon. For early in the 1860s, William Byers had successfully defeated his early opponents in the Denver newspaper business. He was an ambitious man and his ambition would not allow Longs Peak to remain unclimbed.

Byers's second chance for a Longs Peak climb came in 1868. In that year John Wesley Powell, a one-armed Civil War veteran, a geology professor at Wesleyan University in Illinois, and a self-styled explorer, came on his second trip to Colorado. That summer Powell brought a group of about thirty students, constituting what they called the Colorado Scientific Exploring Expedition (given its pretentious name because it was partially sponsored by the Illinois State Natural History Society). One year earlier, in 1867, Powell

The adventurous editor of the *Rocky Mountain News*, William N. Byers attempted to climb Longs Peak in 1864, but failed. In 1868 he joined geologist John Wesley Powell and together they succeeded in leading the first known ascent to the summit. (RMNPHC)

came West on a similar trip and scrambled to the top of Pikes Peak with ease. There he remarked: "The trouble with climbing a mountain is that you can't stay on top."[7] The euphoria of being atop Pikes Peak and seeing unconquered Longs Peak 103 miles to the north must have given Powell another goal. Professor Powell was just as ambitious as editor Byers.

So in August of 1868, William Byers joined Powell and his students at their camp in Middle Park. From there they decided to ascend Longs Peak. Powell and Byers, along with Powell's younger brother Walter, Byers's brother-in-law Jack Sumner, and three students, left their base camp at Grand Lake on August 20th. Starting on horseback, they took a mule loaded with ten days' rations and "each man carried his bedding under or behind his saddle, a pistol at his belt, and those not encumbered with instruments took their guns." They followed ridges southeastward, gradually moving toward timberline and meeting an "impassible precipice." Forced to leave their horses behind on August 22nd, they moved upward afoot, following ridges that appeared to lead toward the Peak but only ended at "impassible chasms." But finally a route was discovered. Late that day one of the students, L. W. Keplinger, scrambled upward ahead of the rest and scouted a usable route to the summit. Forced to wait until the next morning, the seven men spent a windy, wet night and "shivered the long hours through."[8]

On August 23rd, "the day dawned fair," Byers later wrote, "and at six o'clock we were facing the mountain." Although the route chosen by Keplinger appeared impossible ("a great block of granite, perfectly smooth and unbroken") the climbers "were most agreeably surprised to find a passable way, though it required great caution, coolness, and infinite labor to make headway; life often depending upon a grasp of the fingers in a crevice that would hardly admit them."[9] By ten o'clock that morning they stood on the summit. Capping their success with relief, L. W. Keplinger noted: "There were no indications of any prior ascents."[10]

William Byers found his wish fulfilled; he was among the first party ever to climb Longs Peak. Even more important, he became the first to describe its summit in print. "The Peak is a nearly level surface, paved with irregular blocks of granite, and with out any vegetation of any kind, except a little gray lichen," he wrote. "The outline is nearly a parallelogram — east and west — widening a little toward the western extremity, and five or six acres in extent."[11] Then, according to L. W. Keplinger, a moving event took place on the mountain. "As we were about to leave the summit Major Powell took off his hat and made a little talk," Keplinger recalled. "He said, in substance, that we had now accomplished an undertaking in the material or physical field which had hitherto been deemed impossible, but that there were mountains more formidable in other fields of effort which were before us, and expressed hope and predicted that what we had that day accomplished was but an augury of yet greater achievements in such other fields."[12] After their three-hour stay on the summit, they stuffed mementos and notes in a tin can to be left on top. Then they unfurled a flag and left it waving in the breeze as they began their descent.

The troupe spent another night out in the open, without blankets. That evening they suffered even more, "because we were out of 'grub.' " On August 24th, they returned to their old camp on Grand Lake, weary but basking in their success. William Byers recalled: "We had only been gone five days; had been eminently successful, and of course were satisfied; the more so because the mountain had always been pronounced inaccessible, and ours was the first party that had ever set foot upon its summit."[13]

William Byers became a booster for the region in general while John Wesley Powell gained credit as the first of the "official" government explorers to enter the region. But Powell did not tarry in these mountains; his sights were already set on a trip down the Colorado River, a venture that was to bring him national fame and make his speech atop Longs Peak nearly prophetic. Powell and Byers introduced the era of scientific investigation and geographical exploration, soon to be followed by a series of surveys entering the area.

Within the next several years, detachments from two major government surveys entered the mountains. Following the Civil War, Congress displayed a growing curiosity about the American West, funding extensive geological and topographical surveys. "The results of this quest for knowledge," notes historian Richard Bartlett, "were four geographical and geological surveys conducted over large areas of the West from 1867 until 1879, when the U.S. Geological Survey which is still in existence, took over."[14] In 1867, for example, Congress funded a geological survey of Nebraska, to be led by Ferdinand Vandiveer Hayden. Soon Hayden expanded his efforts to become the U.S. Geological and Geographical Survey of the Territories. Major Powell received $12,000 from Congress in 1870 to continue a survey in the Colorado River country. In addition, two surveys under the War Department were also authorized. One of these, the U.S. Geological Exploration of the Fortieth Parallel, under the direction of Clarence King, tended to overlap the territory covered by the Hayden survey. These great surveys became, to some degree, great rivalries. The leaders, aside from being serious scientists, were ambitious men who tended to be egotistical. One place in the West where these surveys overlapped was Rocky Mountain National Park. Perhaps, as we saw with Major Powell, Longs Peak challenged men of ambition. Clarence King arrived in 1871 and Hayden would follow in 1873.

In 1871, for example, Arnold Hague's party, a subdivision of King's Fortieth Parallel Survey, entered Estes Park. Most members of these teams were young men, mountaineering enthusiasts, and notably literate. With this crew came Henry Adams, a descendant of two presidents and a noted scholar. Slightly in awe of his companions, Adams described the men's work as they "held under their hammers a thousand miles of mineral country with all its riddles to solve, and its stores of possible wealth to mark." While Hague's men pecked and pawed at the flanks of Longs Peak, Henry Adams went fishing. "The day was fine," Adams recalled, "and hazy with the smoke of forest fires a thousand miles away; the park stretched its English beauties off to the base of its bordering mountains in natural landscape and archaic peace; the stream was just fishy enough to tempt lingering along its banks." And it was "lingering"

Above: William Henry Jackson photographed members of the Hayden survey party in 1873. (RMNPHC)

Gathering geographic and geologic data meant scampering to numerous mountain summits. Longs Peak was merely one of many mountains in the area receiving attention from surveyors lugging their triangulation equipment along to determine distance and elevation measurements.

that caused Henry Adams to fish until dark, lose his trail back to camp, and force him to backtrack upon his mule down to Evans's cabin. There Adams found Clarence King and became enchanted with this scientist-explorer of the West. The two men were soon provided with a sparse cabin where they "shared the room and the bed, and talked till far towards dawn." "King's abnormal energy had already won him great success," Adams observed. "None of his contemporaries had done so much, single-handed, or were likely to leave so deep a trail."[15]

Scaling mountains and describing geologic mysteries, not fishing, were the general tasks of these surveyors. Many peaks were climbed, careful maps and geologic charts were drawn, elevations were calculated with barometers, and details of flora and fauna were noted. In 1873, James T. Gardner of the Hayden Survey moved through Middle Park, carefully describing its natural features, observing its infant towns and mining camps, following the Grand (now Colorado) River into its upper reaches. Although scientifically dry reading, Gardner's reports were significant for their collection of details. After men such as Gardner or Hague passed through an area, few could argue that the West remained unexplored.

Working their way through the mountains, Gardner and his men carried their scientific instruments to the summit of Longs Peak as well as to ten other mountains and six passes within the region. Just at that time, another well-known lecturer and writer (and avid mountain climber), Anna Dickinson, happened to be climbing mountains in Colorado and met Gardner and his crew hard at work near Longs Peak. These were "men who ought to be immortal if superhuman perserverance and courage are guarantees of immortality," she wrote. Dickinson watched them go about their tasks in awe of their determination. "I remember that after supper when we were camping at timber line, Gardner took one of his instruments and trotted up the side of the mountain to make some observations. He *expected* to be gone half an hour, and *was* gone, by reason of the clouds, nearer three hours, 'but,' as he quietly said when he came back, speaking of the clouds, 'I conquered them at last.' "[16]

All these government surveys helped bring national (if not Congressional) attention to the mountains and parks of Colorado. For just like William N. Byers, men such as Hayden, King, and Powell were always conscious of publicity. Thus it was not mere chance that led James Gardner and Professor Hayden to invite both Anna Dickinson and William N. Byers to accompany them on their September 1873 climb of Longs Peak. Naturally, these writers eagerly

Dr. Ferdinand Vandiveer Hayden (seated) confers with an assistant in an 1872 camp near Golden. (RMNPHC)

agreed; stories of adventure filled with colorful characters always excite a grateful public readership. But an added reward came to Miss Dickinson for her climbing efforts. For although several other ladies started out on this ascent with the Hayden party, Anna Dickinson was the only woman to make the summit that day and became the first of her sex to claim that achievement. Apparently the climb impressed her less than the men she met, for she barely mentioned Longs Peak at all in her autobiography. Interestingly, a more exuberant Isabella Bird made her ascent only a month later with a small blessing from her predecessor. Finding the boots she had borrowed from Griff Evans too large and uncomfortable, she discovered "a pair of small overshoes, probably left by the Hayden exploring expedition," which she conveniently and happily used, even though they "just lasted for the day."[17]

Aside from assuring that a steady stream of glowing prose poured from both explorers and journalists, Hayden made certain that pictures of the landscape were produced, a practice that characterized

William Henry Jackson's 1873 photograph of Estes Park captured a scene of virtual wilderness. Even though fourteen years had passed since Joel Estes homesteaded this valley, hardly a trace of human habitation is in evidence.

Frontier photographer William Henry Jackson packed his bulky camera equipment throughout the Rockies, recording majestic panoramas on fragile glass plates. (RMNPHC)

most major surveys of the West. The man hired to promote both the West and the Hayden Survey was photographer William Henry Jackson. In late May of 1873 his party of seven men left Denver and headed for Estes Park. There they made their base camp near Mount Olympus, not far from the Evans ranch. In spite of the rainy weather that plagued them, Jackson and his crew tramped into Black Canyon, visited Gem Lake, and wandered into the Bear Lake and Dream Lake regions. Within a few days he managed to capture the essence of the area upon his fragile glass plates. His photography was not only remarkable because he led where thousands upon thousands of camera buffs would follow, but also because of the excellence of the pictures he produced. After a few days, Jackson moved his crew southward, heading toward the mining camp of Ward and other regions of Colorado. In 1874 Jackson toured Middle Park on a similar photographic mission, capturing Grand Lake at that time. William Byers's poignant description was now matched by art. "Imagine a great mirror," Byers had written, "a mile wide and two miles long, bordered all around with thick timber, and beyond that with stupendous mountains, flecked with patches and great fields of snow, except one narrow, scarce noticable notch through which the river escapes, and you have Grand Lake."[18]

While Grand Lake received accolades from the press, a steadily increasing number of fishermen, and summertime visitors, and while Longs Peak brought explorers and climbers, Estes Park itself drew a man who helped to shape the destiny of the entire region. Just after Christmas in 1872, a party of English sportsmen visiting Denver decided to try hunting in the mountains above Estes Park. Leading this band of gentlemen was Windham Thomas Wyndham-Quin, also known as the fourth Earl of Dunraven and Mountearl in the Peerage of Ireland, second Baron Kenry of the United Kingdom, Knight of the Order of St. Patrick, and Companion of the Order of St. Michael and St. George. Aside from being linked to English nobility, the Earl of Dunraven was enormously wealthy. In 1872, at age thirty-one, he already owned forty thousand acres of land and four homes, including Dunraven Castle at Glamorgan. Prior to his Estes Park visit the Earl had traveled widely in Europe, the Middle East, and in Africa. He served in the First Life Guards, was an excellent horseman, and had a nervous energy that led him to become a war correspondent during a conflict in Abyssinia and during the Franco-Prussian War.

He first came to the United States on his honeymoon in 1869, visiting only the East Coast. In the autumn of 1871 he returned to America, this time to venture into the West. The completion of the transcontinental railroad in 1869 made his trip a bit easier. There he hunted elk in the region of the North Platte River under the guidance of Buffalo Bill and Texas Jack Omohondro. Like other English aristocrats who ventured into the wilderness, the Earl traveled in style, even bringing a personal physician, Dr. George Henry Kingsley. The Earl planned to live an adventurous life. As historian Dave Hicks notes, he "enjoyed a good pipe, good liquor, good food, women and sports. But not necessarily in that order."[19]

Once again, in 1872, the Earl of Dunraven returned to hunt, this time in Nebraska, Wyoming, and in Colorado's South Park. While relaxing among the night spots of Denver, the Earl met Theodore Whyte. Mr. Whyte, then twenty-six years old, had arrived in Colorado during the late 1860s. Originally from Devonshire, England, he had trapped for the Hudson's Bay Company for three years and had tried his hand in the Colorado mines. During some of his earlier rambles, Whyte became familiar with Estes Park. Whyte, much like Isabella Bird and the Earl of Dunraven, represents a then developing English interest in the Rockies. This was a distinctly curious generation of people, investigating regions for adventure or excitement as eagerly as Hayden or Powell explored for science.

Dressed in his yachting uniform, the Earl of Dunraven displayed the aristocratic demeanor of a man of wealth and position. Here was a man who nearly succeeded in owning all of Estes Park. *(Estes Park Trail-Gazette)*

In *Westward the Briton*, historian Robert Athearn claims that "the state of Colorado drew more of these curious observers than any other western state or territory. So many of them came to visit, and even to stay, that the state has been called 'England beyond the Missouri.' "[20]

"It was sport," the Earl later recalled, "or, as it would be called in the States, hunting—that led me first to visit Estes Park."[21] Theodore Whyte sang the praises of the area, telling the Earl about the abundance of deer, elk, and bear just perfect for "sport." But very little convincing was necessary. Soon the Earl and a few friends were heading into the foothills, following the crude cattle trail leading toward Estes Park. Once there, they stayed with Griff Evans, another of their countrymen and a man eager to please the nobility of his homeland. In the ensuing days, the Earl hunted elk in Black Canyon, along the Fall River, and in the Bear Lake area.

"Sport" and the mountains themselves combined to impress this well-traveled man. "Everything is huge and stupendous," he observed. "Nature is formed in a larger mould than in other lands. She is robust and strong, all her actions full of vigor and young life."[22]

The attractions of Estes Park brought the Earl back for a second trip in 1873. Its atmosphere proved addicting. "The air is scented with the sweet-smelling sap of the pines," he wrote, "whose branches welcome many feathered visitors from southern climes; an occasional humming-bird whirrs among the shrubs, trout leap in the creeks, insects buzz in the air; all nature is active and exuberant with life."[23] "The climate is health-giving," he argued, sounding much like a local booster, "unsurpassed (as I believe) anywhere—giving to the jaded spirit, the unstrung nerves and weakened body a stimulant, a tone and vigor so delightful that none can appreciate it except those who have had the good fortune to experience it themselves."[24]

At some point during his visits, the Earl decided he would attempt to acquire ownership of all of Estes Park. Fits of greed, after all, strike at most people; many have had similar desires to possess this land, perhaps wishing to exclude others and control it for selfish purposes. But only the Earl of Dunraven had both the wealth and the will to try to buy it. Only a handful of squatters stood in his way and within a few short years the Earl came close to owning everything.

Assisted by his new friend Theodore Whyte and several Denver bankers and lawyers, the Earl first arranged to have the park legally surveyed. Once that formality was accomplished, the Earl and his agents used a scheme, common among other speculators, exploiting the Homestead Law to their advantage. They found local men in Front Range towns willing—for a price—to stake 160-acre claims throughout the park. More than thirty-five men filed claims using this ploy. Then, Dunraven's "Estes Park Company, Ltd." (or the English Company as it was called locally) proceeded to buy all those parcels at a nominal price, estimated at five dollars per acre. Between 1874 and 1880, the Earl managed to purchase 8,200 acres of land. In addition, the Company controlled another 7,000 acres because of the lay of the land and the ownership of springs and streams.

Exactly what the Earl intended for his Estes Park estate is not clear. The most obvious future for the land was its continued use for ranching. At that time Griff Evans herded about a thousand head of cattle there, some of which belonged to two Denver investors. But Griff Evans, just like a number of other homesteaders, quickly traded his land for English cash. The Earl explained his goal simply: "Herbage was plentiful, and cattle could feed all winter, for the snow never lay. It was an ideal cattle-ranch, and to that purpose we put it."[25] Whether it was going to be developed as a private hunting preserve for the exclusive use of the Earl and a few of his English friends was a subject for much speculation and popular debate.

Soon additional plans were announced in the Denver newspapers. In July of 1874, reports came that a sawmill would be built, Swiss cattle were to be introduced, ranching would be expanded, and a hunting lodge would be constructed in Dunraven Glade on the North Fork of the Big Thompson. Theodore Whyte was chosen to serve as the Earl's agent and manager in Colorado.

As soon as the Earl began his effort to acquire and develop Estes Park, a bitterness developed between those settlers who had no intention of selling and leaving and the powerful forces of the English Company. Reverend Elkanah Lamb, for example, had earlier chosen a homesite just east of Longs Peak. He loudly voiced his disgust at those who sold out. "Griff Evans," Reverend Lamb recalled nearly four decades later, "being of a good natured genial turn of mind, liking other drinks than water and tempted by the shining and jingle of English gold, Dunraven very soon influenced him to relinquish his claim and all of his rights in the park for $900." Lamb also believed that the Earl's land-grabbing was fraudulent: "Dunraven picked up men of the baser sort, irresponsible fellows not regarding oaths as of much importance, when contrasted with gold." Those who cooperated with the Earl, according to Reverend Lamb, "prepared to sell their souls for a mess of pottage at the dictation of a foreign lord."[26]

Bitterness led to outright confrontations and violence became inevitable. A man reportedly antagonistic to the English Earl and his scheme was James Nugent, better known as Rocky Mountain Jim. Typical of some frontiersmen, Rocky Mountain Jim had a shady, somewhat mysterious past, so conflicting in detail that it is now impossible for us to construct his tale with accuracy. Isabella Bird took care to describe his looks. "His face was remarkable," she began. "He is a man about forty-five, and must have been strikingly handsome. He has large grey-blue eyes, deeply set, with well-marked eyebrows, a handsome aquiline nose, and a very handsome mouth." Her elaborate description included the fact that half of his face and one missing eye had been repulsively mauled by a grizzly bear only a short time before. "Desperado," she concluded, "was written in large letters all over him."[27] Furthermore, he bore the kind of reputation a mother could easily use to frighten her children.

Like other squatters in the area, Jim trapped for a living and also kept a small herd of cattle. Unlike the others, he controlled some very important real estate: his cabin sat at the head of Muggins Gulch, dominating the main entrance to Estes Park. Ill feelings began developing between Griff Evans and Mountain Jim, probably over the idea of land being sold to the Earl, possibly over Jim's glances toward Evans's teenaged daughter, and perhaps enhanced by liquor in both men. Isabella Bird realized the discord between these two men. "For, in truth," she wrote, "this blue hollow, lying solitary at the foot of Long's Peak, is a miniature world of great interest, in which love, jealousy, hatred, envy, pride, unselfishness, greed, selfishness, and self-sacrifice can be studied hourly, and there is always the unpleasantly exciting risk of an open quarrel with the neighboring desperado, whose 'I'll shoot you!' has more than once been heard in the cabin."[28]

No less than five different versions have been told regarding the shooting of Rocky Mountain Jim. None can be regarded as unbiased accounts, since factions had already formed both for and against the English Company. And Englishmen were involved in the shooting. That shots were fired on June 19, 1874 seems fairly certain; that Griff Evans probably pointed the shotgun and pulled the trigger seems equally true. The immediate cause is a mystery. Reverend Lamb, clearly hostile to the Earl, argued that Jim asked for trouble when he "declined to permit this fraternity of English snobs and aristocrats to pass through his sacred precincts any more, there being at the time no other way in or out of the Park."[29] Dunraven himself presented the killing differently: "Evans and Jim had a feud, as per usual about a woman—Evans' daughter."[30] Dr. George Kingsley, the Earl's physician, described the scene when Mountain Jim came toward the Evans ranch that day in June. "Jim's on the shoot!" someone yelled, hoping to warn Evans. Griff Evans, rudely awakened from a nap, bounded to his feet, grabbed his double-barreled shotgun loaded with "blue whistlers," charged out of the cabin, aimed at Jim, and blasted away. But he missed Jim completely. An associate of the Earl, a Mr. Haigh, then cried, "Give him another barrel!" and Evans obliged. This second blast killed Jim's horse outright and knocked "the great ruffian" to the ground. Five of the "blue whistlers" found their mark in Jim's head.[31]

Jim was down but not dead. In fact, he lived for three more months, lingering with a pellet lodged in his brain. While Jim was being tended by Dr. Kingsley, Evans supposedly rode thirty miles to sign out a complaint against Jim for assault. Later, Evans himself was arrested and charged with the shooting. Mountain Jim remained alive until September, being nursed in Fort Collins but finally dying of his wounds. Evans's trials was not scheduled until

July of 1875 and then the case was speedily dismissed for lack of witnesses. Not surprisingly, the Earl treated the matter of Jim's lingering lightly: "But it is hard to die in the wonderful air of that great altitude . . . and before many weeks had passed he was packed down to the settlements, where some months later he did die." On Evans's escape from trial, the Earl interpreted "the result of the verdict to the effect that Evans was quite justified, and that it was a pity he had not done it sooner."[32]

So it really did not matter whether it was land ownership or a personal squabble that led to Mountain Jim's death; he was conveniently removed from the scene. Jim, after all, was only a minor annoyance. The English Earl had plenty of power to continue with his plans. But the continuing arrival of more settlers by the mid-1870s — people who would dispute English Company claims — helped produce a more realistic plan for Estes Park. Any dreams of a private hunting preserve soon vanished. "I well remember the commencement of civilization," the Earl recalled in 1879. It arrived with "an aged gentleman on a diminutive donkey." The Earl sat enjoying a hot summer's evening on the stoop of a log cabin. There this stranger approached the Earl and asked, "Say, is this a pretty good place to drink whiskey in?" The Earl replied, "Yes" and then continued, "naturally, for I have never heard of a spot that was not considered favorable for the consumption of whiskey, Maine not excepted." So the fellow queried, "Well, have you any to sell?" "No," the Earl replied, "got none."[33]

As the old codger disappeared, "puzzled at the idea of a man and a house but no whiskey," thoughts of building a hotel and catering to a growing public demand for shelter and sustenance must have taken form in the Earl's mind. Ideas about serving travelers in Estes Park were not original with Dunraven. The Estes family assisted the handful of people who visited the region in the 1860s, especially those parties attempting to climb Longs Peak. Mrs. Estes prepared a few meals for guests. Griff Evans continued that sporadic service and even thought about building a hotel in 1871. But Evans opted for smaller, cheaper cabins placed near his own. It was the Earl of Dunraven who decided upon a grander project. In 1876, Colorado attained statehood; perhaps the Earl responded to this vision of a new era with his own view of what progress should bring.

In the autumn of 1876, the Earl again returned to Estes Park, this time bringing the noted artist Albert Bierstadt. The Earl commissioned Bierstadt to paint a large landscape of Estes Park and Longs Peak. Once completed, the Earl reportedly paid Bierstadt $15,000 and the painting was transported to Europe to adorn the

Although cattle ranching was the main enterprise on the Earl of Dunraven's domain, the resort business also received attention. The Estes Park Hotel, called The English Hotel by local residents, began catering to vacationers in 1877. (RMNPHC)

walls of Dunraven Castle. While in the area, Bierstadt was also asked to use his artistic eye to help select a site for the Earl's hotel. Dunraven made his decision and had the wealth to insure speedy construction. By mid-January of 1877, Bierstadt had completed the sketches for his painting and had helped select a hotel site on the eastern side of Estes Park, near Fish Creek. Soon after, work was under way on the building of The Estes Park Hotel, locally called The English Hotel. The lodge opened in the summer of 1877 and the tourist industry of the area entered a new phase.

Within a few fleeting years, Estes Park had changed from a primitive ranching area to the scene of a publicized resort. "The marks of carriage wheels are more plentiful than elk signs," the Earl soon boasted, "and you are not now so likely to be scared by the human-like track of a gigantic bear as by the approaching impress of a number eleven boot." Dunraven believed that the beauties of Estes Park destined it to become a pleasuring ground. "There is plenty of room elsewhere for wild beasts," he argued, "and nature's beauties should be enjoyed by man."[34]

In her own eccentric fashion, Isabella Lucy Bird slipped into Estes Park just before the Earl started bringing progress, before Mountain Jim met his violent death. And, in a way, she became an ideal tourist, not worrying whether there was a fancy hotel available. She stayed at the Evans ranch, renting a small cabin for $8 a week and gamely assisted with the chores, tending cattle when asked to help out. Soon she realized that Griff Evans only appeared jolly; problems plagued him. "Freehearted, lavish, popular, poor Griff loves liquor too well for his prosperity," she observed, "and is always tormented by debt."[35] When she wrote those words, Evans must have already realized that the Earl might become his economic salvation.

During her stay Isabella Bird absorbed everything about life in the mountains. She noted everything new or unusual and did not appear eager to move on. "This is surely one of the most entrancing spots on earth," she wrote.[36] Born in Yorkshire, England, in 1831, much of her early life revolved around her father, an Anglican clergyman. Because she suffered a chronic spinal disease, her father and physicians advised her to travel, hoping she might regain her health. Early in the 1850s she made her first trip to Canada and the eastern United States. She returned in 1857 to study an American revival movement and made a third trip to the East Coast shortly thereafter. It was during her fourth journey to America that she visited the Rockies. Letters home to her sister Henrietta described scenes and adventures so skillfully and dramatically that in 1878 an English weekly, *Leisure Hour*, published them as "Letters from the Rocky Mountains." In 1879, the collection of letters became a book entitled *A Lady's Life in the Rocky Mountains*.

In 1873 Isabella Bird was a "quiet, intelligent-looking dumpy English spinster," according to biographer Pat Barr.[37] Fearlessly,

Isabella Bird sketched a self-portrait, displaying her attire and her horse Birdie as they appeared during her 1873 visit to Estes Park. (From *A Lady's Life in the Rocky Mountains*, by Isabella L. Bird. Copyright 1960 by the University of Oklahoma Press)

she traveled by train to Cheyenne, then by horse and wagon to Longmont, and finally by horseback to Evans's ranch. Primitive travel conditions and seedy hotels found on Colorado's frontier failed to bother her; she delighted in adventure; she enjoyed her escape from the stifling propriety and conventions of her Victorian homeland.

And strangely enough, she delighted in the company of Rocky Mountain Jim. Somehow the demeanor of this desperado enchanted her. "He was very agreeable as a man of culture as well as a child of nature," she noted.[38] Unlike others who openly despised or simply avoided him, she found "his manner was that of a chivalrous gentleman, his accent refined, and his language easy and elegant."[39] His language alone "places him on a level with educated gentlemen, and his conversation is brilliant, and full of light and fitfulness of genius."[40]

Rocky Mountain Jim seemed to be equally enchanted with this English lady. Her civil tongue, if not her simple kindness, must have drawn his attention. Furthermore, women of any type were in short supply on Colorado's frontier. Within a day or two of her arrival, Jim appeared at the Evans ranch and offered to guide Isabella on a climb of Longs Peak. Two young men also staying at the ranch were invited as well.

The four proceeded to timberline on horseback, well stocked with food and supplies by Mrs. Evans. Isabella even borrowed a pair of Griff Evans's boots, regardless of the fact that they were too large. That first night they camped "under twelve degrees of frost, hearing sounds of wolves, with shivering stars looking through the fragrant canopy, with arrowy pines for bed-posts, and for a night lamp the red flames of a campfire."[41]

All the details of Isabella's climb cannot be recounted here, but in her opinion the experience proved quite harrowing. "Never-to-be-forgotten glories they were," she later recalled, "burnt in upon my memory by six succeeding hours of terror." During this struggle, the two young men regarded Isabella Bird as "a dangerous encumbrance," but Jim insisted he would guide no further if they left her behind. Ultimately, she made the summit, even though Jim "dragged me up, like a bale of goods, by sheer force of muscle."[42] While it took terror, difficulty, and "much assistance," to make the climb end in success, few people ever appreciated the conquest more. "A more successful ascent of the Peak was never made," she concluded, "and I would not now exchange my memories of its perfect beauty and extraordinary sublimity for any other experience of mountaineering in any other part of the world."[43]

Climbing Longs Peak apparently strengthened a bond of friendship between Rocky Mountain Jim and Isabella Bird. Many writers have already speculated about the genesis of a romance between the two. Since we can only judge from Isabella's imaginative letters, it is impossible to tell exactly what transpired. She did describe a scene on November 18th when they went for a ride through the Park. "It began on Longs Peak," she reported Jim confessing. And his emotional revelation of being "attached to me" made her terrified. "It made me shake all over and even cry," she told her sister. "He is a man whom any woman might love but no sane woman would marry." Many times the Rockies have been referred to as a romantic setting; Isabella Bird provided a rare his-

In her drawing entitled "My Home in the Rocky Mountains," Isabella Bird displayed Griff Evans's ranch with Longs Peak looming in the distance. This was the scene soon to be acquired by the Earl of Dunraven. (From *A Lady's Life in the Rocky Mountains*, by Isabella Bird. Copyright 1960 by the University of Oklahoma Press)

torical example. But she quickly recovered her composure during this conversation, realizing her feelings for this man could only lead to an impossible future. Rather coldly, she rejected his affection, although admitting, "My heart dissolved with pity for him and his dark, lost, self-ruined life. He is so lovable and fascinating yet so terrible."[44]

Early in December of 1873, Jim accompanied the dauntless Englishwoman back down to the prairie. The temperature was twenty degrees below zero and "the air was filled with diamond sparks."[45] There she caught a stage to Greeley and Mountain Jim was soon left behind. Arriving on the same stage that carried her away came Mr. Haigh, "dressed in the extreme of English dandyism," the man who would play a fateful role in the shooting of Mountain Jim only seven months later. The dandy asked to return with Jim to Estes Park in order to hunt.

Isabella Bird saw Estes Park while it was still a primitive ranch on the verge of becoming a resort. The mountains kept a wilderness flavor. At the same time, she also saw settlers hard at work, struggling to make a living much like the Estes family of a decade before. She also exemplified the casual influx of curious English people coming to Colorado, arriving for adventure and sport. She followed the very footsteps of official government explorers. Longs Peak drew her attention, just as it had attracted Powell and Byers, Hayden and Dickinson. Eventually, her letters helped publicize the area, much like the articles in Byers's *Rocky Mountain News* and the development of Dunraven's hotel. Like the Earl himself, she must have realized that the area was changing rapidly, just like any other frontier newly found. And as a tourist, biographer Pat Barr noted, Isabella Bird became Estes Park's first ideal guest: she told exciting tales, seldom retraced her steps, and what's more, never overstayed her welcome.

4

DREAMS WITH
SILVER LINING

"To the West! To the West! There is wealth to be won."
Charles Mackay, as quoted by F. V. Hayden in The Great West.[1]

ESTES PARK saw a second wave of pioneer settlers arriving during
the mid-1870s and the grip of total English ownership was quickly
challenged. At about the same time a tide of prospectors also began
sweeping across the mountains when tales of hidden wealth struck
men with mineral on their minds. Meanwhile, the hunters,
mountain climbers, and curious tourists continued to wander
about, depending more and more upon the few local settlers for
shelter and sustenance. But within a couple of decades, most of
the prospectors would wander away and subsistence ranchers
would start resorts. Mountain-loving tourists rather than miners
established the principal use for this stretch of Rockies: recreation.

A man who lived through the decades of change after 1875 and
took the time to record his memories before his death in 1943 was
Abner E. Sprague. A dark, handsome fellow then aged twenty-four,
Sprague climbed Longs Peak for his first time in 1874. He and a
partner, Clarence Chubbuck, returned in May of 1875 and proceeded to become squatters on the public domain, building a cabin
in today's Moraine Park (then called Willow Park). Together they
joined a handful of settlers willing to challenge the Earl of
Dunraven's claim to most of Estes Park. Only a month later,
however, Chubbuck was murdered during a cattle roundup out on

the plains. That left Sprague and his sixteen-year-old brother Fred to develop their homestead in the heart of the Rockies.

Having crossed the plains from Iowa to Colorado in a prairie schooner at age fifteen, Abner Sprague was not the first of this new wave of Estes Park settlers. Alexander Q. MacGregor, a lawyer from Wisconsin, saw the park as a profitable business opportunity. He obtained land on the northern fringe of Estes Park around 1874, at the very same time the Earl of Dunraven was attempting to gain full ownership. Meanwhile, Horace Ferguson and his family home-steaded near Marys Lake. J. T. Cleave arrived and would later start a store at the junction of the Fall and Big Thompson rivers early in the 1880s; the site eventually became today's village of Estes Park. Soon these men were joined by half a dozen other pioneer families. Further south, at the base of Longs Peak, a United Brethren missionary, Reverend Elkanah Lamb, established a homestead in 1875. There he rapidly developed a lodge for visitors called the Longs Peak House. He and his son Carlyle began guiding people up Longs Peak for five dollars a trip.

Abner Sprague, his parents, and his brother Fred discovered that their newly claimed land had some drawbacks. Building a cabin from rough-hewn timber became one of their simplest problems; furnishing it with "Carrie Nation furniture" ("made with a hatchet") as Sprague called it, seemed to be even less trouble. By August the family was able to live in reasonable comfort. But then Abner was struck down with "mountain fever," a mysterious ail-ment that kept him in bed for over a month. Home remedies— including warm salt water, doses of tobacco, dashes of ice water, and opium—were given in lieu of proper medical treatment. All failed to produce immediate relief but despite the home medicine, he gradually recovered. That autumn when their parents departed to spend winter on the prairie, Abner and Fred decided to watch over their herd of cattle and spend what proved to be a brutal season in Moraine Park.

On September 22nd, 1875, snow fell to a depth of two feet. Although some nice weather followed, periodic blizzards kept the brothers confined to their cabin, once for a solid two weeks. One day Hank Farrar, a well-known guide and hunter in the region, stopped by and offered to fill the Sprague's larder with some game. Tramping up a nearby ridge, Farrar killed two deer with a single shot. One animal he gave to the grateful Sprague brothers. At that point Abner vowed to purchase a rifle of his own, promising to avoid any future possibility of hunger. Farrar, together with Horace Ferguson, continued the occupation of hunting elk for the Denver market that winter. But by the late 1870s, Sprague recalled, "the

A native of Dundee, Illinois, Abner Sprague came to Colorado in 1864 at age fourteen. He worked as a locating engineer for the Missouri Pacific railroad and later served as Larimer County Surveyor. In 1875 Sprague joined the handful of settlers then claiming land adjacent to the Earl of Dunraven's Estes Park holdings. (RMNPHC)

meat of our wild animals became so cheap in the valley markets, that it did not pay for the haul."[2] Maintaining a food supply continued to be a worry as a volley of blizzards kept coming all winter long. Then cold and windy weather persisted through late spring. The final blizzard of that memorable season started on May 20th, lasted thirty-six hours, and dumped three feet of snow on the region. Regardless of all the hardships, isolation, and harsh weather, Sprague noted that they lost only one cow from their herd of cattle, the rest managing to forage on wind-swept meadows. By June of 1876, Abner Sprague must have wondered whether Moraine Park was such a choice location after all.

At the time Sprague completed his first cabin, the Earl of Dunraven controlled at least six thousand acres of Estes Park land. Settlers such as the MacGregors, Fergusons, James, and Spragues located sections of the park overlooked by the English Company or took advantage of mistaken claims following a hurried survey. Theodore Whyte, manager of the English interests, expected to run five or six hundred head of cattle in the park, using every corner of pasture land, whether it belonged to Dunraven or not. The

Located in scenic Moraine Park, Abner Sprague's homestead proved to be in an ideal location to serve travelers. (RMNPHC)

arriving settlers crimped those plans. As Abner Sprague explained: "Estes Park did not furnish grazing lands sufficient to make the cattle business pay; the settlers confined the company to their own lands by surrounding them with their claims, thus cutting off the larger part of the pasture lands of the region." Whyte also put on the airs of an aristocratic Englishman, building even more resentment among his American neighbors. "Whyte came bringing his race horses, hunters, dogs and guns," Sprague recalled somewhat bitterly, "in fact all the paraphernalia of an English gentleman; for was he not sent here to establish and keep up all the customs and usages of such an estate: purely English, nothing American was supposed to creep in? So it looked to us."[3] The coming of these settlers and the restrictions that they placed on the Earl's domain probably made Dunraven and Whyte change their plans from ranching to developing a resort, The English Hotel.

Sprague claimed that the English Company harassed these "Pioneers of 1875." The company ignored their claims, trying to discourage any permanent residence. Soon after Sprague arrived to homestead in Moraine Park, Whyte and two of his cowboys rode up and ordered them off the land. Sprague and his father stood their ground. They informed Whyte about errors in the company's claims and about the legality of their own. One of the "annoying methods" Whyte then used was to round up his cattle and drive them onto the settlers' land. One day Whyte and his cowboys drove two

The Earl of Dunraven's ranch extended throughout Estes Park and into adjacent valleys. The Earl's cattle grazed everywhere, with friction developing between the monopolistic English landlord and the pioneers of 1875. (Lulabeth and Jack Melton Collection)

hundred head of cattle into the Moraine Park meadow and placed salt there to keep the herd from straying. Sprague simply waited until the Earl's men left and then dispatched his "good shepard dog" after the cattle. The thundering herd arrived back in Estes Park before Whyte and his men had themselves returned. Whyte tried the same trick a second time, but Sprague chased them off once again. He followed the cattle back to Estes Park personally. There he met Whyte and "had it out with him." "We had quite a wordy row," Sprague noted, but the issue was settled. "We had no further trouble with the company stock up our way."[4]

Other settlers were not so fortunate. George I. Bodde, for example, was a German immigrant who homesteaded in 1876 and gained his patent in 1881. His land sat closer to the Earl's main pasture, causing more friction. Bothersome cattle forced Bodde to fence his property. Apparently Whyte had his cowboys rip the fence down and soon the cattle were again grazing across Bodde's land. The German became infuriated, but there was little he could do. When Bodde met Theodore Whyte at a stream crossing a short time later rage gained the upper hand and Bodde grabbed Whyte, prepared to toss him in the creek, but then lost his nerve and released the rascal. Mr. Bodde became the only pioneer to physically vent his disgust at Whyte and the company and their tactics. Shortly thereafter, George Bodde sold out and moved away.

According to Abner Sprague, the English Company expected that

For several decades, herds of cattle roamed where resorts, recreation, and revelry would later predominate. *(Estes Park Trail-Gazette)*

Branding cattle on the Earl of Dunraven's ranch offered his guests a spectacle of the American West. (Lulabeth and Jack Melton Collection)

all the settlers would eventually starve, sell out cheap just like Bodde, and leave all of the park to the Earl. "Perhaps he would have been able to do so," Sprague admitted, "only for the visitors to the Park, who were glad to pay for accommodations while in the Park, and forced us, or most of us, to go into that business."[5]

The exact number of tourists arriving in Estes Park during the summers of the 1870s and 1880s is unknown, yet there is plenty of evidence of the region's growing popularity among vacationers. Among those adventurous travelers, Carrie Adell Strahorn offered us a glimpse into tourist travel in 1878. In her book *Fifteen Thousand Miles by Stage*, she describes riding by stagecoach from Longmont through Lyons and into Estes Park upon a newly improved toll road carved only four years earlier by Alexander MacGregor's Estes Park Wagon Road Company. "The stage ride was one of grandeur," she remembered, "from the very first turn of the wheels, up, up, up, along the zigzag trail until the day was nearly spent. . . ." Her initial impressions of Estes Park, "a veritable Eden," were only enhanced by a lengthy stay centered at the twelve-hundred-acre MacGregor Ranch.[6]

Her "days of exploring" on horseback were highlighted by trips to Lily Lake, Willow (Moraine) Park, and into "the mysterious depths of Black Canyon, with its thick growth of pines and black and gloomy shadows."[7] Hank Farrar served as her party's guide, but his fame briefly waned when he lost the trail upon their return trip from Emma Lake (today's Potts Puddle). Several people in the group became "decidedly uneasy" about spending the night out. But Farrar quickly rediscovered the trail and had the visitors back at MacGregor's shortly after nightfall. Strahorn also noted other tidbits of historical interest: such as making a brief stop at Sprague's for a cool glass of milk, seeing summer cabins and camps dotting the landscape, shooting a few bighorn sheep, spotting the Earl of Dunraven's famed resort, and offering a critique of a camping party from Boston dressed as "reminders of the Aztecs in their barbaric costumes . . . of outlandish design." As was the case with many visitors, Strahorn left the park reluctantly, believing "as we turned our backs upon its enchantments, the sun never shown more brilliantly, the flowers never blossomed more beautifully, and the waters never chanted more hypnotic music, all luring us to stay."[8]

Around 1890, J. S. Flory made a vacation journey into the region slightly different from that of Strahorn's. His observations were reported in *Thrilling Echoes from the Wild Frontier* published in 1893. Flory and his five companions were probably typical campers of their day, quite self-sufficient. They took a two-horse wagon with its canvas cover pulled back in order to view the scenery as

Vacation trips to the mountains became ever more frequent as the nineteenth century progressed, with camping out always popular. (RMNPHC)

they drove. Reasonably well equipped, they took "a camp tent, camp stove, buffalo robes, blankets and other necessary bedding, overcoats, rubbers , umbrellas, boxes and sacks of provisions, cooking utensils, table furniture, guns and ammunition, fishing tackle, feed for our team, picket ropes," as well as other items "too tedious to mention."[9]

Two days were spent traveling from the plains to Elder Lamb's resort. While passing The English Hotel they spotted the Earl "who was out with two ladies riding." Flory tersely noted that "he passes much of his time hunting with his friends." Soon they embarked upon a climb of Longs Peak, camping at timberline. That evening the light of their campfire "attracted to our camp a jack rabbit," Flory observed, making first mention of wildlife, "which served as a target for our camp artillery."[10] A lucky shot dispatched the rabbit, but Flory admitted that he "had a sore arm for the rest of that night owing to the back action of the gun."[11] Longs Peak was surmounted the next day without incident and as they descended they met several other parties heading upward. Returning to Lamb's resort, Flory recalled that "we got some of the best milk and butter we ever tasted," inferring that their climb or the mountain air produced ravenous appetites.[12]

With very few establishments catering to vacationers' needs, turn-of-the-century campers had to be self-sufficient. Occasionally travelers called upon people like the Spragues for a taste of fresh food. (Lulabeth and Jack Melton Collection)

The men quickly retreated to the trout streams of Estes Park. There they began angling with great success, hardly bothered by rainy weather. "What piles of fish around that camp!" Flory exclaimed. "What beauties they were, fresh from those icy waters." Feasting on fish, singing around their campfire, and watching pitch pines shoot sparks at the stars brought their vacation in Estes Park to a successful conclusion. "Oh! how we love to steal awhile away from the busy haunts of the noisy world," Flory said, rationalizing his leisure, "and recuperate our tired brain, revive our weakened energies and then come forth anew to the battle of life."[13] Many campers, climbers, and fishermen who followed Flory's tracks would certainly agree.

Sad to say, despite the pleasures of camping, climbing, and cavorting in these mountains, tragedy visited a few vacationers. On September 23, 1884, Miss Carrie J. Welton, a wealthy young lady from Waterbury, Connecticut, climbed Longs Peak with Carlyle Lamb as her guide. While descending the mountain near the Keyhole she collapsed from exhaustion, imploring Lamb to go for help. When Lamb and a rescue team returned, they found her dead from a combination of exhaustion and exposure. A few years later, on August 28th, 1889, four members of the Stryker family of Tipton, Iowa, father, son, and two uncles, embarked upon a similar climb with Carlyle Lamb again guiding. When on the summit two of the men produced pistols, probably to help celebrate their mountaineering achievement. Soon after, just as they began their descent, a pistol carried in the pocket of the Stryker boy hit a rock and discharged a bullet through his neck. Lamb hurried for help but the boy bled to death on the Longs Peak summit. A long list of grim accidents in these mountains had begun. And tragedies in such a beautiful natural setting seemed even harder to accept since the people involved were pursuing pleasure. The Welton and Stryker deaths of the 1880s were only precursors of dozens of accidents and deaths befalling vacationers either lulled into carelessness or simply unfamiliar with the strains and hazards of mountain travel.

But it was not really the growing influx of tourists or the squabble of settlers with the English Earl that became the major event of this era. Instead, perhaps more symbolic of that era of exploitation was the drama of a mining boom played out on the western side of the Continental Divide. Along the headwaters of the Colorado River, in the mountains north and west of Grand Lake, optimistic prospectors, miners, and speculators thought they had discovered an avenue to wealth—a pattern repeated many times in Western American history. Within the scope of Colorado history the brief excitement on the North Fork is barely worth mentioning; by comparison, strikes at Cripple Creek, Central City, or Leadville led to real, sustained wealth. Yet the bare skeletons of ghost towns along the North Fork, especially the log bones of

An 1889 party visiting Sheep Lake displayed the trappings of civilized travel within a panoramic setting of wilderness. (RMNPHC)

decaying Lulu City, seem to epitomize the Western heritage of mining: hopes and dreams, boom and bust, realities and ruin.

Compared with the changes happening around Estes Park, settlement near Grand Lake had been proceeding at a glacial pace. Indian problems lasting until 1879 helped to discourage permanent settlement. Too many high mountain passes also served to isolate the region, prompting historian Robert Black to term all of Middle Park an "Island in the Rockies." Coming from the east, a road over Rollins Pass was not established until 1873 and became unusable in the wintertime. Although it was located in 1861, Berthoud Pass did not boast a road until 1874, finally providing Middle Park with better connections with Georgetown and civilization. So meanwhile only a handful of hunters, trappers, and prospectors spent much time in the Grand Lake region. A few lonely dreamers struggled with the hope of making Hot Sulphur Springs into a major western spa, but its isolation and the lack of good transportation retarded that scheme.

Hunting for elk rather than for silver or gold seemed to dominate Middle Park life. Ranching appeared to hold the only promise for the future. But all that changed quickly. On July 10th, 1875, prospectors Alexander Campbell and James H. Bourn staked a promising claim and called it the Wolverine. Its ore gave hints of being rich, containing silver, copper, and lead. Word of the strike spread quickly and a rush to the Rabbit Ear Range (today's Never Summer Range) followed.

The Wolverine Mine, like others staked nearby, promised more than it paid. Within a year Campbell and Bourn were forced to sell,

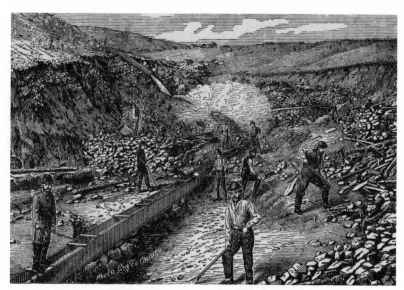

Prospectors saw Colorado's gulches produce gold and its mountains promise a bonanza in mineral wealth. (RMNPHC)

still in debt to a Georgetown grocery firm. That proved to be an ominous precedent for a fledgling mining region. But regardless of low-yielding ore, dozens of footloose prospectors invaded the region.

Famed geologist and explorer Ferdinand Vandiveer Hayden once noted: "The most successful prospectors are those who know comparatively little about minerals." A simple desire to get rich was more important. "Pluck, perserverance, and a pick are the three requisites to success," he cautiously added, "supplemented by pork and provender."[14] Only later did he admit that considerable knowledge of geology and mineralogy might be helpful. Hayden helpfully listed the steps toward a successful discovery. First the prospector must find the "blossom" which indicates some trace or presence of mineral in the vicinity. Next, he "tries to find out where it comes from." If the blossom rock edges are sharp and defined indicating a recent fracture, then "he is satisfied the vein is near at hand." Finding that vein was the final step. Hayden advised men to hunt patiently, "often for a long time," concluding that they might be better off earning three dollars a day as a miner for a surer livelihood.[15]

Thus the prospector became a familiar figure throughout the Front Range and Never Summer Range for decades to follow. From the upper reaches of the Colorado River clear across the Divide all the way to the slopes of Longs Peak, hardly a promising outcrop of rock was ignored. In his book *A Mountain Boyhood*, early Estes Park resident Joe Mills described meeting some of these lonely figures. The slopes of Longs Peak, he reported, were "gophered" by these men who believed they saw favorable traces of gold in the rocks. Mills described meeting "Old Mac," a virtual hermit digging at a dozen claims on Longs Peak. After an initial visit in December, Mills returned the following spring to find the man still alone, still digging. "What sort of a winter have you put in?" Mills asked. Old Mac returned a confused glance. "Winter?" he replied. "It's sure settin' in like it meant business. But I'm plannin' to start a tunnel—I got a rich vein I want to uncover— think come spring I'll have her where somebody'll want to build a mill an'—"

"But you told me you were going to Reno," Mills reminded the fellow.

"Yep; I am, come spring," he replied.

A bit surprised, Mills then asked, "Do you know the date?"

Old Mac gave a sheepish look, "No-o-o, don't reckon I do." And after pondering a few minutes he took a guess, "Must be about Christmas, ain't it?"

Mills noted that it was the eighth of May. "Old Mac was a typical prospector," Joe Mills concluded. "They are all queer, picturesque characters, living in a world of golden dreams, oblivious to everything but the hole they are digging, the gold they are sure to find."[16] Loneliness was an occupational expectation; forgetfulness became a real hazard.

Even forgetting the location of a rich specimen of ore apparently happened more than once. Abner Sprague, in an article entitled "Lost Mines," argued that several rich discoveries had been located with prospectors soon forgetting where the outcroppings or veins appeared. Those deposits were never rediscovered. One fellow, combining a hunting trip with prospecting, stuffed his coat with likely samples of ore. Some months later an assayer told him that one rock was extremely rich in gold, "thousands per ton in fact." But the poor man could never remember where he picked up that blossom. For years he continued to return to Glacier Basin hunting for his lost mine. Among other tales Sprague recounted, one even involved the drawing of a map by a prospector convinced of his success yet breathing his last on his death bed; it detailed a supposedly rich strike on Specimen Mountain. That mineral treasure, like other "lost mines," was never found. But they served to excite the imagination. Overall, it is likely that more prospectors got lost than mines.[17]

So throughout the late 1870s prospectors filtered into the mountains, especially into the Rabbit Ear Range. Promising finds of carbonate ore soon brought many claims. The Wolverine Mine led the way for such strikes as the North Star, the Jim Bourn, the Silent Friend, and the Sandy Campbell. Up neighboring mountains, along gulches and creeks, throughout the upper reaches of the North Fork, the prospectors searched. Quickly added were such cleverly named strikes as Miners Dream, the Ruby, the Cleopatra, the Cross, Hidden Treasure, Living Wonder, Wild Irishman, Excelsior, Silver Queen, Eureka, and several dozen others. In an aura of discovery, optimism and dreams of future riches played dominant roles.

Businessmen in Georgetown and Fort Collins quickly realized that more immediate profits could be made in supplying the new mining region. Improved transportation routes and rudimentary merchandizing followed the miners. Much nearer the center of activity, however, the village of Grand Lake was born. It changed from Judge Wescott's infant resort into a growing village within a few short years. Three hundred and twenty acres were established as a townsite in August of 1879 and by June of 1880 the community could boast thirty-one residents and nine cabins.

Recurrent Indian scares and primitive transportation routes had kept a real boom at bay during the late 1870s. But finally, by 1880, the Utes started leaving and the country seemed safer. One old miner expressed relief: "I am glad to see that the Utes must go, as the rich discoveries now made in our State must, of their natural attractiveness in point of wealth, draw a large and enterprising white population to our State, and drive out the good-for-nothing and unruly savage."[18]

A number of North Fork mines were extensively developed during the early 1880s. Even though mineral-bearing ores were found, their low grade quality clouded the boom with a specter of failure. (RMNPHC)

Added to the good news of the Utes' departure was the knowledge that mines in Colorado's Leadville region contained an enormous amount of silver. Starting in 1877, Leadville's boom revived a general interest in mining throughout the state. As one historian noted: "Wherever the ore resembled the Leadville product there was excitement."[19] Some people believed that carbonate ores found in the strikes along the North Fork could rival booming Leadville. Although containing far less silver, copper, or lead than the ores of Leadville, at least the North Fork mineral offered a promise of greatness. Only two problems appeared to loom over the Rabbit Ears district in 1880: most ores were of poor quality; and a reducing mill would be required for the ore, necessitating great capital investment. In those two hard facts were planted the seeds for the boom's bust.

But into the North Fork streamed dozens, even hundreds, of people. Some were prospectors; many were miners; a few were merchants; all were seriously intent on searching for wealth. Among them were a handful of promoters and speculators. Very few were women. All of Grand County showed a population of 417 in 1880 and by 1883 it was estimated that 2,000 people lived there.

Fortunes imagined as "A Ton of Pure Silver" vanished as soon as investors decided the North Fork mines were worthless. (RMNPHC)

Most of these people had roots elsewhere and many would move on within a year or two, just as soon as other mining booms appeared more promising. The North Fork boom followed a classic Western pattern and people followed predictable paths as soon as dreams of fortune disappeared.

Some men, such as Edward P. Weber, came as representatives of Illinois capitalists. He helped form the Grand Lake Mining and Smelting Company. Among other properties in Bowen Gulch, Weber quickly purchased the Wolverine Mine. He became superintendent of those mines and embarked upon an ambitious program to exploit them. He hired Lewis D. C. Gaskill as a foreman. Well known in the region, Gaskill had helped develop the road over Berthoud Pass only a few years earlier. He was a Civil War veteran, a mining engineer and promoter, a surveyor, an accountant, a man of stability and many talents. Such people as Weber and Gaskill represented a serious effort to probe the mineral wealth of one of the North Fork's most promising prospects. Miners were hired and shafts began to penetrate the mountains.

Meanwhile other men came to establish businesses. Just like the merchants settling at Grand Lake, Al G. Warner built a log cabin at the foot of Bowen Gulch and began offering miners provisions and liquor. Farther up the Gulch, nearer some of the high country mines, a spot named Fairfax appeared. It sported only a double log cabin and served as a post office for the miners from June of 1884 until July of 1885.

Businesses in these key locations spawned schemes among promoters about building towns, finding that real estate speculation could sometimes be just as profitable as mining. Men like Weber were soon developing surveys and plats for potential townsites. At the foot of Bowen Gulch, for example, a town named for Gaskill's hometown of Auburn, New York was planned. Ambitiously drawn to contain 161 blocks each divided into 32 lots, Auburn never became more than a rustic enclave in the wilderness, boasting only a few cabins and a post office called Gaskill.

A more dramatic venture at creating a town began some ten miles farther north. There, with Lead Mountain rising in the west and Specimen Mountain towering on the east, Fort Collins promoters William B. Baker and Benjamin Franklin Burnett created Lulu City. In June of 1879 a party of four prospectors from Fort Collins had wandered up the North Fork, hunting as much for mammals as minerals. There they made two claims on Mount Shipler where there appeared to be rich lodes of silver. Upon their return to Fort Collins, news of their silver strikes stirred considerable interest. Parties of other prospectors, with Baker and

Burnett among them, went to investigate and make claims of their own. Sometime later that summer plans for Lulu City, located in the midst of mining excitement, started to take shape. At the same time Burnett began to seek capital for mining machinery and for the construction of a smelter. Together with a handful of other pioneer prospectors, Baker and Burnett then organized the Middle Park and Grand River Mining and Land Improvement Company, specifically to form Lulu City.

All the details of Lulu City's three-year boom cannot be recounted here. But even a bare outline may demonstrate that this mining camp bore many characteristics of rapid rise and decline so common to our Western mining frontier. According to some reports, Burnett named this budding city after his daughter, supposedly a beautiful, raven-haired lass; she was "the most beautiful girl I ever saw" according to "Squeaky Bob," a man who visited the camp and later developed a resort in the region. By 1880 Burnett and his Improvement Company had a 160-acre townsite astride the Grand (or Colorado) River surveyed and platted. Their plans for Lulu City included 100 blocks each with 16 lots; it was divided by 19 numbered streets and 4 avenues named Howard, Riverside, Trout, and Lead Mountain.

Life around Lulu City, "The Coming Metropolis of Grand County," became ever more hectic throughout 1880 and 1881. Miners' tents dotted the valley and newly built cabins appeared "with crowds of people and the bustle and bang of hammers and saws."[20] Two hundred men were reported to be prospecting and mining on the slopes nearby. "Miners are busy doing assessment work on their claims," one observer noted. "Blasts can be heard at any time of the day from mines in hearing of Lulu City."[21] By July of 1880 a number of businesses catering to the miners had already taken root. The Burnett brothers ran a butcher shop; a real estate agency and mining exchange appeared, with city lots selling briskly; a hotel, a general store or two, and some forty houses testified to the activity of the construction business. Two saw mills ran day and night. By 1881 a clothing store, a barber shop, an assay office, and several grocery, hardware, and liquor stores supplied miners' needs, along with a dairy, offering butter and milk from twenty cows herded in from Denver.

"There is level land for a population of from 3,000 to 5,000 people," read a booster's report, in case anyone was worried that Lulu City was filling up too quickly. But all the businesses and business of town-building seemed to overshadow the produce of the mines. "The great need of Lulu to-day," noted the Fort Collins *Express* of July 1881, "is men with enough money to dig down in

Prospectors proved to be a transient breed, many living in tents while only a few bothered to build cabins. Mining camps such as Lulu City could boast of a population of several hundred people, but none were permanent residents. (RMNPHC)

the ground; men with enough money to go there and work a year or perhaps two years, need not, I think, be afraid of the result."[22] Getting men to invest either time or money, however, proved far more difficult than writing optimistic reports.

If a person actually believed every newspaper story about Lulu City or the future prospects of the rest of the North Fork mining regions during the 1880s, a tale of its rapid decline would seem shocking. Nearly every report offered promises of "immense richness" and a booming future, if not at Lulu City then at Gaskill. A report from the Wolverine, a bellwether mine, in April of 1880 assured 350 ounces of pure silver and $40 worth of gold per ton of ore. Many other mines offered accounts noting similar yields. Evidence of wealth seemed to insure continued development of both the Campbell Mining District around Bowen Gulch and the Lead Mountain Mining District around Lulu City.

To miners, isolation was only a minor problem soon to be overcome; it was expected that new roads soon would be built. A road north from Grand Lake through Lulu City and on to the mining camps of North Park was projected, and in fact commerce came in 1880 from a toll road built by S. B. Stewart linking Lulu City with Fort Collins by way of Teller City in North Park and the Cache la Poudre route. Later, Lulu City boasted three stagecoaches per week coming from the distant plains and two per week from Grand Lake. Georgetown and Fort Collins merchants both vied for the North Park trade, and wagons filled with supplies rumbled toward Lulu. City lots continued to sell at between twenty and fifty dollars each. There was even talk of building railroads into the area.

Wintertime came with a force strong enough to curb the boom's momentum. Travel nearly stopped. Many miners, seeking warmer climes, deserted their claims. Roads and trails soon became impassible and the region's isolation increased. Among all the strikes, only ten mines were active during the winter of 1881–1882. Work slowed in even the richest claims such as the Tiger, owned by pioneer Joseph L. Shipler. Only in the Eureka, the Bonanza, "which turns out some of the finest looking ore in Colorado," in the Godsmark brothers' Triumph, and in a handful of others did miners keep busy during those months of loneliness, blizzard, frost, and avalanche.[23] Mines worth all that trouble, toil, and sweat were eventually supposed to satisfy everyone with a decent yield. Certainly then Grand County would prove itself rich to those "who never believed there was anything here but Utes, a few damphools and jack rabbits."[24]

Ore began piling up at the mouths of many mines. Mine owners could not make a profit on low yielding ores if they had to transport tons of rock sixty miles or more to the nearest concentrating mill. All the optimistic talk about silver, lead, copper, and gold, carbonates and sulphurates, millions of dollars in hidden mineral wealth, all centered on those growing piles heaped near the mines. At one point the Wolverine miners claimed to have a thousand tons ready for processing. But building a smelter cost too much and investors were in short supply. For a while, miners kept on blasting and digging. They were not easily discouraged and were convinced a concentrator was coming.

The summer of 1882 saw the boom continue, but by the end of the season people admitted that little profit would ever be seen unless a smelter was built. "The long-looked-for and many-times-promised smelter," one caustic writer noted, had not been built that year and put a real "damper" on further mining in the region. Then, in April of 1883, the famed Wolverine mine was shut down and its crew of miners laid off. Enough ore sat waiting, but some people believed that E. P. Weber and his company closed their mine merely to trigger a depression in local mine values. Some thought that the company planned to acquire more mines before building the smelter. Ore of low quality, however, was really the basic issue. And it is quite likely that Chicago investors finally tired of pouring

In the decades following Lulu City's decline, only crumbling cabins remained as evidence of the North Fork boom. (RMNPHC)

cash down ill-producing holes. Regardless of whether work on the Wolverine stopped, smaller mining operations continued during 1883. When winter arrived once again, the mines were abandoned. By December of 1883 Lulu City finally lost its mainstay, J. R. Godsmark, who left to winter at Grand Lake. The boom had ended and Lulu City began to decay.

For a few years it looked like the boom would simply shift elsewhere in the North Fork. Sometime in the early 1880s, for example, Lulu City spawned yet another mining camp called Dutch-town. But Dutchtown, located at timberline high on the flanks of Lead and Cirrus mountains, hardly sat in an ideal site for expansion. It merely served as home for a number of former Lulu City residents no longer welcome there because of an evening's drunken brawl. "Some of the more peaceful citizens of Lulu City were pretty badly damaged," read one account, "including one woman who came out of the fracas with a broken arm, one man with several broken ribs, and one fellow lost an eye."[25] Dutchtown owed its existence to a handful of miners sentenced by brute force into exile. These unruly miners stuck with their Dutchtown camp through 1884 and then their cabins too were vacated.

The tiny settlement of Gaskill, close to Bowen Gulch, and the Wolverine Mine held on for a year or two longer than Lulu City. Boosters argued that this was the spot that would keep on growing, although its population never exceeded fifty. Some of Lulu's businessmen settled there, but most left after a year or two. Gaskill faded as hope for a smelter disappeared and as work on the mines finally stopped. By late 1886, Gaskill joined Fairfax, Dutchtown, and Lulu City as a site of abandoned mines, rotting cabins, and faded dreams.

One town not fading from the map was Grand Lake. The mining boom helped make it a supply center as well as a transportation link to Georgetown. It also gained status as a recreation site for men grown weary of work in the mines. Fishing, boating, and swimming entertained the miners by day; dinners, dancing, and drinking entertained them by night. According to historian Robert Black, a number of hostelries appeared in the early 1880s. Foremost among them were The Grand Lake House, offering "Spring Beds, Mattresses and Everything," as well as The Garrison House and The Fairview House.[26] Grand Lake grew in population and in popularity; its citizens numbered 31 in 1880 and had increased to some 300 by 1883. Catering to both the miners and its own growing population, a variety of businesses took permanent root.

Mining activity brought prosperity to Grand Lake, but prosperity produced a touch of haughtiness. Those living around Grand Lake argued that their new town, growing rapidly and seen as the center of excitement, should also become the county seat. For them, Hot Sulphur Springs lay too far west, too distant from the growing population of the North Fork or North Park mines. In 1880 petitioners requested an election on the issue and the November results showed 83 votes for keeping Hot Sulphur Springs as the county seat and 114 in favor of growing Grand Lake. These election results were immediately disputed, fostering bitterness that went

The settlement of Grand Lake prospered during the mining era as the village catered to miners' needs, especially in the form of rest and recreation. (Colorado Historical Society)

Grand Lake's jaunty western image was tarnished by the Fourth of July shoot-out and by the failing North Fork mining district. (RMNPHC)

went well beyond the scope of a friendly rivalry. Political squabbling continued over the next several years, eventually culminating in one of Grand Lake's most infamous and tragic events: the shoot-out of July 4th, 1883.

The bloody incident at Grand Lake hardly fits any Hollywood script of classic gunplay between good guys and bad. It resulted from a web of discord too complex, too enmeshed in personalities and political infighting, too entangled in years of feuding and bitterness to satisfy our perceptions of a classic, western shoot-out. Many of the facts surrounding the incident remain debatable, so a bare outline must suffice. On the morning of July 4th, shortly after eight-thirty, Edward P. Weber, superintendent of the Wolverine Mine and a county commissioner, set out walking from The Fairview House with two associates, fellow commissioner Barney Day and Captain Dean, the county clerk. The three strolled along the west shore of Grand Lake heading for town. When only a few minutes away from the hotel, they heard the report of a rifle. Weber cried, "Oh! I am shot!" Day and Dean immediately caught hold of Weber, assisting him as he fell to the ground. Just then several masked men jumped from their hiding spots in a nearby clump of trees, unleashing a hail of bullets at Day and Dean. Barney Day was hit but he pulled his revolver, shot and killed one of the assailants at close range, a fellow wearing a cloth mask with holes cut for mouth and eyes. Then he wounded another attacker before falling dead himself. Quickly the ambushers withdrew, heading through the woods where horses had been tied, and made their escape.[27]

Some folks thought the gunshots were merely part of the local Fourth of July celebration, fireworks and shooting being commonly heard. The reality of a deadly shoot-out came, however, as people saw Weber groping his way back toward The Fairview House. Only then did people rush to the scene. There Barney Day was found dead. Captain Dean, like Weber, had been mortally wounded. They unmasked the dead assailant and found it was John G. Mills, a Teller City attorney and the leader of a political clique opposed to Weber. Later, someone recalled Mills saying, "We are going to give Weber a little scare and scare him so good he will have to get out of Grand County for good and never come back!"[28] Only much later did the mystery of Mills's colleagues in crime become evident, although the exact number has always been in dispute. Some have argued that Mills had eight associates; others claimed that only two or three helped with the killings. Charles Royer, a much admired sheriff, and William Redman, his Grand Lake deputy, were both implicated. Redman simply disappeared. Royer turned up in

Hot Sulphur Springs later that same day, his horse well lathered. In the days that followed, Royer faced the obvious questions about his behavior. Only seventeen days after the ambush, the Georgetown *Colorado Miner* carried the headline, "More Blood: Charley Royer Blows His Brains Out In Georgetown. . . ."[29] Royer had committed suicide, apparently after telling a friend that he could not live with a murder on his conscience. The elusive William Redman was finally found murdered in October, at least according to one report, after being tracked by a relentless killer. That death brought the bloody toll in Grand Lake's shoot-out to six—three county commissioners, a county clerk, a sheriff, and a deputy.

Because of the shoot-out, Grand Lake's reputation suffered a setback. Violence and gore proved to be poor advertising for a brand new town. "For a decade," wrote local historian Nell Pauly, "Grand Lake tried to recover from the embarrassing damage caused by this tragic occurrence which was not the fault of any of its inhabitants."[30] Political bloodshed combined with poorly producing mines in the North Fork helped to curb Grand Lake's boom. Growth tapered off. By 1886 almost all mining in the North Fork had stopped. Gaskill and the other camps were abandoned; the miners moved elsewhere. A declining, shifting population also meant that the contested county seat was removed from Grand Lake and returned to Hot Sulphur Springs in 1888—and without a fight. Life around Grand Lake quieted down. Catering to fishermen and summer visitors rather than to miners became its major prospect for the future.

Over on the other side of the mountains, the 1880s saw Abner Sprague developing his ranch in Moraine Park. Like his contemporaries, however, he had also been bitten by the prospecting bug. He told of meeting men such as M. B. V. Gillette and John Baker as they returned from Lead Mountain filled with stories of newly discovered mineral wealth. He decided to join them when they headed back for the North Fork. Always afoot, he had to trudge for miles. He told of being forced to camp in a snowbank on Trail Ridge for two days as a blizzard swept across; he described making snowshoes out of pine. He carried forty-pound packs, killed mountain sheep for food and suffered severe snow blindness. Yet all his pains seemed to pay when he finally located a promising ledge of mineral. Only a short time later his claim was jumped by two rough characters, but Sprague and his partner were successful in defending their rights, armed only with geologists' hammers. Later, offering a share in the mine, Sprague hired a miner to dig a 100-foot tunnel to test the claim. "There was too much rock and not enough

By the 1890s, Abner Sprague and his wife Alberta understood that their Moraine Park ranch displayed promise as a resort as more people came to visit. (RMNPHC)

mineral," he concluded.[31] "All hopes of a fortune were soon dispelled."[32]

Like other disappointed prospectors, Sprague returned home, accepting life without quick riches. His Moraine Park ranch gradually proved to be more profitable as it catered to summer visitors. Eventually its thousand acres became one of the best-known guest ranches in the central Rockies. In 1904 Abner Sprague sold his Moraine Park homestead to J. D. Stead. Sprague then developed a smaller resort in Glacier Basin and remained a pioneer in both ranching and the resort industry. Sprague took pride in the progress of the area as a popular resort; in the 1930s he considered it an honor to be one of the first to purchase an entrance permit for Rocky Mountain National Park. In 1936 Sprague's old homestead was sold to Will and Myra Lewis and in 1950 Edgar and Dorothy Stopher took over the ranch. In 1962 the National Park Service acquired the land. Eventually, all the buildings were destroyed and Abner Sprague's Moraine Park ranch land was returned to the way he first found it. Once Sprague's generation disappeared, most dreams with silver lining went with them.

Until his death in 1943, Abner Sprague remained one of Estes Park's pioneers, both in terms of ranching and the resort industry. (RMNPHC)

5

FOR THE BENEFIT
AND ENJOYMENT
OF THE PEOPLE

"From the wilderness the traveler returns a man, almost a superman."
Enos Mills, in Your National Parks (1917)[1]

THE DAY marked a milestone. Some two or three hundred people gathered in Horseshoe Park to celebrate. There a panorama of spectacular mountain scenery provided photographers with a dramatic backdrop as they recorded the occasion. Automobiles, horseback riders, and a motorcycle or two formed a haphazard circle around the crowd. Above them fluttered a banner reading "ROCKY MOUNTAIN NATIONAL PARK—DEDICATION, SEP. 4, 1915." People stood ready to hear a handful of dignitaries offer appropriate remarks. Men from Washington, D.C. mingled with state officials, testifying that another slice of Colorado now deserved greater national attention. Five-minute speeches from each official kept the ceremony brief; people applauded; everyone sang the national anthem; photographers snapped their shutters. Cameras caught the bewhiskered F. O. Stanley, inventor of the Stanley Steamer automobile and a leading Estes Park citizen, as he gallantly posed with a tiny American flag. Seen next to Stanley was the man serving as master of ceremonies that day: Enos Abijah Mills. Mills wore a serious expression, seemingly unable to crack a smile. Perhaps his solemn demeanor betrayed the hard work that led to that moment. For years he had been at the center of the fight to create Rocky Mountain National Park; he had written more than 2,000 letters and given 42 lectures promoting the park idea; he had provided 430 photographs and penned 64 newspaper and magazine articles, all to promote the cause. Somber as he looked, Mills must have relished his victory. But that day was more than a personal

With a somber expression bare-headed Enos Mills stands beside the successful entrepreneur of Estes Park, F. O. Stanley (holding flag). Joining them at the September 4, 1915 dedication ceremony for Rocky Mountain National Park were national park publicist Robert Sterling Yard (next to Mills), Congressman Ed Taylor (next to Stanley), Mrs. John D. Sherman of the National Federation of Women's Clubs, and Governor George Carlson. (RMNPHC)

triumph. For in dedicating a park to future generations, that crowd of people really marked the end to an era of pioneering.

Enos Mills and his generation had watched the frontier pass away. Before their eyes the West changed from being truly wild to a reasonably civilized condition. Mills could stand there on that September day in 1915 and look back over thirty years' experience in these mountains. During the 1880s he had lived in its raw wilderness. By 1915 wilderness had become something to cherish rather than conquer. And like the West, thirty years' time had changed Mills too. In both Enos Mills and in Colorado, ideas leading toward preservation developed slowly.

The 1880s taught men that mineral wealth had to be found elsewhere. In that regard the mountains from Longs Peak to the Never Summer Range proved to be poor. A few people still believed that cattle raising could be profitable, but more serious stockmen used the expansive Great Plains and not restrictive mountain parks. Certainly timber could be harvested, but mines and boom towns had failed and most lumbermen moved their sawmills closer to their markets. Hunting became ever more difficult as bear and elk started to become scarce. Only people seeking the pleasures of summer pastimes appeared to be encouraged by what they discovered. Fishermen, mountain climbers, and other summer visitors continued to invade the Estes Park and Grand Lake regions, returning each season in increasing numbers and with increasing regularity. Summer cabins and camps had become commonplace by the Gay Nineties.

For nearly a decade, Enos Mills had acted much like the rest of those summertime visitors. He was born near Fort Scott, Kansas on April 22nd, 1870, the son of a farmer. Ill health plagued him as a child and any future as a farmer became unrealistic. He needed a healthier climate. His parents had been to Colorado before, joining the gold rush in 1859, only to return to Kansas. But apparently they remembered the beautiful mountain scenery and the healthful mountain air. They encouraged young Enos to strike westward on his own in 1884. So the fourteen-year-old Mills visited Fort Collins, found work on a ranch, and, later that summer, helped trail a herd of cattle to the very base of Longs Peak for Carlyle Lamb. The Rocky Mountains quickly captured Enos Mills's attention.

He soon found employment that allowed him to stay in the area, working at the Elkhorn Lodge run by W. E. James. Wintertime forced him to leave Estes Park, however, and he found work as a cowboy out on the plains. In 1885 he returned and began helping around Lamb's Ranch as Carlyle Lamb catered to people intent upon climbing Longs Peak. Like others enchanted by this region's beauty, Mills decided almost immediately that he wanted to own some land and build a cabin. He spotted a site across Tahosa Creek from Lamb's Ranch, claimed it, and started constructing what he called his "Homestead Cabin." At about the same time, Carlyle Lamb introduced him to Longs Peak. That summer Mills made his first climb. The impression of that ascent was indelible. Over the years he would repeat that ascent over 250 times. Watching Carlyle Lamb must also have made him consider a career as a climbing guide. Over the next few summers, Mills completed his log cabin and began working as a guide for the Lambs. Each winter he would wander, earning money as a cowboy or even as a miner. Like other westerners of his time, Enos Mills "was a curious mixture of the wanderer and the home-lover."[2] His roaming eventually took him to Butte, Montana, a booming mining center of that era. There, during the late 1880s and throughout the 1890s, mining became his trade. Summers he guided tourists; winters found him working for good wages deep in the Montana mines.

A native of Fort Scott, Kansas, Enos Abijah Mills first came to Estes Park at the age of fourteen. He fell in love with the Longs Peak area, later acquired land there, and eventually became a major spokesman advocating the preservation of the region. (RMNPHC)

Just like the pioneers before him, Enos Mills's initial reaction to this country was to possess it, to use it, to build a cabin, and to own it. In fulfilling that desire, Mills was typical of his era. In fact, the 1890s saw many men looking at Colorado's mountains not for their scenic value, but for their practical use. It was a time when the resources of the West faced full exploitation. Farmers living out on the parched plains east of the Rockies eyed the snowy summits, seeing not only dramatic vistas but water waiting to melt. Their soil was rich, but their prairie was dry, averaging only

Surveyors followed the contours of western slope mountains, charting the course canals or ditches would run as they diverted streams and melting snow into eastern drainages. (RMNPHC)

Below: Gangs of workers using picks and shovels built mile after mile of the Grand Ditch, a diversion project that eventually spanned 14.3 miles in length. The Grand Ditch was just one of many such water conservation projects developed throughout these mountains. (RMNPHC)

fifteen inches of rainfall or less each year. Projects to store or divert water for irrigation began with the farmers who followed the Fifty-Niners. The only force fighting the farmers was gravity. Nature inclined much of that Rocky Mountain water to flow westward; it was lost to farmers around Fort Collins, Greeley, and a dozen other communities where agriculture had prospered with irrigation. All along the Front Range reservoirs and canals were constructed. Dams and diversion projects directed the water more where men needed it than where nature intended it to flow.

Building the Grand Ditch reflected this effort to divert water for agriculture. According to historian D. Ferrel Atkins, this project was one of the largest of all the early engineering efforts to divert water from the western slope and send it eastward. La Poudre Pass in the northwest corner of today's Park at an elevation of 10,175 feet above sea level was seen as a perfect focal point for diversion canals. According to the plan, water from melting snow could be caught in ditches carved along the contour of the mountainsides. Those canals could be angled slightly downward toward La Poudre Pass. Once those canals emptied their liquid cargo into Long Draw Creek, the eastern flow of the Cache la Poudre River would do the rest. With that basic plan in mind, the Larimer County Ditch Company was formed in 1881. Work got underway and on October 15, 1890 the first diverted water moved across La Poudre Pass heading east.

Progress on extending the Grand Ditch proceeded slowly, while the number of farms increased and the demand for irrigation water grew more intense. The 1890s saw increased efforts by a number of companies to compete with the Larimer County Ditch Company. For a few years, competing survey crews worked across the slopes to the south of La Poudre Pass and a "water war" seemed to be in the offing. But ultimately the Water Supply and Storage Company of Fort Collins, the successor to the Larimer County Ditch Company, gained ownership and construction rights. Efforts to extend the Grand Ditch began in earnest. Slowly its earthen canal, some twenty feet wide and six feet deep, snaked outward from La Poudre Pass along the contours of the eastern flank of the Never Summer Range. A second and shorter canal called Specimen Ditch captured water along the northwestern side of Specimen Mountain.

Building and extending the Grand Ditch became the main effort. Each summer season from 1894 onward men cut into the slopes with picks and shovels and moved rocks and dirt with wheelbarrows. Several construction or "ditch" camps were built at spots beside the canal. Teams of Japanese workers were employed, hiring on as "companies" rather than as individuals. Similarly, other companies of ditch diggers were also hired, ready to perform this rigorous labor. The willingness of these people to live and work in such an isolated region and the primitive nature of their shelter and food helped set them apart from other workers. Toil at elevations above ten thousand feet above sea level also set the whole project apart from normal construction efforts.

Across the slopes above decaying Lulu City came this growing furrow marking man's newer demands upon nature. Gradually the crews worked their way westward to Bennett Creek, then past Lady Creek, on to Lulu Creek, beyond Sawmill Creek, to Little Dutch Creek and Middle Dutch Creek. The Grand Ditch captured more water each year. By 1904 Big Dutch Creek had been reached. By

Running like a scar across the Never Summer Range, the Grand Ditch demonstrated the urgent need for irrigation water on Colorado's arid eastern plains. (RMNPHC)

1911 Lost Creek, Mosquito Creek, and Opposition Creek were all included. Then for a few years work was intermittent or merely maintenance. It was not until September of 1936 that machinery helped complete the 14.3-mile canal ending at Baker Creek.

Visually, the Grand Ditch made a 14.3-mile scar while the Specimen Ditch was largely concealed from public view. Although both projects "stole" water from the Grand (later Colorado) River, demands for water simply outweighed any concern about unsightliness or the disruption of natural watercourses. Future problems caused by dumping water into unnatural drainages, erosion, scarring, landsliding, seepages, and other damages created by such an ambitious project were largely ignored until the 1960s, when critics began expressing concern. Clearly, aesthetics were less important than water in the 1890s. Getting water for farms meant that nature must yield. Water remained something to be diverted, dammed, stored, sold, and used. The mountains could not escape being surrounded by arid land and ambitious men who intended to make that land produce. For these mountains, the Grand and Specimen ditches merely marked the beginning of water projects.

While Enos Mills, Carlyle Lamb, and a few other landowners eked out a living, they began to see the mountains a bit differently than the ditch diggers. Meeting people bent on recreation taught these pioneers a basic lesson: the mountains also produced pleasure. One of the people Mills and Lamb met during the late 1880s was Frederick H. Chapin of Hartford, Connecticut. He was a member of the Appalachian Mountain Club and he had already climbed in Europe. While certainly not the first mountain climber to enter the Rocky Mountain National Park region, he was an effective writer and a popularizer. Tales of his climbs up Longs Peak, Mummy Mountain, and Ypsilon appeared in *Appalachia*, a journal of the Appalachian Club. A well-known national magazine, *Scribner's*, also published Chapin's accounts. His book, *Mountaineering in Colorado*, was published in 1889 and began to turn the attention of other mountain climbers and sportsmen toward the Rockies. His photographs, adventures, portraits of wildlife, glaciers, flowers, and natural grandeur, all made the Rocky Mountains rival the Alps of Switzerland. His criticism that "the first difficulty which presents itself to the mountaineer in Colorado is the lack of guides" must have been heard by Enos Mills, then in his late teens.[3] Though Chapin could kill a bear just for fun or shoot seven ptarmigan while descending Mummy Mountain, he could also wax ecstatic about the sights seen from summits or the "dancing flames" of a campfire. Chapin brought an attitude of enjoyment without possession, a simple sense of appreciation. Chapin and visitors like him may have sparked a sense of aesthetics in people such as Lamb and Mills. At the very least, the sport of mountaineering had officially arrived. "The lover of high mountain ascents finds a good field for novel expeditions throughout the range," Chapin concluded, and people came to follow his lead.[4]

While Chapin climbed, Lamb catered, and Enos Mills completed his cabin and pondered Longs Peak, greater forces were in motion well beyond the horizon of Estes Park or Grand Lake. The idea of conservation began to take shape, nearly ready to invade the region

People seeking pleasure or a respite from economic pursuits and daily toil discovered sport and adventure in the mountains. (RMNPHC)

and alter its future. By the 1890s Americans realized that a line of frontier settlement could no longer be drawn on a map: our pioneering population had finally scattered all the way across the country. Formerly considered limitless, land itself gradually seemed more precious. Forests, minerals, grazing land, and water could no longer be considered abundant, free for the taking. Years of advancing into the wild West, years of homesteading and conquering the wilderness were ending. Giving people easy access to timber, wildlife, water, and other resources in the public domain came to be questioned. Laws regulating the use of public lands had to be refined. Many practices common to frontier life were now defined as abuses. People realized that lumbermen stole timber from land they never owned; forests had been recklessly cut from Maine to California; reforestation hardly existed; stockmen ruined the range, herding too many cattle upon it; rampant logging brought erosion and flooding; forest fires raged unchecked; miners dumped tailings helter skelter. Following an era of exploitation, a few people reacted, perhaps as a national conscience, expressing concern for the future of the land.

Natural resources seemed unlimited to most people in the nineteenth century. Only a handful of visionaries urged conservation when abundance ruled the day. (RMNPHC)

Earlier naturalists and philosophers offered plenty of intellectual leadership for developing an attitude of land protection. Men such as Henry David Thoreau and Ralph Waldo Emerson were often quoted as leaders of this new consciousness. "Nowadays," Thoreau had written in his essay "Walking," "almost all of man's improvements, so called, as the building of houses and the cutting down of the forest and of all large trees, simply deform the landscape, and make it more tame and cheap."[5] Nature had a champion. Emerson suggested that rather than simply chop and saw, people should study and enjoy the forest. "Here is sanctity," he wrote in "Nature," "which shames our own religions, and reality which discredits our heroes. Here we find nature to be the circumstance which dwarfs every other circumstance, and judges like a god all men who come to her."[6]

A bevy of similar advocates followed Thoreau and Emerson. Concerned spokesmen such as John Muir of Yosemite, Interior Secretary Carl Schurz, forester Franklin B. Hough, naturalist John Burroughs, and President Theodore Roosevelt all helped draw national attention to the need for better management of the nation's natural bounty. Later these proponents of wise management were termed "conservationists" and called for a much sounder, careful management of public lands. For example, efforts to regulate hunting and fishing through limits, laws, and licenses were initiated in many states. An honest concern about rapidly disappearing forests and endangered watersheds led to the establishment of the American Forestry Association in 1875. That generation also saw efforts at preservation, with unique natural spots such as Yosemite Valley granted protection in 1864 and Yellowstone National Park set aside from settlement in 1872. Conservationists began to urge that dozens of other natural features be protected, suggesting sites as diverse as Niagara Falls and Mount Rainier. Congress, however, acted with random wisdom. Public pressure took time to build. In 1881 a Division of Forestry finally appeared in the Department of Agriculture and in 1886 Congress finally granted it ten thousand dollars to help curb forestry abuses.

On March 3rd, 1891, Congress passed one of its many bills attempting to revise and reform land laws. Somewhat more by fluke than foresight, that bill contained a minor section allowing the president to "set apart and reserve . . . public land bearing forests. . . ." Conservationists had lobbied hard for a power to "reserve" certain lands with the idea of protecting them. Influenced by an attitude of urgency, President Benjamin Harrison wasted no time; he set aside the Yellowstone Forest Reserve in Wyoming on March 30th, 1891. The tempo of conservation increased. By 1892, a total of 15 reserves protected some 13 million acres of forest, at least on paper.[7] Four of those reserves were in Colorado, with the White River Plateau Forest Reserve being created first on October 16th, 1891. Eventually the Estes Park and Grand Lake regions caught the attention of conservationists. On May 17th, 1905, President Theodore Roosevelt extended Wyoming's Medicine Bow Forest Reserve southward into Colorado, a reserve that included the land of today's Rocky Mountain National Park. In July of 1910 that section of the Medicine Bow Reserve in Colorado became the Colorado National Forest. Later, in 1932, it was renamed the Roosevelt National Forest. But names, boundaries, and legislative protection meant little until 1897 when Congress finally appropriated $75,000 for administration of these forests by a Forest Reserve Service. Rangers began their patrols, but they had no police power; rules and regulations to stimulate a climate of conservation had a force of law, but they were rarely enforced. During the 1890s many westerners could be described as "wholly antagonistic" to the entire idea of reserves. And the people of Colorado were no exception.

As historian G. Michael McCarthy demonstrates in *Hour of Trial*, conservation in Colorado proved to be somewhat controversial between 1891 and 1907. As long as forest regulations went unenforced, the temper of protest remained in check. But after 1897, with the congressional appropriation funding enforcement, with rangers patrolling the lands, with stockmen finally required to obtain permits to graze their cattle on public land, with lumbermen and miners facing restrictions, only then did protests against the Forest Reserves grow louder. McCarthy offers a typical example of this early backlash with the remarks of spokesman H. H. Eddy in 1892. "The aesthetic Eastern people [who] are not interested in the country," Eddy argued, "will plaster the West with reservations that will retard and cripple the hardy pioneers."[8]

The idea of conservation hardly appealed to hardy pioneers busy extracting their livelihood from the soil or from grazing land. Similarly, hunters, loggers, and miners believed the government was interfering with their right to nature's bounty. (RMNPHC)

In the minds of many westerners, conservation and forest reserves meant locking away any chance for economic growth. Settlers and miners saw free use of timber and water as essential to their lives. For decades it seemed the government encouraged people to come West, to settle and develop the land. Now it appeared as if the government had shut the door, putting resources they needed out of reach. Yet forest reserve policies, issued in 1897, looked quite reasonable. Prospecting and mining were allowed to continue; water for irrigation and other useful purposes could still be taken; livestock could still graze upon forest land, although permits were required and sheep were forbidden; and timber could be cut. The goals were simple: end destructive abuses and stop waste. But it was not a more lenient set of rules that Westerners demanded, they wanted freedom from all regulation. Arriving rangers symbolized interference.

Regardless of objections, the forces of conservation grew stronger. Even in Colorado some agreed that the Federal Government had to assume control. "I think," said William N. Byers of the Colorado State Forestry Association, "that the general government is the only authority that can protect the public forests."[9] Similarly, Enos Mills's interest in conservation started to develop in the late 1880s with his ascent of Longs Peak. According to his biographer, he also spent long winter hours in the library at Butte, satisfying a growing appetite for natural history and the literature of travel. The works of Dickens, Parkman, Huxley, Darwin, Spencer, and Ingersoll all cultivated his interest in popular scientific and philosophic notions. But even more important to his development was his enthusiasm for travel. A fire in the Butte mines in 1889 set him free to explore sections of the West he had not seen before. During a trip to California he met John Muir. This well-known naturalist and preservationist deeply impressed Mills, motivating him to become a spokesman for conservation. "You must tell them," Muir was quoted as directing the twenty-year-old Mills, "tell them that we are cutting down and burning up the forests of the West so fast that we'll lay this continent as waste as China, in a few generations."[10] Within only two years, Mills attempted his first public speech on forestry, later admitting that the results were premature and dismal.

Mills continued to roam about the country, exploring the Sierras, Yosemite Valley, Death Valley, and other sites in California. In 1890 Mills returned to California to enter a business school, expecting to use knowledge of bookkeeping and accounting for a career in mining. The lure of the outdoors and wanderlust proved stronger. Over the next decade he took extended trips to Yellowstone, to Alaska, down the Mississippi, eventually exploring every state in the Union. In 1900 he visited Europe. Even though he traveled widely, each summer found him guiding on Longs Peak. Answering questions from curious climbers helped hone his skills as both a speaker and a naturalist. Gradually his travels, his reading, and his experience with people combined to make him effective and popular both as a guide and later as a spokesman for conservation. At the same time he began writing articles about the Estes Park region for the Denver newspapers. Working winters in the mines merely provided him the means to travel; mining was not his career. Beavers and bears, forests and flowers, interpreting the scenes of nature and describing his own adventures occupied his thoughts more than the mines.

But conservationists such as Enos Mills could not take all the credit for changing the way Americans viewed their land. As the nation's middle class grew ever larger and demanding of leisure time, the concept of the vacation crept into American life. Previously, only the very wealthy could afford extended time at play; vacations were hardly a regular experience for most people. But increasing prosperity combined with a growing rail network made remote, scenic areas such as the Rockies accessible to those of even the most modest means. And, once experienced, the cool, dry climate of Colorado's mountains became addictive for Americans seeking refuge from the hot summers of the East and Midwest.

As in the past, Colorado's established and more fashionable resorts catered to these new seasonal vacationers. Places such as Colorado Springs had long cultivated a reputation for being accessible and affording stylish comfort. Somewhat more difficult to reach in the 1890s, Grand Lake and Estes Park started to attract fun seekers in the same way. The Kaufman House, built at Grand Lake in 1892, matched the Grand Lake House, the Fairview House, and the Garrison House in supplying summertime accommodations, along with a growing number of small cabins. Up along the North Fork, Robert L. Wheeler, or "Squeaky Bob," established one of the first dude ranches in that region. Called Camp Wheeler or "Hotel de Hardscrabble," Wheeler's ranch opened in 1907. Although often described as primitive, resorts such as Camp Wheeler proved more than sufficient for visitors in a holiday mood. The atmosphere was perhaps exemplified by signs on Squeaky Bob's cabins that read, "Blow your nose and clean your shoes. Use all the grub you need and leave things as you find them." Dudes spending days on horseback hardly ever complained of crude food or lumpy beds. Resort owners with a sense of humor helped make vacations memorable. According to historian Lloyd Musselman, Squeaky Bob ran a camp more memorable than most; he was notorious for not changing the sheets on his beds, merely scenting them with talcum powder.[11]

Around Estes Park ranches, guides, and hotels all catered to the turn-of-the-century surge westward. Small rental cabins began to dot the landscape. More resorts appeared: in 1902 the Wind River Lodge was opened, soon followed by the Horseshoe Inn and the Timberline in 1908, Moraine Lodge in 1910, and the Brinwood in 1911. In 1910 the Western Conference of the Y.M.C.A. acquired the Wind River Lodge and began an extensive development on its adjacent grounds.

Along with these developing resorts, private summer cabins appeared in greater numbers. Numerous families became seasonal residents spending each summer of their lives in the Estes Park region, generation after generation. One example of these long-term

Fishing always ranked high on everyone's list of enjoyable Rocky Mountain sports. (RMNPHC)

summertime vacationers was the family of William Allen White. Late in the 1880s, White spent most of one summer with some of his Kansas college chums exploring the region from the doorstep of a rented cabin on the Big Thompson River in Moraine Park. Memories of those good times drew him back. In 1893 he returned to Moraine Park with his bride to spend his honeymoon. Later that decade his wife's health dictated that they escape the summer heat of Emporia, Kansas where White served as editor and publisher of the *Emporia Gazette*. They spent many summers in the Colorado Springs area, the hours of leisure allowing White to engage in numerous writing projects. In June of 1911, the Whites decided to rent a cottage in the Estes Park region. "I set up a tent a hundred feet up the hill," White wrote in his *Autobiography*, "put my cot and typewriter there, and every morning after breakfast went up to write." The result was his second novel, entitled *In the Heart of a Fool*. Of his 1911 experience, he concluded: "It was a summer of pure delight."[12] As a vacationer turned resident, in 1912 he purchased a summer hideaway perched at the eastern end of Moraine Park. For around three thousand dollars he acquired a main cabin built in 1887 and another that had been added about 1900 as well as two additional "bedroom" cabins. There the Whites, their relatives and friends, spent many pleasant summers. Among their neighbors were university professors and Kansas political leaders, adding an element of suitable intellectual companionship.

In this atmosphere of leisure, conversation, and creativity, with the tonic of mountain air and scenes of natural beauty, White was able to cultivate his passion for politics and his talent for writing. Over the years White's editorials gained national fame. He reflected the thinking of small-town America, of people on Main Street. Gradually his conservative opinions of the 1890s became more progressive, influenced by close contact with men like Theodore Roosevelt. White's many articles appeared in national magazines, carrying his influence across the country and earning him a reputation as "The Sage of Emporia." As an articulate and well-informed editor, leading political figures of the day visited White, both in Emporia and in Estes Park, eager to discuss his views on vital issues. Over the years he produced dozens of editorials, articles, and short stories as well as several novels, biographies of Presidents Wilson and Coolidge, and an autobiography. His writing won him two Pulitzer Prizes. At the time of his death in 1944 he had earned a reputation as a national spokesman for common sense. Just like White's Moraine Park place, dozens of similar cabins appeared in Estes Park around the turn of the century. These vacation homes served to give people a different perspective, a place to think and relax, and a place with a touch of solitude.

Summertime residents such as White and the growing number of his fellow vacationers helped hasten the birth of the village of Estes Park. Visitors needed supplies and hardly a store existed. Only John T. Cleave sold a few provisions. This honest and eccentric Englishman held a 160-acre homestead at the junction of the Big Thompson and Fall rivers. Some years earlier Cleave obtained that property from the Earl of Dunraven, opened a store, sold a few goods, and acted as postmaster for the area. The central location of his land made the site quite natural for a town. In August of 1905, Cornelius H. Bond, formerly of Loveland, organized the Estes Park Town Company along with four associates. The Company bought Cleave's land for $8,000. Bond and his Company then hired Abner Sprague to survey the property. The resulting lots were sold, with a twenty-five-foot frontage on Elkhorn Avenue selling for fifty dollars while less desirable lots a bit further east sold for thirty-five dollars. Businesses took root almost overnight. Although it was not officially incorporated until 1917, the village of Estes Park began to grow. Enterprises boasting "Everything for the Tourist" started to appear. According to historian June Carothers, general stores, photography shops, a laundry, a stage station, the Hupp Hotel with "twenty-three rooms with steam heat and . . . baths with hot and cold water," and a handful of other businesses brought a taste of civilization.[13]

A panoramic view of Estes Park in 1905 shows a settlement barely emerging from its pastoral heritage. (RMNPHC)

Around the same time, an equally significant land exchange occurred that was destined to help shape Estes Park's future. In 1905, succeeding where others had failed, B. D. Sanborn of Greeley negotiated the purchase of the remainder of the Earl of Dunraven's Estes Park holdings. Prior to that sale, Sanborn had owned two cabins in the area as well as Bierstadt and Bear lakes. He had also secured water rights with the hope of developing hydroelectric power on Fall River. In Sanborn's view, Estes Park could be developed as one of the nation's great resorts. Sanborn soon learned that another investor, F. O. Stanley of Newton, Massachusetts, was also interested in acquiring the Dunraven property and building a resort, so the two men joined forces.

During a particularly inventive era in American history, Freeman Oscar Stanley and his twin brother Francis were regarded as geniuses. Together they developed a sensitive dry emulsion for photographic plates. Selling that discovery to the George Eastman Company brought them a fortune. They also invented, perfected, and manufactured the Stanley Steamer automobile. At the time, their steamers were powerful rivals of gasoline-powered vehicles. In 1906 one of their cars, clocked at 127.62 miles per hour, gained fame as the world's fastest auto.

Stanley first visited Estes Park in 1903. Fifty-three years old and suffering from tuberculosis, his doctor had advised him to visit

F. O. Stanley, "The Grand Old Man of Estes Park," boosted the reputation of the region as a resort by building his grand hotel. (Frank and Judith Normali, The Stanley Hotel Collection)

Colorado and not to make any plans beyond that autumn. Stanley's summer vacation in Estes Park, however, put him back on the road to health. In the next year or two he made his own plans for an Estes Park resort, then found it convenient to join B. D. Sanborn in his efforts. Together, Stanley and Sanborn paid some $80,000 for Dunraven's 6,400-acre estate as well as 600 acres in litigation, the old Estes Park Hotel, the Earl's cottage, and a few other holdings.

Almost immediately F. O. Stanley turned his energy and money into making this Estes Park property into a premier resort. On September 10, 1907, work began on a luxurious hotel, designed by Stanley himself and costing more than half a million dollars. At the same time a hydroelectric plant was designed and built on the Fall River, allowing the hotel to claim it was the first in the country "to heat, light, and cook meals exclusively with electricity. . . ."[14] The massive, dominating, five-story hotel opened in June of 1909 and began hosting the wealthiest of vacationers. Here was a resort genteel by design, clearly the rival of every spa in the Rockies. Its size, conveniences, and scenic location earned it an instant reputation. Stanley expected his guests to stay a month or more and, with a wealthy clientele, that was not an unrealistically long vacation.

In September of 1910, the Stanley Manor was started nearby. This second hostel was intended to stimulate year-round visits since rooms in the Stanley Hotel had not been designed for winter use. F. O. Stanley also planned to transport his guests, for his Stanley Steamers were able to carry visitors from the railheads at Lyons, Longmont, or Loveland with a touch of modern ease. Naturally, he recognized the need for better roads, just as other Estes Park enthusiasts had years before. In 1907 he donated funds for the improvement of the North St. Vrain highway to Lyons. Only three years earlier a road carved up the Big Thompson canyon brought better connections with Loveland and Fort Collins. In 1906 the Loveland-Estes Park Transportation Company, using eleven-passenger Stanley Steamers, started making the five-hour trips from Loveland. But Stanley was not merely content to see the success of his own resort, for he helped organize a bank for the village in 1908, sold electricity to the growing number of villagers, and donated property for a park and school buildings. Most important, publicity advertising the Stanley Hotel put Estes Park on the map as one of America's foremost "playgrounds." Within just a few years, influential F. O. Stanley earned a reputation as "The Grand Old Man of Estes Park."

The region's resort business grew more popular each year.

Vehicles like the Stanley Steamer started appearing, bringing demands for better roads. An eleven-passenger version of the Stanley Steamer soon carried vacationers from railheads at Lyons or Loveland to Estes Park in a matter of hours, ending the days of rigorous travel. (RMNPHC)

There is no question that the Stanley Hotel—and F. O. Stanley—put Estes Park on the maps of vacationing America. Few resorts could match such an expansive structure and such a dramatic natural setting. (Norlin Library, University of Colorado)

Enos Mills developed his techniques as a naturalist, a public speaker, and as a writer. *(Estes Park Trail Gazette)*

One man watching it grow was Enos Mills. In 1901 he finally stopped watching and began to negotiate with Carlyle Lamb for the purchase of Longs Peak Inn. Finally in 1902, Mills bought the Lamb property. Until his death in 1922, the task of running that resort became Mills's prime responsibility. His summers were busy; his business became a success. Having that lodge also allowed this budding naturalist to offer his own ideas about how Longs Peak and this region could be presented to visitors. Croquet, tennis, or golf hardly fit his style of outdoor recreation. Instead, mountain climbing, hiking, viewing birds or beavers, or merely getting alone

Longs Peak Inn served as Enos Mills's base of operations, first when he acted as guide for Carlyle Lamb and then, from 1902 until 1922, when he owned and operated this hostel at the base of Longs Peak. (U.S. Geological Survey)

with nature, could all start at his doorstep. "They need the temples of the gods," said Mills of his urban visitors, "the forest primeval, and the pure flower-fringed brooks."[15]

Tending Longs Peak Inn (and rebuilding it after a fire in 1906) meant that Mills no longer returned to work as a miner each winter. Instead, he took a job with Colorado's Irrigation Department as its "Snow Observer." Beginning in 1903, he tramped throughout the Rockies during wintertime to test the snow depths. The Irrigation Department needed such information to predict water supplies for the coming season, and this was a job Mills relished. It gave him a practical excuse to exercise his wanderlust and curiosity. Into the winter wilderness he went, alone. He explored much of Colorado's high country, meeting blizzards along the way. He ventured across the Divide on snowy routes such as the Flattop Trail to Grand Lake; climbed Longs Peak in February, the first ever attempt at such a feat; and dared avalanches. One winter, according to his biographer, "he walked the crest of the continent—the 'snowy range of Colorado'—from the Wyoming line to close upon the New Mexico."[16] The same curiosity that had sent him wandering across the nation in earlier years now focussed on the mountains in his own backyard. Mills soon discovered that his tales of adventure while alone in the wilderness delighted every audience, whether at Longs Peak Inn, while making a Longs Peak climb, or at some public meeting. In an age rapidly growing accustomed to comfort, people were amazed to hear of Mills's feats in the face of the elements. "The dangers in such times and places are fewer than in cities," Mills told his eager listeners. "Discomforts? Scarcely. To some persons life must be hardly worth living. If any normal person under fifty cannot enjoy being in a storm in the wilds, he ought to reform at once." Nature could be a tonic for us all. According to Mills, even a storm could "furnish energy, inspiration, and resolution."[17]

The inspiration he found resulted in writing and more public speaking. In 1905 he published *The Story of Estes Park and a Guide Book*. That book displayed an interesting composite of local history, a bit of poetry, tales of Longs Peak, and a touch of personal aggrandizement. Fifteen more books followed, ranging from *Wild Life in the Rockies* (1909) to *Bird Memories of the Rockies* (published posthumously in 1931). In addition, he wrote dozens of articles that appeared in national magazines, offering readers details about forests, the Rockies, wildlife, and geology. At the same time he was becoming a popular public speaker, traveling throughout the country telling about life in the forests and mountains. In 1907 President Roosevelt recognized his ability to deliver a conservationist message and appointed him Government Lecturer on Forestry, a position he held until May of 1909. Just as Estes Park was growing more popular with its new resorts, Enos Mills was gaining a national audience with his pen and personality.

The creation of the Medicine Bow Forest Reserve in these mountains in 1905 came without the apparent efforts of Mills, F. O. Stanley, or any other residents of Estes Park and Grand Lake. Much earlier, in 1892, John G. Coy of Fort Collins had proposed to the Colorado Forestry Association that a reserve be created "on the

Sawmills, like the one in Hidden Valley cutting lumber for the Stanley Hotel, dotted Colorado's Front Range. The creation of Forest Reserves (later called National Forests) helped regulate such operations on the public domain. *(Estes Park Trail-Gazette)*

Cache La Poudre, Thompson, and St. Vrain watersheds."[18] A public meeting held in Fort Collins expressed approval of that idea, but soon after opposition developed and the proposal was delayed. In 1898, conservationists at Fort Collins again pushed the idea, "badly needed for the protection of the watersheds feeding agricultural lands. . . ." Again, opposition to a reserve was heard, this time from a sawmill operator. "My home is in the reserve," he protested, "and I earn my bread with a little 10-horse power sawmill, running the saw myself. If you wonder why I object to the reserve, it is because I love liberty, hate red tape, and believe in progress."[19] Years of wrangling and debate followed, but conservationists never let the issue die. Then, with the stroke of a pen, President Theodore Roosevelt settled the issue. He established the reserve by proclamation on May 17th, 1905.

Only a few months earlier, in February of 1905, jurisdiction of all forest reserves had been transferred to the Department of Agriculture. Running the reserves now became the task of the newly formed United States Forest Service, and later that year all reserves were renamed National Forests. Also announced was a basic principle of management, "that all land is to be devoted to its most productive use for the permanent good of the whole people and not for the temporary benefit of individuals or companies."[20] National forest advocates held an idealistic goal of producing the "greatest good" for the greatest number of people. But that was still

As agents of conservation, forest rangers began protecting the resources of the region. Cabins along patrol routes allowed the rangers a degree of comfort as they roamed the Rockies. (RMNPHC)

a concept conservationists might dispute. Some wondered whether "productive use" for the "greatest good" ruled out preservation.

On July 20th, 1907, H. N. Wheeler took charge of the new Medicine Bow National Forest (later named the Colorado National Forest). He established a government headquarters in Estes Park and hired a handful of rangers. Soon such men as Warren Rutledge and Shep Husted were patrolling the new national forest from the Estes Park office. Other rangers were stationed at Allenspark to the south, Manhattan to the north, and Grand Lake to the west. But after spending a single lonely winter at Estes Park, "and having almost no users of the Forest come to the office to see me,"

Colorado National Forest Supervisor H. N. Wheeler believed the region received adequate protection in its status as a National Forest. Yet he also suggested a "game refuge" idea that fostered the proposal for a park. (U.S. Forest Service, Regional Office Historical Collection, Denver)

Wheeler decided to move his office to Fort Collins. He believed that Cornelius Bond and other town promoters were "incensed" by his decision. "It was freely stated that they wanted a Government headquarters at Estes Park," Wheeler contended, "and if they could not have a Forest headquarters, they would create a National Park so as to have the headquarters there."[21]

Exactly who first suggested the creation of Rocky Mountain National Park may be endlessly debated. Wheeler's name is mentioned; Enos Mills is a prime candidate; a number of prominent Estes Park businessmen might qualify. According to historian Patricia Fazio, the formation of the Estes Park Protective and Im-

Building a useable road across the Continental Divide was discussed for years. By 1913 the State of Colorado agreed to fund the project, dispatching convicts to begin a seven-year effort that developed the Fall River Road. (RMNPHC)

provement Association in September of 1906 marked a milestone in efforts to promote preservation of the local natural scene. Men such as F. O. Stanley and Cornelius Bond took leading roles in that group's decision to publicize the beauty of this mountain valley, to build roads and trails, contruct and maintain a fish hatchery, enforce game laws, and even protect the wildflowers. By that time Enos Mills had also become a close friend of Stanley and perhaps his influence as a naturalist made a strong local impact.

Over the next few years a fish hatchery built along Fall River began producing millions of trout for nearby streams. Numerous trail building projects such as those on Prospect and Deer mountains made hiking a bit more enjoyable. Beginning in 1913, elk were reintroduced, transplanted from Montana. That same year, members of the Association finally convinced the state to initiate construction of the Fall River Road across the Continental Divide.

The Fall River Road served its purpose as a route across the Rockies, but its narrow and winding course made improvement or replacement essential. (RMNPHC)

In September convicts from the Colorado State Penitentiary moved into cabins along Fall River and started a major seven-year highway project. Most unusual, perhaps, was a posted "wild flower notice," intended to guard against wanton plucking. It read: "You can keep Estes Park a beautiful wild garden. Spare the Flowers! Thoughtless people are destroying the flowers by the roots or are picking too many of them. Neither the roots nor the leafy stocks should be taken, and flowers, if taken, should be cut and not pulled. What do you want with an armful of flowers?" Then the notice concluded with a stern warning: "Those who pull flowers up by the roots will be condemned by all worthy people, and also by the Estes Park Protective and Improvement Association."[22] Conservation consciousness had arrived.

Community leaders were clearly sensitive about the natural scenes around them. In October of 1907 the Association asked H. N. Wheeler of the Forest Service to address them on the topic of wildlife protection. "I told them that one of the biggest assets of any recreation area is the game," Wheeler remembered, "and if they wished to increase the value of their playground they should create a game refuge."[23]

Talk of that type certainly appealed to Enos Mills. In the spring of 1908 he wrote Wheeler asking where a "game refuge" of that sort might be located. Sometime later that summer, the game refuge idea was transformed into a "national park" in the mind of Mills. And the park idea Mills had in mind grew much grander, both in size and in preservationist sentiment, than Wheeler or the Forest Service ever expected. Mills proposed a refuge or park running forty-two miles from east to west and twenty-four miles from north to south—over a thousand square miles of land with Estes Park as its heart.

In Mills's view, national forests failed to offer enough protection for nature. Here he reflected an ideological split that was occurring nationally. Utilitarian conservationists such as Forest Service head Gifford Pinchot argued a "productive use" viewpoint and preservationists such as John Muir fought for aesthetic preservation. Mills could not agree with lenient Forest Service policies in regard to grazing or timber cutting. He watched cattle trample flower-filled meadows right in his own backyard. "A Forest Reserve," he wrote, "is established chiefly for the purpose of using it to produce trees for the saw-mill and grass for the cattle—a place where trees are harvested, where woodmen do not spare the trees but fell them by the thousands to keep numerous saw-mills at work." "Though a Forest Reserve, like a farm, has beauty," Mills concluded, "it is not established for its beauty but for practical use."[24]

Once considered a harmless pastime, picking flowers was ranked as injurious to the natural scene by people who expressed a conservationist consciousness. (RMNPHC)

In September of 1909, the Protective Association voted unanimously to support a game refuge plan for the area. Later that organization backed the Estes National Park idea and, by 1911, the concept of Rocky Mountain National Park. Every detail of all the debates, squabbles, and arguments relating to the proposed park need not be examined here. It is enough to say that the Forest Service in general and H. N. Wheeler in particular supported neither Mills's plan nor the park idea. Wheeler believed that Forest Service efforts toward regulating stockmen and sawmill owners were working; forest fires were being fought; trails and ranger cabins were being built; water development projects, such as dams at Sandbeach, Bluebird, and Lawn Lakes, offered progress; mines, such as the newly discovered Eugenia on the side of Longs Peak, were still being dug. Furthermore, national forests now had a solid advocacy within the Department of Agriculture. National parks, on the other hand, had no such constituency. Those that existed appeared to be run in a haphazard fashion. No National Park Service had been formed.

Enos Mills cared little for the type of protection the Forest Service offered. "It deals almost entirely with the business world and is as plainly and severely a business proposition as is the growing

While many other individuals contributed to the success of the national park proposal, Enos Mills adopted the issue as a personal quest. (Colorado Historical Society)

of wheat and potatoes or the raising of hogs."[25] From 1909 on Mills embarked upon a personal crusade to establish a preserve. At first he gained the support of F. O. Stanley, the Protective Association, and many other Estes Park citizens. His speaking tours allowed him to carry his idea to the nation. In 1910 he convinced J. Horace McFarland of the influential American Civic Association to back the project. The Denver Chamber of Commerce declared its support that same year and as early as January of 1910 Congressman Edward Taylor of Fort Collins prepared a bill to create Estes National Park and Game Preserve.

By early 1911, opposition of the Forest Service became louder, with people such as H. N. Wheeler often quoted by newspapers. Some of Mills's closest neighbors living near Longs Peak Inn also opposed the idea and formed a small but vocal group called The Front Range Settlers League. Their concern about a loss of private property as well as a general distrust of Mills's motivations made their protest especially bitter. In response, that July Mills spawned his own "Mountain Climbing Organization" to support preservation, patterned after John Muir's Sierra Club. He enlisted the aid of Denver attorney James Grafton Rogers and in April of 1912 the Colorado Mountain Club held its first meeting. Helping to create Rocky Mountain National Park became one of its prime objectives. Rogers and his law partner, Morrison Shafroth, also helped by supplying more accurate maps of the region and drafting and redrafting bills presented to Congress over the next three years. Meanwhile, Mills served as chief propagandist for the park idea. He crisscrossed the nation each winter giving speeches, enlisting the support of newspaper editors, various organizations, and politicians.

In early September of 1912, Robert B. Marshall of the United States Geological Survey was dispatched to evaluate the proposed park and to determine whether its features deserved national park status. His conclusion delighted all the park advocates. His report, issued early in 1913, recommended "that Congress be asked to create for the benefit and enjoyment of the people a National Park in the Rocky Mountains of Colorado in the vicinity of Longs Peak, to be known as 'Rocky Mountain National Park.' "[26] But rather than presenting Mills's thousand-square-mile preserve, Marshall scaled the preserve down to seven hundred square miles. Active mining regions, in particular, kept his proposal smaller.

On February 6, 1913, the first park bill was presented to Congress. Soon after, the Colorado State Legislature and numerous other local, state, and national organizations voiced their support for the legislation. But a speedy decision did not come. More compromises had to be made. Claims regarding water usage, grazing rights, private land ownership, use of timber, and mineral extraction, all reflecting previous decades of pioneering, needed to be resolved. Mills's original thousand-square-mile dream shrank even smaller than Marshall's modest seven hundred-square-mile proposal. The first two park bills died in congressional committees. Eventually five major revisions were necessary.

On June 29th, 1914, the third and final bill was presented. Over the next several months Congressman Edward Taylor carefully guided it through the House of Representatives and Senator Charles S. Thomas helped it through the Senate. On December 13th, 1914, the House Committee on Public Lands began its final hearings. Showing a unity of purpose, former Governor John Shafroth, retiring Governor Elias Ammons, and Governor-elect George Carlson all testified in behalf of the bill. There, too, was Enos Mills. Through those years of debate and compromise, Mills never lost sight of his goal, never stopped lecturing or promoting. Now he stood ready to make a final emotional plea in behalf of Rocky Mountain National Park. Between Mills and his colleagues from Colorado every argument regarding recreation, natural beauty, patriotism, "Seeing America First," and the proposal's nearly universal popularity came forth once again. That the region was already a major recreational area Congress could not deny. Backers claimed that fifty-six thousand people visited the region in 1914 alone; ten thousand automobiles traveled the highways into the mountains each year. Following all that powerful testimony, success seemed assured.

Congressman Taylor kept the bill moving. On January 18th, 1915 the final legislation passed Congress and on January 26th President Woodrow Wilson signed the bill into law. Over five years of discussion, debate, and compromise finally produced a park. Less than a dream, the final bill created only a 358.5-square-mile park, a third the size Mills had envisioned.

Nevertheless, the *Denver Post* proclaimed a victory. And it publicly thanked Enos Mills for his vision and efforts, calling him "The Father of Rocky Mountain National Park."[27] For those involved, years of debate, frustration, and strenuous effort were not without cost: friendships were strained, quarrels flourished, and bitterness sometimes resulted.

Still, there was cause to celebrate on September 4th, 1915 when citizens gathered to dedicate the "nation's newest playground."[28] Clouds loomed overhead as the festivities began. A light rain started falling just at two in the afternoon when Enos Mills, acting as master of ceremonies, opened the program. A mountain-style

The *Denver Post* congratulated Mills for his efforts in January of 1915, just after President Wilson signed the bill creating Rocky Mountain National Park. *(The Denver Post)*

downpour pounced upon the later speakers, but dampened speeches could not drown the strong feeling of progress pervading this assembly. Every path of the past seemed to lead to creating this new park. Mills may have looked back, thinking of the changes he had seen. "My youthful dream had been to scale peak after peak," he later recalled, "and from the earthly spires to see the scenic world far below and far away."[29] One of the last changes Mills and the passing generation of pioneers produced was a park, helping to insure that those coming after might also scale the peaks and see the scenic world.

Bidding farewell to "The Eve of Estes," Enos Mills and Superintendent L. Claude Way offer Miss Agnes Lowe their best wishes as she prepares to spend a week in the "paradise" of Rocky Mountain National Park. (Lulabeth and Jack Melton Collection)

6

PARADISE FOUNDED

"Many thousands are bound to find their way to this glorious
country, yet reached by relatively few. We are trying to do our part
to bring the thousands here."
Stephen T. Mather, Assistant Secretary of the Interior
4 September 1915[1]

THE NEWSPAPER headline blazed: "Naked, Unarmed and Alone, 'Eve'
Goes Forth Into Forest." An eye-catching story, complete with
photographs, described a twenty-year-old college co-ed from Ann
Arbor, Michigan, Miss Agnes Lowe, as she waved good-by to a
crowd of well-wishers. She was leaving to spend a week with nature
in the wilderness of Rocky Mountain National Park. It was Monday, August 6th, 1917, when Miss Lowe's tale appeared in *The
Denver Post*. This "modern Eve" had donned a suitable "cave
woman" costume, resembling an abbreviated leopard's skin, before
entering the newly created "Garden of Eden." Enos Mills and Park
Supervisor L. Claude Way joined the bevy of reporters, photographers, local dignitaries, and "nearly 2,000 persons" to watch the
girl dash into the woods near the base of Longs Peak, supposedly
heading into the Thunder Lake country. With farewells completed
and photographs taken, rangers restrained the crowd as Miss Lowe
began her adventure. Enos Mills had the honor of escorting Miss
Lowe, "The Eve of Estes," as far as the beaver ponds on the Roaring
Fork. From there, Mills "left her to pursue her barefooted way
alone. . . ."[2]

A girl attempting to live alone in the wilderness was hardly a
new idea in 1917. Others had recently experimented with the same
adventure at several locations in the East. Yet no one would really
have classified living "without clothing, food, weapons, or shelter"
as a national fad. It was new to Colorado. And it was certainly

unusual enough to attract the attention of most readers. Almost at once newspapers across the country started carrying the story, providing their readers with the latest details about "Eve." At the same time that news of the World War captured page one, the Eve of Estes kept reports coming from Rocky Mountain National Park. As she worked her way through a week in the wilderness, tidbits about her progress enchanted the public and drew attention to the new Park.

The creation of Rocky Mountain National Park in 1915 meant that many people started to look at these mountains differently. Conservationists such as Enos Mills saw the region as a preserve, a place to be guarded from cattle yet enjoyed by people. Businessmen believed the new Park would enhance the reputation of their area, now starting to prosper from growing numbers of tourists. Most ideas about developing hotels, roads, and recreation as well as publicizing the Park could not be called new in 1915, but with the establishment of a national interest in the area further development was intensified. Work was already under way on the Fall River Road, connecting Estes Park and Grand Lake with a scenic route across the Divide. Like building projects of former years, this road symbolized only the latest effort to draw more visitors into the region. And just like Fall River Road, the newly created Park was seen as another way to promote the area, a way to make the region even more famous as a resort. For years, however, promoting and developing this stretch of the Rockies had been a local effort. Occasionally a few other people within Colorado offered some kind words. Rarely did outsiders take the trouble to promote or advertise the area. Little seemed to change while the region was a national forest. But once Congress created the Park in 1915, a new era of promotion and protection began. Determining how these mountains and the new Park would be promoted, protected, developed, and enjoyed now became a federal task.

Forging a national park out of territory already explored and somewhat settled for over fifty years was not easy. Over the next decade and a half, well-meaning people worked hard to decide what direction this new park should take. Between 1915 and 1929, Rocky Mountain National Park became a little like a stage, its magnificent horizon serving as a backdrop, upon which a variety of actors argued about which play should be presented. Upon the scene came familiar local players such as Enos Mills, eager to recite old scripts for new audiences. Soon other characters arrived, upstaging those more familiar. And other scripts also appeared, some sent from places as distant as Washington, D.C. Everyone

C. R. Trowbridge
served as Acting
Supervisor from July
1, 1915 to September
18, 1916, introducing
national park admin-
istration into the re-
gion. (RMNPHC)

wanted to please the audience. Once in a while a comedy act came
along, like that of the adventuresome Miss Lowe, providing a touch
of levity. But from 1915 onward, those people intent on producing
a national playground took their roles very seriously.

A new era began on July 1st, 1915 when C. R. Trowbridge arrived in Estes Park and took charge as Acting Supervisor of Rocky
Mountain National Park. A New York native and veteran of the
Philippine insurrection, Trowbridge also worked with the Secret
Service until 1913 when he became a field representative for the
secretary of the interior. Based on that experience, he was selected
to organize the administration of this new park. During the months
that followed, Trowbridge watched work proceeding on the Fall
River Road; followed trails to Bear Lake, Lawn Lake, and Bierstadt
Lake; and inspected resorts run by Abner Sprague in Bartholf Park,
by W. H. Ashton at Lawn Lake, by the Higby brothers at Fern Lake
and the Pool, and by E. A. Brown at Bear Lake. He issued numerous
permits for guides. He examined timber cutting sites and posted
a number of "Fire Warning" signs. He also bought furniture and
opened an office in Estes Park on July 10th. From there he directed

the efforts of his three rangers, R. T. McCracken, Frank Koenig, and Reed Higby. Paying them each a salary of $900 per year, Trowbridge dispatched these men to patrol the Park, repair old Forest Service ranger stations and telephone lines, and work on the trails. They also fought a forest fire during their first month on the job. Watching the dedication ceremonies must have been an enjoyable task that September, but soon after the whole squad spent "considerable time" searching for a Dr. R. T. Sampson, reportedly lost along the Continental Divide. For Trowbridge and his men there was always plenty to do.

During his fifteen months as acting supervisor, C. R. Trowbridge managed the Park with the dual goals of protection and regulated use. Fighting forest fires, patrolling for hunters or trappers, or chasing neighboring cattle out of the Park were acts of protection. Having brush and rubbish cleared from roadsides displayed some common sense regarding aesthetic guardianship. Opening trails and repairing roads merely augmented the work already being done by local guides, packers, horsemen and residents. Issuing permits for guides, resorts, and reservoirs testified to the continuation of practices familiar even before the Park's creation. But some less common activities, no longer identified with today's national parks, also surfaced in 1915 and 1916. Trowbridge issued several timber cutting permits, meaning local people continued hauling lumber from the Park just as if it were still a national forest. Firewood could also be taken, using the dead or down trees, at a cost of only fifty cents per cord or less. In fact, with the exception of regulating grazing and hunting, it seemed as if few changes really took effect in the management of these mountains as it evolved from a national forest into a national park.

Most people applauded the protective efforts of the rangers, but if they had promptly enforced a list of rigid rules or regulations, immediately restricting common practices in the area, the rangers might have created a furor. In 1915, however, few rigid rules had even been considered, much less written. Even a centralized bureau in Washington offering a uniform administration for all national parks had yet to be created. Only in August of 1916 when Congress organized the National Park Service did a consistent philosophy and uniform policy for the national parks appear. Soon the administration of Rocky Mountain National Park began to reflect the goals mandated by Congress for all the parks: "to conserve the scenery, the natural and historic objects and the wildlife therein and to provide for the enjoyment of the same in such manner and by such means as will leave them unimpaired for the enjoyment of future generations."[3]

Many elements of national park philosophy had yet to be refined. Paying hunters to eliminate predatory animals so elk and deer could thrive was thought to be an essential part of "protection." (RMNPHC)

Exactly what national parks meant and what they were for took some time to clarify. Whether campers would predominate or resorts would continue or more roads would be built, someone needed to chart a course for Rocky Mountain National Park's future. (RMNPHC)

Prior to the development of the National Park Service, management of each park or monument depended upon who was in charge, the whims of Congress, and local pressure. Each of the thirty-one areas set aside by 1915 tended to have its own special set of rules. No clearly stated purpose for all of them existed until Congress formulated the dual goals of preservation and "enjoyment."

The national park idea had evolved in a haphazard fashion. Historians offer many reasons for the birth of this unique, wilderness park concept. Some have suggested that a European heritage of hunting reserves kept by the nobility took root in a more democratic American environment. Others link the idea to the town commons established for public use in villages of the East. The beginnings of nationalistic pride during the 1820s and 1830s might also have contributed to an appreciation of the nation's natural wonders. Feeling competitive with an older European culture, Americans boasted about the natural grandeur of their country. In the absence of any native literature or art, self-conscious Americans tried to "show up" Europe by extolling the virtues of American geography.

Influential writers such as Thoreau and Emerson helped contribute an intellectual justification for appreciating and protecting objects of nature. They also insured that mere thoughts of conservation would be strongly linked to a sense of aesthetic appreciation. Proposals for parks and preservation soon came from other spokesmen, such as Frederick Law Olmstead, landscape architect and park planner. Olmstead argued for government control of scenic land, claiming the advantage of "protection for all its citizens in the pursuit of happiness."[4] And happiness meant preserving areas that permitted the "contemplation of natural scenes of an impressive character." Once designated as a public park, such an area would bring people "relief from ordinary cares, change of air and change of habits . . . favorable to the health and vigor of their intellect beyond any other conditions which can be offered them." In the view of visionaries such as Olmstead, recreation in such grand natural settings offered metaphysical benefits, something like a spiritual quest, with a "pilgrimage" to a park providing the "means of securing happiness."[5] Preservation and recreation were seen as ideological companions. The images of freedom, adventure, wildness, independence, vigor, rest and play, all helped augment the idea of parks.

The audience for such ideas was small but receptive. Other intellectuals agreed with the need for a more sensitive attitude toward nature. That sympathetic attitude became an urgent desire to guard especially scenic spots from being despoiled. Active efforts toward preservation began. In 1864, Congress granted Yosemite Valley and the nearby Mariposa Grove of redwoods to the state of California "for public use, resort, and recreation"[6] and established a precedent for setting aside large tracts of undeveloped land simply in the name of "recreation."

In 1872, a massive forested plateau surrounding the headwaters of the Yellowstone River and dotted with unique thermal basins, deep canyons, and jeweled lakes received similar protection. With this two-million-acre reserve — Yellowstone National Park — set aside "as a public park or pleasuring ground for the benefit and enjoyment of the people," historians mark the official beginning of the American national park movement.

During the following decades additional parks joined Yellowstone in its elevated status as a national treasure. Among them were Yosemite, Sequoia, and General Grant, all created in 1890. Mount Rainier followed in 1899, Crater Lake in 1902, and Glacier in 1910. Along with those large parks sites of historical interest such as the ancient ruins at Mesa Verde received protection through the 1906 Antiquities Act. By 1915, when Rocky Mountain gained its national park designation, thirty-one parks and monuments had been created.

As the number of preserves grew, a clear policy for managing them all had to be developed. In some, such as Yellowstone and Yosemite, the U.S. Cavalry worked as guardians; in others, civilians with political influence took charge. Compounding an inconsistent management was a penurious Congress that voted very little money for improvements. Visitors to those early parks sometimes found rules unenforced and vandalism rampant. A wide gap existed between intellectuals who encouraged an appreciation of nature and the average traveler, called "the great unwashed" by an unsympathetic observer. Viewing heaps of litter in Yellowstone, one traveler reported: "Society in general goes to the mountains not to fast but to feast and leaves their glaciers covered with chicken bones and eggshells."[7] Yet national park administrators continued to be idealistic about preserving nature "unimpaired." One could almost understand that an ill-informed public, not displaying aesthetic sensitivity, might bring its rapacious attitudes, destructive tendencies, sloppy manners, and careless attitudes to the parks. Just as it took work to create preserves, similar efforts had to be directed toward educating people to appreciate the parks without destroying them. John Muir served that purpose for Yosemite in particular and the West in general. Enos Mills followed Muir, promoting first forests and conservation and later the ideals

Grand Lake offered aquatic pastimes, the type of activities many people associated with national parks. (RMNPHC)

of preservation in the Rockies. "Go to the trees and get their good tidings," Mills urged the public, paraphrasing Muir who had paraphrased Emerson. "Have an autumn day in the woods, and beneath the airy arches of limbs and leaves linger in the paths of peace."[8] Dozens of other writers followed that theme, encouraging turn-of-the-century travelers to discover "the healing powers of nature."[9] "Elsewhere man must live by the sweat of his brow," one national park advocate wrote. "Here let him rest and play."[10] By 1915 national parks were becoming the "playgrounds of the people." Exactly how these playgrounds were to be managed or used remained a question.

For years the national parks lacked a cohesive organization or philosophy. They needed direction. Intellectuals saw parks simply as wilderness preserves. Years earlier, Thoreau had observed: "To preserve wild animals implies generally the creation of a forest for them to dwell in or resort to. So it is with man."[11] Parks afforded that physical space offering wildness. At the same time, parks served as a source of nationalistic pride, "crown jewels of the continent." The railroads encouraged Americans to "See America First," especially before spending dollars in Europe. Advertising grand scenery of the parks helped convince people to spend their vacations seeing sights within the nation. Always able to make a case for wilderness, Enos Mills claimed that national parks promoted every positive attribute a person could imagine, from health to knowledge, from thinking to suppressing prejudice, from stimulating patriotism to ending vice and crime. Put simply, national parks offered what was good for people.

Since national forests protected watersheds and promoted wiser use of timber and other resources, Americans felt that national parks needed a similarly practical justification. Convincing people to have fun took work. Seeking pleasure in an acceptable manner and in the right frame of mind took education. So once parks were created, promotion and publicity followed. People had to be encouraged to experience life in a wilderness preserve. "I wish that everyone might have a night by a campfire at Mother Nature's hearth stone," Enos Mills suggested. "A campfire in the forest marks the most enchanting place on life's highway wherein to have a lodging for the night."[12]

Whether visitors entering Rocky Mountain National Park would sit by a campfire, ride a horse down a trail, meander through a meadow, or lounge at a lodge would not be decided by Enos Mills alone. Nor would Acting Supervisor Trowbridge make every decision affecting future travelers. How people entered the Park, what they saw, who they spoke with, how long they stayed, what impressions they gained, all these basic issues took park planners and promoters years to consider. Obviously, some people made these decisions for themselves. On August 7th, 1917, *The Denver Post* announced that George Desouris, self-styled as "the new Adam," intended to enter the "new Garden of Eden," searching for Eve. Wearing a primitive robe, "Adam" claimed to have had "a vision from heaven" directing him to enter the Park and join the Eve of Estes in her quest of living with nature. Supervisor Way, quoted by the *Post*, merely retorted: "Adam won't think he's in the Garden of Eden if he comes here." He said his rangers would not tolerate anyone molesting the adventurous Agnes Lowe.[13] Like Miss Lowe before him, Adam thought he had discovered the best method of enjoying a national park.

Adventurers pretending to be Adam and Eve in paradise were not quite what national park idealists had in mind. More typical perhaps was a journey made by J. W. Willy and his son Knight in 1916. Their trip through the Park that summer began with a stay at the Stanley Hotel. In Estes Park father and son went on short hikes and made a special trip to meet the great naturalist, Enos Mills. Their second night was spent at the Horseshoe Inn where they met

Always a popular inkeeper, Squeaky Bob Wheeler poses with his dog Jack. Wheeler personified the hospitality common among owners of small resorts, many predating the Park's establishment. (RMNPHC)

Shep Husted, "the famous guide of the Rocky Mountain region." Joined there by another tourist, Daniel Tower of Michigan, Willy, his son, and Husted mounted horses and embarked upon a journey across the mountains. They traveled along the Ute Trail, crossed the Divide, and reached Poudre Lake where they spent the night in a ranger cabin. The next day they rode their horses up Specimen Mountain, Shep Husted offering tidbits of geological history along the way. Then they descended to the western slope, spending the evening at "Squeaky Bob's." There they discovered that many other people had made the same journey. "They keep a-coming and a-coming," Bob complained, "and I can't turn 'em away (in) this weather." Bob Wheeler's resort reminded Willy "of country hotels of a century ago" with all its frontier flavor. Among its rustic elements, he noted that the "toilet paper fixture at Squeaky Bob's carries a big mail order catalog."[14]

After sleeping two to a bed in one of Wheeler's tents, the men rode northward to the headwaters of the Colorado, crossed Thunder Pass, and ascended Lulu Peak. After a second night at Squeaky Bob's, they traveled to Grand Lake. There they stayed at the Nowata, one of five hotels in operation. It featured "hot and cold running water in the rooms, bath, and a very good table; the rate $3.00 a day." Willy and his son explored nearby sights afoot, later complaining that trails needed to be cleared. He also noted that automobile travelers were bringing changes to these resorts, with more mobile travelers inclined to spend only one night rather than a week as guests had in previous years. Willy saw hotel keepers inconvenienced and higher prices resulting from such quick visits. The next day Husted guided his party across the Flattop Trail, down to Bartholf Park (today's Glacier Basin), then over Storm Pass to Longs Peak Inn, making a thirty-two mile ride. From there, Willy and his son departed for home. Their seven-day stay in the region encompassed a hundred miles on horseback and seventy-five miles hiking. Following their ambitious excursion, Willy offered a suggestion. "Whenever there is an automobile road in a national park," he urged, "it should be paralleled with a trail for the exclusive use of those who go afoot or on horseback. . . ."[15]

Not every proposal or plan for the uses of the Park were as reasonable as Willy's, however. In January of 1915, for example, Congressman Albert Johnson of Washington suggested that Rocky Mountain National Park would be an ideal spot for a "leprosarium," by which he meant a national leper reservation. "The national parks are intended for recreation," *The Denver Post* snapped in reply. That "pinhead from Washington," the *Post* argued, totally misunderstood the purpose of having parks.[16] Less controversial requests came from hay fever patients who wished to build cabins, "to seek asylum above the weeds every season for about two months."[17] But those proposals met a similar fate. Interior Department officials replied tartly that no cabins would be constructed, nor would cattle be grazed, nor prospecting allowed, nor farming permitted, nor summer resorts built. Clearly, national parks could not satisfy everyone.

On September 19th, 1916, Supervisor Trowbridge completed his organizational assignment and turned Park administration over to L. Claude Way, designated "Chief Ranger in Charge." A former Army captain and forest ranger, Way had worked at the Grand Canyon prior to his Rocky Mountain appointment. Some of his later critics claimed he brought an "arrogant" military style too harsh for a national park. Others said that he failed to communicate park policies to local residents, leading to disharmony. In fair-

Supervisor L. Claude Way, taking charge of the Park in September of 1916, displayed the new national park uniform, apparel adopted from the U.S. Army's Cavalry. (RMNPHC)

Whether protecting visitors or wildlife, park rangers covered miles of trail, frequently camping out in isolated regions of the Park. (RMNPHC)

ness to Way, it should be noted that few policies existed for him to communicate.

Chief Ranger Way discovered that the Park was already immensely popular. Trowbridge earlier estimated that 51,000 people entered the Park in 1916. In 1917, Way reported that some 120,000 visitors arrived, bringing with them nearly 20,000 automobiles. Two years later his report showed 170,000 people entering the area. Officials boasted that Rocky Mountain National Park drew more people "than the combined tourist patronage of Yellowstone, Yosemite, Glacier, and Crater Lake Parks."[18] Rocky Mountain's easy accessibility from the East and Midwest made it an instant success.

The need to serve so many visitors led L. Claude Way and other Park Service officials to ask Congress for increased appropriations. More rangers were needed, the public demanded better roads, camping areas had to be developed, the trail system was deemed "incomplete," and quarters for the Park staff had to be constructed. None of this could occur without more money, and a promise to hold spending at $10,000 annually, made during the passage of the Park's organic act, quickly proved to be a liability. Joining other citizens, Enos Mills sympathized with the Park Service. "I am starting a campaign to have an increased appropriation for this Park," he wrote in 1918. Yet the Park Service still gloried in Rocky Mountain's early popularity, and the increasing enthusiasm for national parks in general put pressure on Congress to increase funding. In March of 1919 Congress removed the $10,000 spending limit, finally making money for improvements available in 1920. Until then, Chief Ranger (later Superintendent) Way did his best to maintain the Park with the limited money and manpower available.

Like the need for money, regulations grew from necessity. Increasing numbers of automobiles entering the Park, for example, necessitated some rules, even though Park roadways totaled only sixty miles in 1919. Aside from demanding "careful driving of all persons," the regulations issued in 1918 limited speeds to twelve miles per hour, or ten miles per hour when "descending steep grades." Horns had to be sounded at every curve and "before meeting or passing other machines, riding or driving animals, or pedestrians." Every vehicle had to be "in first-class working order," capable of making the trip, with "sufficient gasoline in the tank to reach the next place where it may be obtained." Meeting horse teams along the roadways demanded extra caution. Regulations of this type helped, but accidents still happened. "Numerous collisions occurred between automobiles," Superintendent Way reported in 1918, "and between automobiles and saddle horses, none of which resulted in more than slight damage."[19]

A new regulation in 1919 restricting the public conveyance of visitors exclusively to Roe Emery's Rocky Mountain Park's Transportation Company gave Superintendent Way a real taste of controversy. That regulation resulted from the desire of National Park Service Director Stephen Mather to provide reliable public transportation services for visitors. Just outside the boundaries of many national parks, independent drivers offered to transport travelers to local hotels or to take them on sightseeing excursions. Visitors complained that some of those operators cheated the public, provided "indifferent service," failed to keep their schedules, or would not run unless their vehicles were full. Park Service officials concluded that a public transportation system would best operate through one company in each park. Applying that new policy to Rocky Mountain National Park, the Park Service granted the Transportation Company a virtual monopoly.

Local entrepreneurs around Estes Park and Grand Lake were incensed. In an era of free enterprise and of "trust busting," granting a local monopoly in the name of "efficient service" appeared to be almost tyrannical. Among the most critical was Enos Mills. Angered by the granting of this new concession with exclusive privileges, which now applied to an area long used by local resort owners, Mills fumed: "Our national park policy governs without the consent of the governed." "The Director of the National Park Service," he concluded, "is farming these parks out to monopolies." Years of debate verging on acrimony followed. Mills championed the rights of "numerous resident local people who earned their living serving visitors."[20] Superintendent Way found himself caught in a crossfire, defending a national policy he had not created. Nevertheless, the new National Park Service would not recant; it flexed its muscles by emphasizing its concern for the greatest good for the greatest number of visitors.

This controversial regulation also proved to be difficult to enforce. People like Mills were willing to challenge Superintendent Way, his rangers, and the National Park Service in more than just debates. Unauthorized vehicles carrying passengers were deliberately sent into the Park to test the new policy. Rangers arrested offending drivers, court cases resulted, and the noisy controversy lingered. Not until 1926 did the state of Colorado dismiss suits against the federal government related to this issue. And by then a larger issue had surfaced: who controlled the roads in the Park? The state, and Grand and Larimer counties built those roads before 1915, with the Fall River Road not completed until 1920. Colorado

A noisy public dispute regarding a transportation concession for the Park lingered on for nearly a decade. (RMNPHC)

had not ceded jurisdiction to the federal government. Granting a monopoly grew more complex, and it was a concept some local businessmen felt they could not accept. At the same time, idealists in the new National Park Service merely planned to provide better transportation for the public. While less than 15 percent of all Park travelers used Transportation Company services, the imposition of a national policy that upset local economics raised serious questions.

While wrangling over the monopoly issue, Superintendent Way might have written the phrase, "Tempted to give up but didn't," a cryptic message that in fact came from the Eve of Estes, Miss Agnes Lowe. Etched with a piece of charcoal upon bark and placed upon a trail in a conspicuous fashion, that phrase joined the words, "Nearly froze last night." She was keeping a curious world informed. "Have fire now. Feeling fine," completed her words from the wilderness. According to *The Denver Post* of August 9, 1917, those notes and a brief sighting by four parties of tourists confirmed that Miss Lowe was alive. She was spotted "roaming thru the sunshine 'a la Nature.'" Reportedly, she quickly donned her leopard's skin, displayed a good sized string of trout, and paused only long enough to describe an encounter with a brown bear.[21] Four straight days of such reports, with a tale or two about Adam, meant that readers across the country could pinpoint Rocky Mountain National Park on their maps.

Advertising this new park became one of many tasks undertaken by the National Park Service between 1915 and 1929. One of their recurring advertisements during that era brought the latest news about roads as vacationing by automobile flourished in the post-war period. Promoters saw the completion of the Fall River Road as providing a vital link for tourist travel through the region. Superintendent Way met constantly with state officials between 1917 and 1920 urging this project toward completion. Based upon prior agreements, when the state finished the Fall River Road it was to be turned over to the federal government. Late in 1920 the National Park Service proudly announced that "the outstanding event of the year was the completion of the Fall River Road connecting the east and west sides of the park." News that a new route over the Rockies had opened spread quickly. Visitation to the Park jumped accordingly, "reaching the enormous total of 240,966 visitors" in 1920.[22]

While this roadway beckoned thousands of travelers, its rugged and narrow nature made it more challenging than enchanting. Numerous switchbacks "with exceedingly sharp curves" as well as steep grades and a "roadbed too narrow to admit of safe two-way traffic" were combined with long sections of bogs and bumps."[23] Almost immediately Park officials started working to make improvements. Removing snow each spring proved to be one of the most laborious tasks. In 1921, for example, crews spent more than a month clearing snow to insure that travelers could use the route by mid-June. Near Fall River Pass, crews encountered a drift 1,200 feet long, 25 feet deep. That season alone, two tons of dynamite were used to clear the road. Soon the Park acquired a steam shovel to assist the crews shoveling tons of snow by hand. Even then, early in the season teams of horses had to drag many of the first busses and autos across some sections of the road. Costs of keeping this road passable became a major item in the Park budget. While national park officials heralded the scenic aspects of this route across the Rockies, it demanded a continuous drain on money, manpower, and maintenance.

Dozens of lesser activities, many promoting recreation and preservation, also got a boost in the 1920s. Rangers kept a concerned eye on Park wildlife, attempting to provide accurate counts of sheep, deer, and elk. They lured some animals closer to roadways by placing salt blocks at certain locations, believing that these "tame" animals served an educational function for the public. In 1918, Superintendent Way reported: "The frolicking lambs are especially interesting to travelers and convince the great majority of them that the kodak furnishes more real and lasting pleasure in game hunting than the gun."[24] An Interior Department biologist

Somewhat narrow in spots, the Fall River Road proved to be immensely popular throughout the 1920s. (RMNPHC)

The route across Fall River Pass made for an adventurous passage, especially as the road opened each spring. (RMNPHC)

linked wildlife and Park publicity more directly: "The greatest advertising any national park obtains is the number of pictures taken by visitors and given wide distribution. This is the most effective method of advertising—the more so because the intent is not apparent." He suggested that fenced enclosures be placed near roadways, keeping animals of various species on display. "An exhibition inclosure of wild animals," he concluded, "greatly increases the number of pictures taken by visitors."[25]

Though rangers worried about protecting some animals, they worked toward the destruction of others. For example, they watched over the herds of sheep, elk, and deer like guardian angels; they looked for poachers and patrolled the boundaries every hunting season. During the winter of 1917, when food appeared scarce, they even went to the trouble of sawing open a beaver house and dumping in some tasty treats. But meanwhile they waged war on "undesirable" species. Throughout the 1920s such predatory animals as mountain lion, fox, bobcat, coyote, and marten were killed. Some animals were loveable; others made the mistake of preying upon those beloved.

Planting fish in lakes and streams became one of the most active and popular programs of the era. Fishing always ranked high on everyone's recreational list. Park officials hoped to increase the chance that no fisherman would go away disappointed. Through cooperation with nearby state hatcheries, rangers stocked from one hundred thousand to a million trout in Park waters each year.

Diverse forms of recreation also received attention. In addition to extending trails, improving roads, and creating campgrounds, Superintendent Way and his staff assisted the Colorado Mountain Club in its well-advertised winter outings at Fern Lake by building ski trails and toboggan slides and by assisting when accidents occurred or when people became lost. Wintertime use of the "playground" received its first boost when officials noted that "skiing, ski-jumping contests, snowshoeing, skating, and tobogganing were the most popular amusements" among people coming to enjoy winter recreation. Promoting many "improvements" and activities while providing "excellent service" kept Superintendent Way and his rangers busier than ever. By 1921, the rangers numbered four permanently assigned men and six more added each summer season. Helping develop sites that promoted popular forms of recreation fulfilled their ideal of a park. Wilderness and preservation tended to provide a useful backdrop for action. At the heart of most activity ran the Fall River Road, renowned for its "scenery and far-flung panoramas," having "few peers and no superiors."[26]

National park officials promoted the idea that Rocky Mountain National Park could be used year around. When the Colorado Mountain Club made winter outings to Fern Lake Lodge, rangers skiied along. This was the type of healthful recreation park planners dreamed about. (RMNPHC)

Having established some trends toward development and tasting a controversy or two, Superintendent Way decided to return to cattle ranching in Arizona. He resigned on October 24th, 1921. Succeeding L. Claude Way was Roger W. Toll, a popular man who was able to soothe local tempers, resolve a few disputes, and at the same time make National Park Service policies more effective. Throughout the 1920s, Roger Toll committed himself to making Rocky Mountain National Park even more popular with the public.

Born in 1883, Toll was the son of a Denver attorney. Like other Denverites, Roger Toll spent much of his youth exploring the Rockies nearby. His knowledge of Colorado contributed to his popularity among residents of Estes Park and Grand Lake. After obtaining a civil engineering degree from Columbia University in 1906, Toll spent a year traveling around the world. He worked in Massachusetts and Alaska prior to returning to Colorado where he became chief engineer of Denver's tramway company. When the Colorado Mountain Club organized in 1912, Toll joined as a charter member. In the years that followed, he compiled a guide-book about his hobby, later published as *Mountaineering in Rocky Mountain National Park*. That book caught the attention of

Wintertime in the national Rocky Mountain playground. (RMNPHC)

National Park Service Director Stephen Mather. In 1919, Mather asked Toll to become superintendent of Mount Rainier National Park. There Toll proved to be a good administrator, an active mountain climber, and a leader in such local organizations as the Mountaineers. In 1921 he accepted the appointment of superintendent at Rocky Mountain National Park.

Among dozens of people voicing enthusiasm for Rocky Mountain National Park during the 1920s, Roger Wescott Toll was probably the most prominent. Being an adventurous mountain climber, Toll rambled throughout the range, taking photographs and making notes, ascending one peak after another. As an active writer Toll produced numerous articles about the Park and became the Park's chief publicist. He wrote promotional stories describing Park scenes, telling potential tourists what they might find. His articles suggested new development projects, convincing the public that the National Park Service had its welfare in mind. He explored historical topics and described recreational opportunities. His themes helped inform and educate the public, always making Rocky Mountain National Park look exciting and attractive to the potential tourist. In Roger Toll, national park idealism found both a practitioner and a spokesman. "Along with the recreational value of the parks," he wrote, reflecting his own mountaineering experience, "is their health giving value and their inspirational value." He observed: "It has been said that great views create great thoughts and great thoughts create great men."[27] Toll tried mixing his publicity with a philosophy both practical and hopeful.

Under Roger Toll's guidance, Rocky Mountain National Park entered its modern stage as a center for wide-ranging recreational activities. Although rigorous mountain climbing and hiking were among Toll's favorite pastimes, he also recognized that some people might find a mere automobile ride along the Fall River Road equally inspiring. Staying at a lodge within or near the Park, whether at F. W. Byerly's Bear Lake Camp or at Mrs. McPherson's Moraine Lodge or at one of several dozen other resorts, remained the classic way to enjoy the region. Camping at spots such as Aspenglen, Pine-ledge, Glacier Creek, or Endovalley, all developed by 1926, became more popular as visitors sought both inexpensive outdoor vacations and a campfire.

By 1922, ranger-naturalists were conducting "all-day nature study trips" in an effort to provide an educational dimension to national park visits. Evening talks proved to be instantly popular, with lantern slides adding a visual treat. The public gave the naturalists encouraging reviews, expressing an even greater desire "for more accurate and complete knowledge with reference to natural history subjects."[28] A variety of new books helped answer an increasing demand for information, covering subjects as diverse as geology, birds, plants, Indians, and mountaineering. Newly produced maps also appeared. A curious public arriving with probing minds stimulated many avenues of research and education.

Roger Toll also managed an ambitious building program. A new administrative office appeared in 1923, along with a machine shop, a warehouse, a mess hall, and dwellings for National Park Service employees. The main Park utility area started taking shape. Camps for road workers were built at Horseshoe Park and Willow Park; checking stations were placed at the Fall River and Grand Lake entrances. Ranger stations were built at Twin Owls, Bear Lake, Fern Lake, and Horseshoe Park to augment older stations like those at Pole Creek and Mill Creek which had been inherited from the Forest Service. Shelter cabins at Fall River Pass and on Longs Peak were also constructed. Backed by steadily increasing National Park Service appropriations, Roger Toll helped produce a plethora of projects, all viewed as helpful or necessary steps toward progress.

Of course Superintendent Toll was not the sole advocate of building for the future. National Park Service planners contributed many

Roger W. Toll, super-
intendent from 1921
until 1929, actively
promoted and
publicized the Park.
As an active moun-
taineer he knew what
the Park had to offer.
As a practical park
planner, he
envisioned what the
public would come to
appreciate.
(RMNPHC)

ideas. And most of Toll's contemporaries applauded these many
developments. Local businessmen, newspapers, and politicians
welcomed any federal effort to increase the popularity of the Park.
Very few people worried about overdeveloping the region or introducing too many comforts of civilization into an area also intended
as a wilderness preserve. As early as 1922, however, Assistant Park
Service Director Horace Albright responded to an expressed fear
of "over-development of the National Parks in the future by too
many roads, hotels, etc." Albright reported that the national park
superintendents "were unanimous in their belief that certain wild
sections of every park should be forever reserved from any development except by trails, first because the National Parks are destined
to soon be the only sections of wilderness left in America, and
second because wildlife thrives best in untouched wilderness."[29]
Amid the bustle of construction, a few people still pondered the
problem of preservation.

Meanwhile, private enterprise surrounding the Park energetically
prepared for the future too. Trends born in previous decades gained
momentum. The 1920s saw numerous cabins built around Estes
Park and Grand Lake. Additions came to many resorts. More shops
and businesses catering to travelers sprouted. One classic exam-

John Holzwarth helped cater to the tourists of the Twenties. His family's Holzwarth Trout Lodge became the Never Summer Ranch on the Park's western slope. In 1975 that famous dude ranch became part of the Park. (RMNPHC)

ple of resort development occurred on the Park's western slope, at a ranch site first called Holzwarth's Trout Lodge. John G. Holzwarth, a German immigrant, had been a successful Denver saloon-keeper until wartime Prohibition put him out of business. Around 1917, Holzwarth and his wife Sophia decided to move into the mountains, establishing a homestead along the Colorado River north of Grand Lake. There on the North Fork the Holzwarths and their three teenaged children cut timber, built a sawmill, and erected a cabin. Their original idea was to develop a ranch, raising both hay and horses. Trapping for furs and freight hauling helped bring in extra money.

In about 1920 a few of Mr. Holzwarth's "drinkin' friends" from Denver made a visit to the homestead to do some fishing. That group proved to be "so lazy and drunken that they even quarreled over the division of the fish." Once that bunch left for home, Mrs.

Holzwarth and son Johnnie "rebelled" at having to cater to such ill-mannered people. Future guests, they insisted, would have to pay. They christened their homestead the Holzwarth Trout Lodge and began charging two dollars a day or eleven dollars per week. A dude ranch was born. Rental cabins soon offered visitors some rustic shelter and Mrs. Holzwarth provided filling meals. This infant business found a steady clientele and thrived, growing larger during the decade. The Never Summer Ranch, as it was called by 1929, continued as a prosperous example of the 1920s until it was purchased by The Nature Conservancy in 1974 and transferred to Rocky Mountain National Park in 1975. Dozens of other businesses similar to the services offered by the Holzwarths grew as more travelers explored the region.

Not every Park visitor had a good time, however, regardless of people such as the Holzwarths or Superintendent Toll and his rangers. Sometimes nature proved to be a harsh host. In 1922 and again in 1923, for example, lightning struck hikers on Longs Peak. J. E. Kitts was killed outright by a strike as he stood on the summit. Ethel Ridenour, hiking to Chasm Lake, was hit by lightning, burned severely, rendered unconscious, and upon recovering, suffered the permanent loss of one eye. But accidents did not alter the popularity of climbing Longs Peak; in 1929 alone, more than sixteen hundred people signed the register at the summit.

Superintendent Toll and the National Park Service fully recognized the dangers of mountain climbing. Yet all their advice and warnings sometimes went unheeded. In January of 1925, for example, Miss Agnes Vaille intended to become the first woman to scale the east face of Longs Peak in wintertime. Since the east face was an awesome challenge even in good summer weather, she tempted disaster. Vaille made three tries at the summit in the three previous months, failing each time. January found her more determined than ever, although "friends sought in vain to dissuade her from her plans." She found a companion in Walter Kiener, "an experienced mountaineer of Switzerland." On Monday, January 12, 1925, they made that remarkable climb, achieving success by way of the Couloir, Broadway, and a chimney just west of Notch Chimney. But Vaille's hard-won victory was short lived. There on the summit, she and Kiener found the temperature at fourteen below zero and a wind "blowing a terrific gale." Quickly they descended along the easier north side. Soon after, fatigue started clouding her brain. According to Kiener, Agnes Vaille "insisted that she was so sleepy and was going to take a rest and a short nap." Kiener went for help, but when a rescue party found her, she had already frozen to death. For his part, Kiener himself lost most of

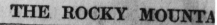

THE ROCKY MOUNTA

AGNES VAILLE DIES IN STORM AFTER CLIMBING LONGS PEAK

Body of Chamber of Commerce Secretary Found Frozen in Snow.

(Continued From Page One.)

Oscar Brown; Jacob Christy and Herbert Sortland, all employed at the inn.

Sortland became exhausted after going about a mile from the house and, suffering from a frozen face and frozen ears, left the party and started back to the shelter. That was the last any of the party saw of the man and it is feared that he fell exhausted in the deep snow and froze to death. Thermometers carried by Kiener showed a temperature of 50 degrees below zero. The heavy snow storm, virtually a blizzard, which raged on the peak yesterday, was accompanied by a strong wind.

Body Found Frozen in Snow.

When the party of men reached the spot where Kiener had left his companion, they found her lying in the snow, dead from the cold and exposure. She had evidently succumbed to her desire for sleep, natural to one slowly freezing to death, and had died but a short time before her rescuers reached her. She had been alone on the mountain saddle from 11 o'clock yesterday morning to 4 o'clock yesterday afternoon, when the men found her body, Kiener's journey to the shelter house and the return trip of the party consuming this amount of time because of the se-

AGNES W. VAILLE.

his fingers and toes as well as part of one foot to frostbite. And compounding the tragedy, Herbert Sortland, a volunteer member of the rescue team, disappeared while returning to Longs Peak Inn. His body was not found until February 27th. A local paper considered the unfortunate Sortland a "martyr to humanity."[30] Yet almost no one publicly criticized either Vaille or Kiener for attempting such a hazardous climb, even though they risked the lives of others. Perhaps people decided that Agnes Vaille had paid the ultimate price for her reckless adventure.

Facing the reality of accidents that came with increasing climbing activity, Superintendent Toll proposed building a shelter cabin high on Longs Peak at the Boulderfield. As a result, in 1927, National Park Service crews constructed a sturdy stone structure that operated as a chalet-type concession until 1935. In memory of Agnes Vaille, another rock-walled shelter was built, this one placed near the Keyhole.

Deaths on Longs Peak and elsewhere in the Park meant more active patrolling by rangers. Rescue work started playing a larger role in their jobs. Nevertheless, enthusiasts publicizing the Park continued to encourage vigorous recreation. "Mountaineering, in its broader sense," Roger Toll claimed, "promotes the health and strength of the body, it teaches self-reliance, determination, presence of mind, necessity for individual thought and action, pride of accomplishment, fearlessness, endurance, helpful cooperation, loyalty, patriotism, the love of an unselfish freedom, and many other qualities that make for a sturdy manhood and womanhood."[31] Accidents were a small price to pay if people truly sought such noble qualities. A number of deaths, caused by carelessness or a lack of caution, would periodically plague the Park in succeeding years. Thus words of advice coming from National Park Service spokesmen mixed a zeal for wilderness recreation with a dose of concern for safety.

Based upon a decade's success as a popular park, Roger Toll proposed an expansion of Rocky Mountain in 1925. The original 1915 boundary lines had already been moved in 1917 to include such areas as Gem Lake, Deer Mountain, and Twin Sisters. The Park grew to include 397.5 square miles. By the mid-1920s, the Park boundaries also surrounded some eleven thousand acres of private land, making administration of the area more complex. Seeing an increasing popularity of the Park, the National Park Service hoped to annex adjacent Forest Service land. Superintendent Toll and other Park Service planners suggested that the Park expand southward to include the region of Arapahoe Glacier. Toll also believed that the Never Summer Range to the West would fit nicely into an enlarged park of the future.

Toll's plans for expansion were not accepted with unanimity. Like the heated transportation controversy or the question of who owned the roads, a larger park was seen by some Coloradans as further endangering their rights to water, private property, mining, and economic prosperity in general. Cooler heads pointed out that tourist dollars meant prosperity too. A local editorialist summed up the opposition to the expansion program: "There is so much that is wrong with administrative policies and regulations of the

A romantic image of the past, the horserider crossed Flattop Mountain as park officials planned highways for the future. (RMNPHC)

National Park Service that Boulder will vigorously fight to be kept from being sacrificed on the destructive altar dedicated to federal red tape and monopoly."[32] Wary of their critical neighbors, Park officials pursued boundary expansion somewhat less zealously.

Contributing to this atmosphere of acrimony was the issue of the state ceding jurisdiction over Park roads. Colorado's concern ranged from a theoretical loss of state's rights to a fear that entrance fees would be charged. Losing control of the roads was also tied to a possible prohibition of future water projects. "It would be unwise and foolish," one opponent of the Park noted, "to let a monopoly-granting, fee-charging Federal Bureau like the National

Park Service become the absolute czar of State-built, State-owned roads leading to and through the Rocky Mountain National Park." With a touch of melodrama, he concluded: "Abolish the Park if you wish! A rose by any other name will smell as sweet! Czarist Federal encroachment on the rights and property of States must stop!"[33] Not until February 16, 1929 did Colorado finally agree to cede its rights to Park roads. Soon after, on March 2nd, 1929, the federal government gladly accepted that cession. Years of debate over that awkward management of roadways finally ended. With the best of intentions, National Park Service planners had helped expedite the conclusion of that debate. They proposed building another scenic road across the mountains, this one by-passing the narrow and twisting Fall River Road. Their proposed route lay along Trail Ridge.

By the mid-1920s, Park Service Director Stephen Mather had little trouble demonstrating the popularity of the national parks; dramatic increases in the number of people visiting the parks proved his case. Congress at last started listening to his budget requests. Soon substantial appropriations were available for improving roadways, an item always greeted enthusiastically by the public. While the jurisdiction question went unresolved, only old roads were fixed. No new construction could take place. Efforts to modernize the Fall River Road proved fruitless, since its narrow, winding course defied improvement. An alternate route soon became a reasonable suggestion. In August of 1926, the Bureau of Public Roads initiated a survey across Trail Ridge. Just as the jurisdiction issue reached its final stages of debate in October of 1928, plans were presented for "one of the greatest scenic park highways in the entire United States." The start of this project, however, depended upon Colorado's willingness to cede its jurisdiction over Park roads. Rather swiftly, that old bureaucratic blockade was cleared. Newspapers lauded this "one-half-million dollar project" as a new sign of federal concern for the region.[34]

The beginning of Trail Ridge Road marked the end of a decade of promotion and development. In January of 1929, the energetic Roger Toll accepted an appointment as superintendent of Yellowstone National Park. When he left Rocky Mountain, it was well established as a booming recreational area. Park boundaries had been adjusted a bit; numerous facilities and services for visitors appeared; modern highways took shape; several sticky controversies were resolved; protection was enhanced for both wildlife and mountaineers. Promoting the Park was paying off in increasing popularity and greater numbers of visitors. In 1929, nearly three hundred thousand people entered the Park.

People spending a carefree day in the mountains rarely considered the elements of risk, danger, or safety, occasionally to their peril. The hazards of driving across the Divide were to be reduced by a new route proposed along Trail Ridge. (RMNPHC)

Publicity was paying off by the mid-1920s, when loaded jitneys plied the road to Bear Lake. (RMNPHC)

On August 13, 1917, *The Denver Post* reported that the Eve of Estes had returned to civilization after her week in the woods. "Sunburned almost of the shade of pine bark, and covered with mosquito bites from the crown of her head to the soles of her feet," came the story, she appeared in perfect health "and weighed a half pound more than when she left civilization."[35] According to the *Post*, her adventure produced dozens of stories in newspapers "from Portland, Maine to Portland, Oregon, and from Hudson Bay to Key West, Florida."[36] After being welcomed back by Park officials and Enos Mills, and posing once again for cameras, Agnes Lowe was given a mail sack containing sixty-four proposals of marriage. With the adventure at an end, she left for a local lodge to rest. She rapidly returned to obscurity, leaving only a week's worth of newspaper columns in her wake.

Whether those columns spelled positive publicity for the Park was debatable. Within a week, Park Service officials in Washington were fuming at this "frame-up for publicity purposes." Called upon by superiors to explain his participation, Superintendent Way immediately blamed "the *Denver Post* and the Hearst Syndicate," although he felt the stories "will result in very valuable publicity and undoubtedly in bringing hundreds of people to this park."[37] Rather than receiving praise for his role, Way then heard from Assistant Director Albright. Albright claimed that stunts of that type "will surely bring adverse criticism upon park management." He added that "a national park is not the proper stage for even this sort of thing."[38]

Faced with a barrage of criticism, Way confessed to being duped into helping reporters from *The Denver Post* arrange the stunt. He admitted watching as "Eve" arrived at Longs Peak Inn and as she posed for photographers in preparation for her adventure. But rather than watch her disappear into the mountains alone, Way arranged for one of his rangers to take her to Fern Lodge. There she stayed until Way himself escorted her back to Estes Park that following Wednesday. He admitted that her emergence from the forest that next Sunday was entirely a staged affair. The whole event had been a fraud. But once again Way argued that the stories "did no real harm and aroused interest in the Park and would bring people here who would enjoy themselves and be benefitted."[39] Like the unamused Park Service officials in Washington, ranger R. A. Kennedy disagreed. Kennedy considered it an unpleasant task to escort Miss Lowe to Fern Lodge. "It is cheap and disgusting, and smacks more of a cabaret than a wholesome advertisement," he concluded.[40]

Whether it was really "cheap and disgusting" or merely amusing, Rocky Mountain National Park had hit the headlines. Trying to make a park for all to enjoy meant making a few mistakes, having a few embarrassments. Success and popularity came regardless, in part because of the efforts of such people as Roger Toll, but mostly because the sublime beauty of Rocky Mountain National Park could not be diminished by ill-conceived publicity stunts. Roger Toll knew this well: "Surely if one can ever grasp the infinity of time and space, it is here, standing on the peak and looking off to the vanishing horizon."[41]

Exactly what publicity the Park needed, only time would tell. (RMNPHC)

7
PUBLICITY PAYS OFF

"American tourist travel is of a swift tempo. People want to keep moving. They are satisfied with brief stops here and there."
Horace M. Albright, Director, National Park Service, 1931[1]

IN 1936, a Rocky Mountain ranger named Bob Flame became an historical phenomenon. Through his eyes and actions Americans discovered the dramatic world of rangering in the Rockies. Readers found Flame and his fellow rangers busy searching for tourists missing in the mountains. Observers soon recognized the courage and daring necessary to effect the rescue of hapless or careless Park visitors. They learned of daily difficulties rangers confronted in weather and wilderness. Like other heroic characters, Bob Flame and his men fought for justice, captured outlaws, and faced death without fear. With Bob Flame offering a literary example, Rocky Mountain's rangers changed from being mere government bureaucrats; their dedication to the principles of preservation and the protection of the public made them worthy of adulation.

But Bob Flame, like a few other heros in history, existed primarily in the mind. He was created by Chief Park Naturalist Dorr Yeager and portrayed in a novel entitled *Bob Flame, Rocky Mountain Ranger*, published in 1936. As one of the Park's key publicists during the 1930s, Yeager believed that rangers offered a popular and romantic image of courage and adventure. Yeager knew he had a subject tailor-made for projecting the pride of the National Park Service, the best it had to offer. Mixing facts with his fiction, Yeager sought to describe the rangers of Rocky Mountain at work. He hoped to record the realities of their job. In developing the character of Bob Flame, he offered a composite of

Symbolic of an ideal, the rangers of Rocky Mountain National Park seemed to personify the preservation of nature and the protection of the park visitor. (RMNPHC)

men he knew, of rangers he saw in action. But a simple story about protection and preservation activities was not enough; idealism and adventure had to be added. In Yeager's novel, Bob Flame came to symbolize a spirit of professional dedication. Having national parks required finding people willing to work for a "good cause." Rangers such as Flame helped the National Park Service achieve its goals, whether in publicity, preservation, or protection. Yet the real Rocky Mountain rangers, like the concept of a national park itself, never existed in an ideal form. Reality played havoc with idealistic notions. Was the Park a preserve or a playground? Was it going to be protected or expected to produce something tangible? Between 1930 and the mid-1950s, Rocky Mountain National Park became a tremendously popular refuge for Americans seeking recreation and relaxation. And it started to face the consequences of that popularity.

In 1929, when Roger Toll left for Yellowstone and Edmund Rogers became the new superintendent, neither man could foresee how events well beyond the Park would affect its future in the coming decades. Toll had worked hard to create an image of progress and popularity for the area. Rogers could only expect that development would continue and tourism would steadily increase. But within a year or two, the Depression changed that vision of the future; later, World War II interrupted vacation plans nationwide; and then, just as unexpected, a boom in post-war travel produced by prosperity brought more tourists than ever. So rather than experiencing the steady development initiated by Roger Toll, Rocky Mountain National Park reflected the pulse of the nation, feeling the tempo of Depression, war, and peace.

As the 1930s began, it appeared as if the publicity efforts and construction programs of the previous decade would simply continue. Edmund Rogers, handpicked by Superintendent Toll, stepped into a park seemingly destined for a bright and busy future. Before his new appointment, Rogers had served with the U.S. Geological Survey and was an officer of the Colorado National Bank. His brother, James Grafton Rogers, had earlier formulated the original legislation that created the Park. A long personal friendship with Roger Toll, active membership in the Colorado Mountain Club, and having national parks as a "sort of hobby," all helped Rogers gain the position of superintendent. And for a year or two, the future certainly looked promising. As National Park Service Director Horace Albright reported about Rocky Mountain in 1931: "Its problems were not pressing. Its organization has been func-

A new highway carved across the tundra of Trail Ridge offered a safer route of travel over the Continental Divide. This "scenic wonder road" was opened for use in 1932. (RMNPHC)

tioning smoothly. Steady progress has been made in all lines of activity."[2]

One form of the "steady progress" Albright described involved the construction of Trail Ridge Road. Congress appropriated $450,000 for the first phase of that project in April of 1929. By October, W. A. Colt of Las Animas, Colorado was awarded the contract for building the eastern portion of the new highway. Colt, a well-known ditch and railroad builder then seventy-two years old, had just completed a contract on the Bear Lake Road. Establishing a base camp at Hidden Valley, Colt soon had his crew hard at work. Among his 185 employees were foremen, power shovel operators, oilers, cooks, blacksmiths, mechanics, and about 150 laborers. The winter of 1929–1930 proved to be mild, enabling Colt and his crew to continue construction activities until March 16th. Even then, blizzards interrupted their progress only briefly. By April 7th, 1930, the men were back at work, proceeding much faster than originally thought possible. By September of 1930 the first phase of the 17.2-mile project was 55 percent completed. At the same time, L. T. Lawler of Butte, Montana was awarded a contract for

Care was taken to minimize the environmental damage that the construction of Trail Ridge Road caused. The decision to build the roadway meant sacrificing some preservationist ideals to allow easier access to the high country. (RMNPHC)

the western section of the road, from Fall River Pass to the floor of the Colorado River valley, a distance of 11 miles.

Both Colt's and Lawler's crews faced a more difficult winter in 1930–1931. Drifts of snow and persistent frosts kept Lawler's men inactive until May and Colt's crew waiting until June. But delays caused by weather failed to dim any enthusiasm for its upcoming completion. "It is hard to describe what a sensation this new road is going to make," Park Service Director Albright predicted, "you will have the whole sweep of the Rockies before you in all directions. It is going to give you the quintessence of the Rockies in one view."[3] Work proceeded rapidly throughout the summer of 1931, helping speed Albright's promise into reality. By July of 1932, the eastern section of Trail Ridge Road was sufficiently completed to allow automobiles filled with curious sightseers to traverse the roadway. In 1933, the entire new route opened for travel, although finishing touches such as paving and rock work would continue throughout the decade.

Here was a highway built to serve as a perfect introduction to the Rocky Mountains, a "scenic wonder road of the world" as the

Rocky Mountain News termed it. Although some potential visitors would wonder whether it was safe, especially "flatlanders" unaccustomed to mountain driving, Trail Ridge provided "a perfect roadbed—twenty-four feet from shoulder to shoulder, providing sufficient room for even the most timid and unexperienced motorists to pass abreast."[4] Promoters of this new road could also boast that ten of its miles ran at an altitude above eleven thousand feet in elevation. Yet at the same time no part of the road exceeded a grade steeper than 7 percent. The *Estes Park Trail* reported that "many cars make the trip from the village to the 'top' without changing gears."[5] Creating an easy approach to the high country offered "one of the most amazing vistas of mountains and forests ever given men the privilege of seeing for only the cost of a few hours' effortless driving."[6]

Constructing this new highway through the heart of a national park brought very few complaints. Voicing one note of concern, landscape architect Charles Eliot argued: "It is much better to build no roads than to run the risk of destroying wilderness areas."[7] Clearly that was a minority opinion. For contrary to Eliot's view, advocates of Trail Ridge road pointed to the simple fact that it replaced the older, more hazardous Fall River route. Any destruction of wilderness could be blamed on the earlier road crossing the mountains, initiated prior to the Park being "preserved." And this was also an era when building roads in national parks gained wide popularity. The National Park Service believed it was responding correctly to a public need. The improved route across Trail Ridge matched the Sylvan Pass road in Yellowstone, Going-to-the-Sun highway in Glacier, the Wawona road and tunnel in Yosemite (as well as the Tioga Road by 1940), the Cape Royal road in Grand Canyon, and others. All these roads provided easier automobile access to national park interiors and all were conceived during this same flurry of development activity. Road construction of this type, Park Service Director Albright believed, "is meeting an obligation to the great mass of people who because of age, physical condition, or other reason would never have an opportunity to enjoy, close at hand, this marvelous mountain park."[8] Both newspaper and National Park Service reports stressed that only minimal disruption of the natural scene occurred as a result of the road's construction. "Everything possible has been done to preserve the beauty of the terrain through which the road leads," claimed one report. Careful supervision by W. T. Lafferty, district engineer for the Bureau of Public Roads, and continuous inspection by Superintendent Rogers helped maintain aesthetic sensitivity. When outcroppings at the Rock Cut had to be blasted with dynamite, for example, care was taken to guard neighboring rock pillars to prevent noticeable scarring. "After each blast of dynamite," a final report noted, "workmen have cleaned up all 'country rock' thrown over the landscape so that there would be no unsightly white rock among the lichen covered boulders that contribute to the scenery."[9] Historian Lloyd Musselman credited Superintendent Rogers with walking the entire length of Trail Ridge some twenty times. Based on his recommendations, the road followed the most scenic route possible, including the dramatic Rock Cut area. But no single individual could have built this "million dollar road." From the laborer who worked with pick and shovel, gasping for breath in the frigid high altitudes, to Park Service officials guiding the project through the corridors of government, many could be proud of their achievement. Historian Musselman concluded simply that the "Trail Ridge project was a triumph of human ingenuity and perseverance."[10] Whether it compromised a wilderness ideal for the Park was another matter.

The immediate impact of opening Trail Ridge Road was far from philosophical. On a purely economic level, a project of such magnitude kept many people from Estes Park, Grand Lake, and other nearby communities employed while other parts of the nation began to suffer the effects of the Depression. In addition to producing jobs, the new highway attracted more tourists. While other national parks watched their annual tide of vacationers dwindle by 25 percent or more during the 1930s, Rocky Mountain's figures kept increasing. In 1929, an estimated 256,000 people entered the Park, and by 1933, with Trail Ridge Road fully opened, the number increased to nearly 292,000. Economic ills could not compete with a spectacular new highway as those 1933 travelers arrived in 83,000 automobiles. By 1938, the number of people entering the Park climbed to nearly 660,000, bringing with them some 200,000 cars. Whether these travelers stayed only briefly or took the time "to rest and play" as expected by national park idealists appeared to be unimportant as National Park Service officials reveled in those numbers and local businesses reaped a harvest of tourist dollars. The annual display of those growing statistics allowed Park officials to link their concept of progress through construction to the economic well-being of the local communities. Whether fulfilling national park ideals or not, this section of the Rockies remained closely tied to the entrepreneurial environment of Estes Park and Grand Lake, just as it had during the era preceding the Park's formation. Superintendent David Canfield summarized this mood in 1941. "In the villages of Estes Park and Grand Lake," he observed, "national park interests are as close to the vil-

By the late 1930s, the village of Estes Park displayed growth enhanced by businesses linked to the recreation industry. (RMNPHC)

lagers as their own interests, and local suspicions of this government bureau are being replaced by a spirit of cooperation."[11]

During the decade preceding Canfield's hopeful report, occasional differences arose with local residents as Park officials promoted a wilder environment for the Park. Along the Park's eastern boundary, in particular, dozens of parcels of private property, many sporting summer cabins, served as an encroaching display of civilization for visitors expecting to see wilderness. Creating an appropriate entrance and environment for the Park meant acquiring private property. Much of Horseshoe Park, Beaver Meadows, and neighboring Moraine Park were occupied by ranches and resorts, this land having been homesteaded prior to the Park's formation. Also private was Bear Lake, the Loch, Mills Lake, and thousands of acres of other key attractions. At Director Albright's urging, the National Park Service started a lengthy program of land acquisition. Their intention was to insure that anyone driving the new Trail Ridge Road would behold scenery "free from unsightly and cluttered up structures." It took some convincing to assure local landowners "that the whole plan is a patriotic one in that the primary interest is to safeguard the general public interest in the protection for all time of the landscape of this wonderfully beautiful park approach."²² But buying property could only be accomplished in a piecemeal fashion, taking decades to accomplish. Removing every trace of old buildings, many in ramshakle condition, took even longer.

An additional concern about the number of businesses sprouting at the very edge of the Park brought statements of cautious admonition, with National Park Service spokesmen gingerly sidestepping any interference with the legal rights of property owners. In a guarded statement, Director Albright suggested that "the establishment of hot dog stands and billboards is frowned upon but there is no reason why the service should seek to curtail legitimate business enterprises."¹³ Practically admitting defeat in that arena, he conceded: "Our ideals contemplate a national park system of primitive lands free from all present and future commercial utilization, but, like all ideals, they can not be uniformly attained in this day and age."¹⁴

Protecting the Park's periphery included more than just decrying billboards and hot dog stands. Officials faced a more dramatic problem in poaching. Guarding the Park's wildlife kept rangers busy throughout the 1930s. Pursuing poachers became an annual challenge, especially when the local hunting season was in full swing and hunters occasionally "strayed" into the Park. Chief Ranger John McLaughlin, who served as the archetype for Dorr Yeager's hero Bob Flame, argued that a modern poacher "is nothing more than a sneaking racketeer." This cowardly villain "carries on his illegal trade in a game refuge," McLaughlin wrote, "where deer browse a few yards from a road and only a minimum amount of physical exertion and hunting skill is necessary." Not only were the poacher's hunting methods scurrilous, but he would shoot "the same deer that have only several months previously given tourists and visitors a real thrill and no little delight." McLaughlin appealed to people of the local communities to assist his rangers in their protection efforts, hoping to stamp out "this Sneak in our midst." He complained that public opinion did not seem overly concerned about poaching "but it is high time that thinking citizens consider it."¹⁵ In the semi-fictional *Bob Flame, Rocky Mountain Ranger*, the damnable poacher got caught. "He'll have six months to think things over," Flame concluded, "and when he comes out I'll bet he'll have reached the conclusion that those three does were pretty expensive meat."¹⁶

Using the latest two-way radio equipment, barricading roads, and making daring automobile chases all helped capture the classic poacher in fiction. While actual pursuits might prove equally

Rangers of the 1930s started forsaking their horses for patrol vehicles with more horsepower. (RMNPHC)

The introduction of mobile radios in patrol cars enhanced rangers' power to perform their duties of enforcing park rules and regulations. (RMNPHC)

Rangers always had to be prepared for any emergency, from fixing flat tires to fighting forest fires. (RMNPHC)

dramatic, many times they were less successful. District Ranger Jack Moomaw recorded one version of a real chase, offering an example of a particularly ambitious effort. The pursuit began when Grand Lake ranger Fred McLaren discovered a poacher's trap line within the Park boundary. Hoping to catch the culprit, he started trailing the fellow's fresh snowshoe tracks. That trail led the determined McLaren clear across the Continental Divide, down into Forest Canyon, all the way to the Pool on the Big Thompson River. Along the way he gathered all the illegal traps as well as a couple of ensnared marten. Exhausted by his trek and unable to catch sight of his quarry, McLaren retired to Park headquarters and reported his evidence. Almost immediately his task was continued by rangers Moomaw and Harold Ratcliff. Heading into the mountains on skis, they first went to Fern Lake, thinking that the devious trapper might have broken into Fern Lake Lodge to spend the night. They were proved wrong. Regardless, they spent that night at the government cabin nearby. Early the next day they rediscovered the poacher's tracks heading westward, back across the

Divide. Cautiously, the two rangers worked their way to the head of Spruce Canyon, climbing a steep pass on crusty snow and ice. "Without knowing it we had been flirting with disaster," Moomaw recalled, "for to have slipped down that slope into the rocks below would have been almost certain death." A gale of icy wind greeted the two rangers once they topped the Divide. Rapidly they began their descent into Tonahutu Creek. Finding shelter among some trees, they built a fire, thawed their canteens, and ate a chilly lunch. "Gosh, he must be a tough egg!" Ratcliff admitted. During the afternoon that followed, the two men continued on, sometimes floundering in soft snow, crashing through down-timber and brush. Nightfall came as the rangers trudged on. Finally, in a dilapidated barn at Big Meadows, they found some shelter for the night. Even though they were exhausted and nearly frozen, they managed to build a fire and fix a warm supper. Through the frigid night that followed, the two took turns tending their fire and sleeping, trying to avoid freezing to death. When morning came, they skied to Grand Lake Ranger Station. There they met ranger McLaren who had returned by automobile. All their efforts proved fruitless. McLaren announced that the poacher had escaped, "left for parts unknown," leaving the rangers with only a set of traps and a memorable chase. A couple of marten McLaren found in those traps soon graced the Park's museum.[17]

Frustrating pursuits of this sort must have angered dedicated men like Ratcliff, Moomaw, and McLaren. As a result, continuous appeals were made for the public to assist in wildlife preservation. "Government protection is of little use, in a community such as ours," Moomaw wrote in a local newspaper, "unless backed by private effort and cooperation, and this means you, and you, and you."[18]

As with their success in attracting more and more tourists, Park Service efforts at protecting wildlife started to look almost too effective. By the end of the 1930s, officials realized that there were more deer and elk living in Rocky Mountain National Park than its natural range could support. With predatory animals almost entirely removed and hunting controlled, the remaining animal population multiplied rapidly. In 1937, naturalists Merlin Potts and Howard Gregg, along with ranger Harold Ratcliff, counted some 648 deer and 263 elk, and their totals were considered only a part of the actual population. By 1939, the elk in particular had overpopulated their grazing territory. Ratcliff observed: "They can no longer sustain themselves in such numbers without irreparable damage to the range."[19] The old practices of simply killing predators and guarding against poachers would not insure a healthy herd of animals within the preserve. Additional "management" to prevent over-browsed feeding grounds and starvation now became necessary. Encouraging hunting on land adjacent to the Park offered a workable solution. So, in 1941, a special hunting season was permitted along the Park's eastern boundary, culling 97 elk from the increasing herd. But not enough animals were eliminated and the problem continued. By 1944 an even more aggressive step had to be taken. Park rangers were forced to shoot some 300 elk and 100 deer. A crisis in overpopulation demanded radical solutions. Throughout the 1940s and early 1950s, numerous studies monitored wildlife populations and their ranges. Park officials hoped to establish a balance between animals and edibles. Live-trapping and transplanting were sometimes substituted for shooting; scientific studies were initiated; wildlife biologists were consulted; officials sought to avoid controversy by basing their decisions upon research. Shooting hundreds of animals, after all, appeared quite contrary to general national park ideals based on pure protection. Ideals changed to irony as problems grew more complex.

Seemingly less complicated, even the transplantation of troublesome animals occasionally produced strange results. In August of 1932, for example, ranger Jack Moomaw trapped a 300-pound black bear that had been rummaging around near his cabin. Soon after, Chief Ranger McLaughlin transported the offending bruin to Chapin Pass, released the critter, and watched it scamper northward. But Moomaw's problem was just beginning. The very next night, five smaller bears started skulking around his station. Apparently the larger bear had kept the others out of that territory. Managing Park wildlife became a learning process for rangers as well.

One pressure forcing poachers to invade the Park in the early 1930s may have been the Depression, although ranger Moomaw argued against that notion. "It is hard for me to believe that anyone in this community is in such dire need that it is necessary for him to kill a deer," he wrote.[20] Regardless of his opinion, economic woes were affecting the communities around the Park. In February, 1933, Superintendent Rogers observed: "There is no activity in the town of Estes Park. 'Old Timers' say it is the quietest year in the history of the region. Business and hotel men are going about with long faces, realizing of course, that the coming season will be a gamble." Expecting the worst, Rogers concluded: "It's our opinion that the community in general has just begun to feel the sting of the depression."[21]

Yet vacationers defied that ominous prediction and continued to stream into Rocky Mountain National Park, the nation's economy notwithstanding. Perhaps the Park offered a temporary escape from the realities of hard times. In the case of hundreds of young men, the Park definitely provided an economic refuge: these were the members of the Civilian Conservation Corps. In March of 1933, President Roosevelt proposed a program to provide unemployment relief by putting people from cities to work in the nation's forests and parks. Based on Roosevelt's plan, Congress swiftly passed the Emergency Conservation Work Act. On April 5th, 1933, Roosevelt signed the bill into law, creating the "CCC." Immediately, state foresters, members of the U.S. Forest Service, and officials of the National Park Service were called upon to integrate this new program into their areas and operations.

Young men who enrolled in the program were to be physically fit, unemployed, unmarried, and between the ages of eighteen and twenty-five. Later, the age limits were reduced to seventeen and increased to twenty-eight. Each enrollee received a dollar a day for his labor, of which twenty-five dollars a month was sent to his family back home. Crew foremen earned a bit more, normally forty-five dollars per month. Every man also received suitable clothing as well as shelter, food, and transportation. The War Department coordinated the selection of men, the construction and supervision of camps, and the delivery of supplies and equipment. Local rangers identified important projects they wished to see accomplished, giving assistance, advice, and occasional supervision once work got underway. Between 1933 and 1942, when the CCC was finally disbanded due to the war, nearly 3,200,000 young men gained employment through this program all across the nation. The total cost of the CCC amounted to some $3 billion, of which $700 million went directly to the enrollees' families. In spite of the cost, President Roosevelt deemed the CCC necessary to relieve "the acute condition of widespread distress and unemployment."[22]

Rocky Mountain National Park received its first contingent of this unemployed army on May 12, 1933. Two officers and 8 men arrived from Fort Logan near Denver and were promptly greeted at Park headquarters by a howling blizzard. Undaunted, however, they recruited an additional 35 local "woodsmen" within a week and started constructing the first of several CCC camps in the region. Although piles of crusted snow had to be shoveled to clear the ground, a camp called "N.P.-C-1" eventually sprouted in Little Horseshoe Park. Built in army style, the camp contained some 24 pyramidal tents for quarters, 4 larger hospital tents, a field kitchen, and other necessary accouterments. Almost immediately, men started arriving: 48 from Fort Sill, Oklahoma; 111 from Greeley;

Nation-wide unemployment during the Depression found hundreds of young men joining the Civilian Conservation Corps, with Rocky Mountain National Park offering one of many sites for outdoor work. (RMNPHC)

Below: Organized by the Army in military fashion, CCC camps provided food, shelter, and clothing for each enrollee willing to work. (RMNPHC)

and 50 more from Fort Logan. Unfortunately, all these men arrived before necessary supplies reached the camp. Chilly weather caught many of them without proper clothing. Shortages of food and bedding soon caused the men to riot. Park officials quickly assisted camp supervisors, providing Moraine Lodge as temporary shelter. Within a couple of days, adequate food and supplies finally arrived and the CCC's future looked brighter. Every man was issued 6 blankets, a mattress, and a cot. In addition, each enrollee received 2 pairs of denim pants, a pair of khaki pants, 2 khaki shirts, a blue-

The CCC camp called "NP-1-C" in Little Horseshoe Park displayed the orderly environment provided for unemployed men between 1933 and 1942. (RMNPHC)

denim hat, 6 pairs of socks, 2 pairs of boots, a toilet kit, and one aluminum mess kit, which included a canteen. N.P.-C-1, rapidly built and inhabited, standing ready for work, held 194 men and 2 officers. But just when everything seemed in perfect shape, another late spring blizzard hit on May 22. Tents were "torn to ribbons," while others collapsed with men inside. Part of the mess tent "was blown into Kansas," and pots and pans were strewn for a mile down the valley. Perhaps this storm helped christen the CCC concept. It certainly made the men of N.P.-C-1 more determined to succeed, for it only took one day for the blasted camp to recover. The following day 100 men were hard at work chopping away at beetle-killed trees as part of "Roosevelt's Green Guard."[23]

At first many of the recruits found forest work difficult. According to CCC enrollee Battell Loomis, "sore backs and blistered hands, sunburn, homesickness, and general misery made us about as stiff-muscled a bunch as you every saw." A few men called it quits, deciding to "go over the hill." But most enrollees preferred the work in the woods to facing depressed conditions back home. Loomis recalled their camp schedule: up at six o'clock; breakfast at seven ("hot and plenty of it"); policing the camp until eight; off to work from eight until noon; lunch at twelve ("we get a pound of bread and a pound of meat per man per day, as well as eggs and plenty of vegetables"); four more hours of work and back to camp by four-thirty. Evening left the men on their own, with athletics, classes, and occasional trips to the village serving as diversions. Army rules were mixed with the knowledge that these men were civilians. "No liquor in camp is the hard-and-fast rule," Loomis recalled. Following a similar pattern, camp life at N.P.-C-1 was copied at several additional locations such as Grand Lake, along Mill Creek, or at various temporary backcountry sites.[24]

Once underway, the CCC workers did more than just cut and remove beetle infested trees. They landscaped government buildings, removed old and unsightly structures, built and improved trails, restored land to its natural condition, constructed telephone lines, improved campgrounds, and completed dozens of other tasks involving both construction and conservation. Some of them worked in skilled occupations, helping the National Park Service with its administrative tasks, assisting as naturalists, photographers, carpenters, trail crews, and the like. Whenever the Park experienced major emergencies, CCC crews offered assistance. They participated in numerous rescue efforts, especially those searches that required many helpers to comb the countryside. They fought forest fires. In all their tasks, CCC manpower was a considerable asset to the Park. Local pundits first called these men "woodpeckers" or "woodticks," terms that riled more than one enrollee. Defending their honor, Battell Loomis saw this "Green Guard of the Roosevelt Revolution" simply as "men who didn't have a chance under the old deal, willing to work, just starting out in life, good cannon fodder for the Communists or the racketeers."[25]

Until July 29th, 1942, when the last enrollees left the Mill Creek camp, the CCC worked to improve the condition of the Park. At the same time, the mountains worked their own magic upon the men. In the words of Battell Loomis, "While we CCC men are doing things to the forests, the forest is doing things to us." What Loomis saw his fellow enrollees gaining most was self-reliance. In addition, they obtained practical experience in the trades of forestry, masonry, and carpentry. Just working at a job, holding employment of any sort, was highly valued. Best of all, Loomis believed their work in Rocky Mountain with the CCC gave them hope for a brighter future, for "the one thing (the CCC) will *not* do is retreat into the bread lines whence Roosevelt recruited it."[26] Rocky Mountain National Park assumed a role as an economic refuge, there for men who needed help.

While park officials were sorry to see the CCC program end, they were even less pleased to see another government project get under-

Rocky Mountain National Park provided plenty of labor intensive projects for CCC men willing to work for a dollar a day. (RMNPHC)

The CCC enrollees took pride in their accomplishments and the aesthetic quality of the Park was improved through their efforts. (RMNPHC)

way. That new undertaking, viewed as endangering the ideals of wilderness and preservation, became known as the Colorado-Big Thompson Water Diversion Project. During the 1930s water remained a very critical issue for farmers living on the eastern plains of Colorado. With the spreading Dust Bowl causing ever greater worries, irrigation advocates around Greeley and other plains communities revived a decades-old proposal to divert Colorado River water directly through the Rockies by means of a tunnel. In 1933, when this idea was again publicly suggested, national park supporters immediately unfurled the banners of wilderness preservation. They challenged any further encroachments of civilization upon the Park. Two basic philosophies regarding public land use once again came into conflict: one that sought to preserve the natural integrity of the Park and one that saw the utilitarian aspect of water, arguing its necessity for agriculture.

Building diversion canals and reservoirs throughout the mountains had become a standard practice in Colorado dating from the 1860s. Farming land that received less than sixteen inches of rainfall each year required the development of irrigation. Ambitious water projects served as the lifeblood for hundreds of farms and dozens of villages out on the arid plains. For western agriculture, dams, canals, and reservoirs meant more than just conservation: they meant survival. Simple irrigation canals of the 1860s and 1870s led to major diversion projects by the 1880s and 1890s, producing such projects as the Grand River Ditch. In 1905, a group of engineering students from Colorado State College examined the Front Range and plotted a potential tunnel from Grand Lake to Moraine Park, and presented a convincing case to water project advocates showing this plan was feasible. At about the same time, the federal Bureau of Reclamation, aggressive in water development and conservation projects, withdrew land around Grand Lake from public entry, eyeing that region for potential diversion projects. When Rocky Mountain National Park was formed in 1915, the Bureau of Reclamation received assurances that "rights of way" for "irrigation and other purposes" would not be disrupted by the new park.[27]

In 1923, Superintendent Toll surveyed all the reservoir and ditch sites then active in the Park, all predating the Park itself. He discovered eighteen such projects, including such entries as Lawn Lake, Sandbeach Lake, the Eureka Ditch to Spruce Canyon, Snowbank Lake, and three Cairns reservoirs. Every section of the Park appeared to have its share of projects. Park officials were fully aware of the expectations Colorado farmers had for the melting snows and bubbling brooks of the Rockies.

When the tunnel idea once again emerged in 1933, Park Service officials argued that their ideals of wilderness preservation were being undermined. So strong was that feeling that the initial reaction of Park Service Director Arno B. Cammerer to the project led him to reject a request from Weld and Larimer county citizens to make a survey of suitable locations for a tunnel within the Park. Sites outside of the Park should be considered first, the officials suggested. When a survey party arrived at Grand Lake regardless in August of 1933, Chief Ranger John McLaughlin was sent there to meet the intruders and block their entry into the Park. But in spite of the rangers, one engineer claimed to have located suitable sites for both the east and west portals of the proposed tunnel: Grand Lake would serve as the western reservoir for a tunnel that would empty some thirteen miles to the east at the Wind River, just southeast of Emerald Mountain. Convinced the project would work, supporters of the tunnel remained undaunted by the challenge of Park Service idealists.

What national park supporters feared most was another scar of civilization, damaging the remaining wildness of the mountains. They believed that a tunnel might pierce fractures in the rock, draining some of the high mountain lakes dry. They argued that reservoirs were unsightly and that power stations and electrical transmission lines ruined the aesthetic quality of wild areas. In general, they believed that the proposed tunnel could "leave a scar on the wilderness character of the park and its environs."[28] Allied conservation groups, many from outside of Colorado, joined the National Park Service in its opposition to the tunnel. "We submit that this project violates the most sacred principle of National Parks," one protest read, "namely freedom from commercial or economic exploitations and that if approved by Congress it will establish a precedent for the commercial invasion of other parks."[29] The Audubon Society, the Izaak Walton League, the Wilderness

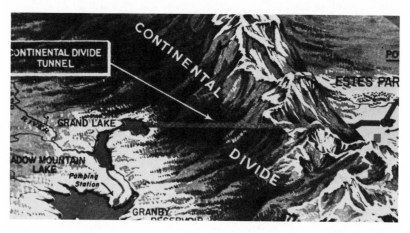

Society, and other like-minded groups campaigned to prevent the project. Yet the proposal would not die. Colorado farmers demanded water and farmers carried political clout. With little difficulty, supporters of the project gained the backing of the Bureau of Reclamation, along with numerous Colorado communities and newspapers, and most of the state's leading politicians. More surveys soon led to legislation proposed before Congress. Once the issue entered the political arena, the tunnel idea found a most favorable climate.

This was a project that appeared to constitute a practically unbeatable formula for one view of conservation: it combined water for irrigation with the production of inexpensive hydroelectric power. Furthermore, farmers would pay for the water they used and customers would pay for electricity, eventually repaying the government for all expenses of construction. Receiving a blessing from the Public Works Administration, a project of this type also created many jobs, helping boost the economic conditions in neighboring communities. That economic promise found particular favor in Estes Park and Grand Lake. And like dozens of other New Deal construction projects, the proposal gained the support of President Roosevelt once the legislation was submitted to Congress by Colorado's Senator Alva B. Adams in 1937. Nevertheless, National Park Service spokesmen still tried to stem this tide of support. Superintendent Thomas J. Allen demanded that "vigorous efforts should be made by the Service to prevent such construction in this or any other national park, in order that these areas may be safeguarded for perpetual preservation."[30] But arguments for preservation would not erase the historic legacy of water projects predating the Park; idealists arguing for wilderness could not defeat ardent pragmatists whose views were based on employment and necessity. Every National Park Service protest failed. On December 27, 1937, President Roosevelt gave his final approval for the Colorado-Big Thompson diversion project.

Following almost two years of preparation, drilling into the mountains began on June 16, 1940. Work continued steadily, but in late 1942 the War Production Board ordered a halt, claiming that the tunnel was not essential to the war effort. By September of 1943, the task of boring resumed. The main tunnel was finally "holed through" on July 10, 1944. When the eastern crews met men drilling from the west, engineers claimed that their 13.1-mile tunnel was off its alignment by only seven-sixteenths of an inch. Regardless of the controversy, here was a marvel of engineering. On June 23, 1947, the first water flowed eastward from Grand Lake through the "Alva B. Adams Tunnel" and by 1954 almost all associated elements of the project, including Lakes Estes and Granby, Shadow Mountain Reservoir, additional tunnels, power stations, dams, and so on, were completed.

Yet the question remained whether national park ideals had been compromised. Arguing their case for wilderness values, the National Park Service spokesmen simply hoped that alternative routes through the Rockies would also be considered. Their subsequent failure to prevent the tunnel did not mean total defeat for their ideals, however. According to Lloyd Musselman, voicing concern about protecting the Park meant that the Bureau of Reclamation

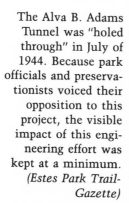

The Alva B. Adams Tunnel was "holed through" in July of 1944. Because park officials and preservationists voiced their opposition to this project, the visible impact of this engineering effort was kept at a minimum. *(Estes Park Trail-Gazette)*

displayed greater care "so that nature's setting was disturbed as little as possible."[31] As one example, the pumping of water into Shadow Mountain Lake helped keep the scenic Grand Lake at a constant level. Thus, the old resort setting of Grand Lake retained its image even though it served as the western portal for a massive water diversion project. On the eastern slope, tourists would have to go out of their way and find the Wind River in order to discover the tunnel's exiting portal. Far less damage resulted from construction because advocates of preservation expressed their fears for the Park. Historian Musselman concluded that "the practical needs of nearby water users resulted in only minor modifications of the Park's primitive character."[32]

The bustle of the 1930s—the completion of Trail Ridge Road, the arrival of the CCC, and the construction of the Colorado-Big Thompson project—tapered off with the onset of World War II. Activity in the Park wound down as numerous Park employees (including Superintendent Canfield) took furloughs to serve in the military and national gasoline rationing curtailed the use of automobiles for pleasure trips. As a result, Rocky Mountain National Park saw a decline in its visitation for the first time. Dipping from around 393,000 tourists in 1942, travel decreased by 67 percent in subsequent years, amounting to only 130,000 people in 1943 and 1944. Seventeen thousand of those 1943 visitors were listed as "men in the armed forces." Changing from its role as an economic refuge of the 1930s, the Park now offered a brief respite from war during the 1940s. And because of war, nearly every program of development, construction, and publicity was halted for the duration. In summary, the war years found the Park affected "by changes in personnel, decline in travel, reduced or curtailed work programs and activities, and with essential functions and activities being carried on by fewer employees with greater responsibilities," according to Acting Superintendent George Miller.[33]

But any doldrums experienced because of World War II quickly disappeared once victory came. In the words of the newly returned Superintendent Canfield: "With the cessation of hostilities and the end of gasoline rationing, visitor travel took a marked jump and brought with it the increased load of protection work which results from heavy visitor use."[34] That "marked jump" soon displayed evidence of a real boom: in 1947 nearly 900,000 visitors entered the Park and in 1948 "an all time record" was reported as visitation finally topped the million mark. Peace and prosperity helped bring more vacationers than ever. And all those numbers meant more work for the Park rangers, their numbers still reduced from economy measures of the Depression and curtailment caused by war. According to Superintendent Canfield, those rangers were "seriously handicapped" because of "accidents occurring frequently along the highways and in the back country," resulting in a situation in which "the few men in the field were kept exceedingly busy."[35]

It was not just accidents that kept rangers busy. Other problems surfaced, too. In 1948, for example, a headline in the *Rocky Mountain News* read: "Vandals Deface Rocky Mountain Park." The vandals of the story were not identified by name nor were they specific individuals. The article did not tell of a particular mountain being defaced or of some feature being stolen. Rather, the general public was the culprit and the "vandalism" was litter. Producing an aesthetic crisis, littering reached beyond the point of tolerance and was termed "the biggest problem" of the Park. "People who give us trouble," Superintendent Canfield declared, are those "who scatter bottles, cartons, and camp refuse around with no regard for sanitation or cleanliness." He claimed that Park crews charged with cleaning campgrounds and roadsides could barely keep up with all the newly deposited trash. Furthermore, inconsiderate vandals also ripped down many of the Park's rustic signs, chopping them up and using them for campfire wood. If firewood happened to be in short supply at campgrounds, Canfield observed, "they'll chop up the furniture or anything else they can find. Or they will tear shingles off the roofs of the shelter houses." In an effort to discourage such barbaric manners, Canfield offered one realistic solution: "We try to build everything so it's pretty hard to tear up."[36] Suggesting that visitors bring along some common courtesy and civilized behavior became part of the Park's publicity.

But for every story that detailed acts of vandalism there was a humorous tale or two from Park workers describing their encounter with tourists. Dorr Yeager once told of a Park visitor who became quite interested in all the glacial boulders strewn around the countryside, and asked a naturalist how they got there. The naturalist gave an elaborate explanation about how the glaciers carried the boulders down from the mountains. After listening intently, the tourist asked the obvious question: "But where are the glaciers now?" Responding with a touch of jest, the naturalist replied: "They've gone back after more rocks."[37]

The growth of wintertime recreation in the post-war years initiated the last major construction project linked to the era of promotion and publicity. A growing interest in winter sports had actually paralleled the entire history of the Park. In February of 1916, members of the Estes Park Outdoor Club invited the directors of the Colorado Mountain Club on a trip to Fern Lake, calling their expedition "a snow frolic." From then on, Fern Lake Lodge, then run by Clifford Higby, opened for about two weeks every winter, serving as a base for snowshoeing, skiing, and other outdoor activities. Every year until 1934 the Colorado Mountain Club members trekked to Fern Lake, discovered the joys of skiing, and proclaimed their enthusiasm for the sport. Businessmen and community boosters around Estes Park and Grand Lake also helped promote the idea of wintertime activities, eager to draw visitors to the region during the "off season." Rangers soon found themselves skiing along with these frolicsome folks, helping clear ski trails and assisting people with their bruises and fractures. National park planners, also eager to advertise this aspect of the playground, agreed with Superintendent Toll's statement: "There are great possibilities for the future development of winter sports in the region."[38]

The momentum of downhill and cross-country skiing popularity grew during the 1930s. In 1931, the Rocky Mountain National Park Ski Club was organized, comprising a mix of National Park Service employees and local villagers, with Chief Ranger McLaughlin serving as director. The club soon urged the building of a ski

The post-war boom in tourism saw frequent overcrowding at spots such as the Bear Lake area. A generation of prosperous vacationers began taxing park facilities and personnel with a burden of too much popularity. (RMNPHC)

hill and toboggan slide at Hidden Valley. In 1932, however, the slopes within Moraine Park appeared more attractive for development. *The Denver Post* quickly voiced its enthusiasm for such an idea, believing that a ski area there would be "of major importance in the winter sports world."[39] But a major ski area failed to develop. Instead, on a less ambitious scale, winter carnivals were held at Estes Park and Grand Lake. Some ski jumping, a few ski races, and some cross-country jaunts remained the style of wintertime sport in the Park. More elaborate proposals for building ski areas equipped with tows remained the subject for local newspaper editorials, government reports, and skiers' dreams. "It has been done in other parks," Director Albright said, offering some hope, "and we will have to find a place for the toboggan slide, ski jump, etc., where it will not mar the natural beauties of the Park."[41]

Marring the Park or "scarring the landscape" with large swaths of trees cleared from the forests made the whole idea of a ski area less attractive to park preservationists. "Quibbles about 'scarring' the park have never seemed to us more than the poor argument of obstructionists," snapped the *Estes Park Trail* in a 1936 reply.[41] In response to such pressure, Park officials stepped up their winter program. They kept the Bear Lake road open for skiers' use, pro-

Attempting to advertise winter sports in the area, local businessmen and park officials tried to portray Rocky Mountain National Park as a year around recreation spot. (RMNPHC)

Somewhat controversial in its origins and location, a winter sports center was finally established in 1955 when the Hidden Valley Winter Use Area opened. (RMNPHC)

vided a skating rink on a beaver pond in Hidden Valley, and plowed the roads to both Willow Park and Hidden Valley.

When David Canfield took charge of the Park in 1937, he brought with him the experience he gained as superintendent of Crater Lake National Park. There he had worked for winter sports development. Once settled in Rocky Mountain, he discovered a booming interest in skiing, with a reported 75,000 wintertime visitors. At Hidden Valley, the unofficial center of action, he found overcrowded conditions and poor ski trails, "rather dangerous for the average skier." Its "perpetual wind blown crust" did not make the Hidden Valley site especially suitable for permanent development in his view. Instead, Canfield suggested that the upper Mill Creek basin could be developed, although he admitted that "meager snowfall seems to be a discouraging factor."[42]

World War II forestalled any major decision regarding developments at Mill Creek, Moraine Park, or Hidden Valley. Meanwhile, in 1941, some local high school boys installed a primitive tow at Hidden Valley. Once the war was over and winter sports were growing ever more popular, the Hidden Valley site had gained almost by default preeminence over the other sites. Slow to proceed with any major construction, Park officials hesitated about building a major ski area, weighing their choices between "landscape losses against the public use benefits." So leadership regarding ski area development passed to local businessmen and community boosters. By the late 1940s, they gained the backing of their Congressmen and the push for better facilities at Hidden Valley entered its final phase. By 1952, an "improvement of facilities" meant the building of a permanent chair lift. "A rope-tow-narrow-trail area appears to have the appeal of kissing your girl-friend's mother," read the *Estes Park Trail*, "just a substitute for the real thing."[43]

That kind of public pressure eventually paid off, much to the delight of down-hill skiers. Park officials soon agreed to construct two T-bar lifts (rather than the larger chair lifts) as well as a ski lodge that offered sufficient facilities to accommodate the increasing crowds of skiers. Yet at the same time, park planners worked to develop the area so it would not appear obtrusive and detract from the view along Trail Ridge Road. Because ski areas already existed in a few other national parks, most notably Yosemite's Badger Pass, lengthy philosophic debates regarding the preservation of wilderness values failed to delay the plan for development. After all, nearby Trail Ridge Road symbolized an earlier invasion of civilization crowding into the wilderness. Surveys for the new ski area began in 1954 and the construction of the lifts and a lodge followed quickly. On December 18, 1955, the Hidden Valley Winter Use Area was officially opened.

Completing the ski area capped years of construction, development, and promotion, a trend that had been going on since the Park was founded. Whether the Hidden Valley project was really desirable or in an ideal location could be questioned. In any case, national park officials had responded to public pressure. In a similar way, the building of Trail Ridge Road catered to a perceived public demand, combining a desire to promote the Park with "improvements." In this era, preservation of the area took a back seat to publicity, and such projects as the Colorado-Big Thompson tunnel forced the Park Service to compromise its ideals in order to accommodate an ever-demanding public.

By the mid-1950s, decades of publicity and development started to show results. If national parks measured their popularity by numbers, then Rocky Mountain National Park was a success. Trail Ridge Road reigned as the supreme attraction of the Park, with a million and a half visitors enjoying its vistas each season. The age of the automobile predominated, insuring easy access to the high country. A two- or three-hour drive across the Park became the principal Park experience for most visitors, and very few people complained that the scenery was less sublime as a result of the road.

The rangers' response to this mobile tourism meant spending more time patrolling the highways, less time hiking the trails, climbing the mountains, or pursuing poachers. Their more romantic image faded as they assumed duties similar to those of other officers of the law. Once in a while the adventurous ranger reemerged to rescue climbers from cliffs or capture a crook or two or patrol the ski slopes of Hidden Valley. But the image of the rugged and romantic park ranger was changing with time. Perhaps, like the Park itself, the image seemed a little less romantic once the horses and trails were forsaken for automobiles and highways.

By the time the fictional ranger Bob Flame left the Park, Dorr Yeager wrote, "He had grown to know its moods and to understand the calm peace of its meadows and the splendid fierceness of its timberline storms."[44] Few would doubt that ideals and images could be forged by people reacting to wilderness, but many of those ideas would also be tempered or tested by civilization. In a similar way, by the mid-1950s, Rocky Mountain National Park displayed a mixture of idealism and reality: its image was both romantic and wild but it faced the reality of a demanding public.

8

THE PRICE
OF POPULARITY

*"We're loved to death. The resource is going to pot. We're supposed
to be an outdoor museum. What we have is an urban park."*
Edgar Menning, Resource Management Specialist, 1980

ON AUGUST 9, 1978, a bolt of lightning struck near Ouzel Lake in
Rocky Mountain National Park and started a fire in a subalpine
spruce–fir forest. In accord with a new philosophy that recognized
the ecological significance of natural fires, Park rangers monitored
the fire continuously as it carried out its "cleansing" role. For days
the fire behaved as expected, spreading slowly and casting only an
occasional puff of smoke into the sky. But then on August 23 and
again on September 1, gusts of wind caused the fire to intensify
and spread rapidly. As public pressure grew Park officials decided
that the fire could remain wild no longer and assigned firefighter
crews to control the blaze. With the help of snow and rain, con-
tainment seemed assured by September 11.

However, on September 15 winds exceeding thirty miles per hour
swept out of the west, whipped the fire back into life and pushed
it eastward toward the Park boundary. Residents of nearby
Allenspark were alarmed at the rapid progress of the fire. People
living in a housing subdivision even closer to the Park boundary
found themselves directly in the path of the fast-approaching fire.
Nearly 350 people prepared to flee or fight for their homes. Facing
this emergency, some 500 firefighters scrambled to prevent the
"Ouzel Fire" from escaping the confines of Rocky Mountain National Park. After days of strenuous effort, the fire crews successfully controlled one of the wildest elements of nature and kept the
Ouzel Fire within the Park.

In 1978 wind-swept flames of the Ouzel Fire tested the preservationist philosophy of allowing natural fires to run their course. (RMNPHC)

Stopping this 1,050-acre forest fire did not silence questions about the wisdom of allowing fires to burn freely. Critics wondered whether every natural condition should really be restored, especially in a region growing ever more populous. Could Rocky Mountain National Park even be considered "wild?" Did its closest neighbors or its millions of visitors really want a wilderness? Or were notions about creating a natural environment in the Park merely idealistic nonsense, spouted by ivory tower eggheads, really impossible to permit or produce? Theories aside, once the Ouzel Fire threatened to leave the Park and endanger private property it ceased being a beneficial force of nature. It became a test for both firefighters and wilderness ideals.

Americans of the late 1950s were a people on wheels. The rapid pace of vacationers, sometimes only driving through the Park in an hour or two, made automobiles and roadways predominant parts of a park visit. (RMNPHC)

Forest fires created very little controversy during the 1950s, for those that occurred were quickly suppressed. Nor were the administrative policies of Rocky Mountain National Park particularly controversial in other respects. An atmosphere of progress and cooperation prevailed as more and more people came to the Park each year.

In this era of prosperity, Rocky Mountain National Park clearly demonstrated its role as a shrewd investment for Colorado businessmen, paying annual dividends in tourist dollars. A study conducted by University of Colorado economists showed that the average tourist party of the early 1950s (comprised of 3.8 statistical people) spent less than three days in the state while visiting the Park. Those mobile travelers expected to see more of the West than just a single park or the central Rockies. Only 10 percent of those vacationers stayed in the Rocky Mountain area for a full two-week period. Yet Park visitors boosted the state's economy, spending some $47 million annually, or an average of $30.78 a person per day. This purely economic analysis as well as the "regional grand tour vacations" of the tourists themselves were approaches to national parks not fully envisioned by idealists at the turn of the century. Yet it was a trend that would continue into the 1960s. "But this is part of the high speed life we live today," admitted one Park official in 1965, "fast cars, fast freeways, and a speed of life which, I'm sure, would have made Steve Mather push back his Stetson and scratch his head in disbelief."[2]

Watching this boom in tourism develop, officials recognized that Rocky Mountain National Park was "suffering from a lag in funds and manpower for general maintenance and modernization of physical facilities."[3] Simple wear and tear had produced shoddy conditions within the Park. In the years following World War II, vacationers had been streaming in, taxing all the roads, trails, museums, and campgrounds. Most other national parks experienced a similar onrush of tourists and also faced deteriorating facilities. As early as 1949, Park Service Director Newton B. Drury saw the pressure from enthusiastic visitors creating a crisis for the parks: roads and trails were badly in need of repair, campgrounds needed expansion, visitor centers and museums proved to be inadequate, and the park ranger and naturalist staffs were undermanned and ill-housed. A decade of neglect and a lack of proper maintenance brought by war and economy measures meant that the national parks appeared unable to meet the growing demands of tourists. By 1953, historian Bernard DeVoto suggested that the national parks simply had to be closed, since "so much of the priceless heritage which the Service must safeguard for the United States is beginning to go to hell."[4]

This widespread deterioration of facilities demanded a major reconstruction program. The National Park Service replied with "a forward-looking program" called Mission 66. It planned to remedy many older problems and to prepare for the future, providing "maximum enjoyment for those who use the parks" as well as "maximum protection of the scenic, scientific, wilderness, and historic resources that give them distinction."[5] When this ten-year program began in 1956, over $9 million worth of improvements were projected for Rocky Mountain National Park alone. With other parks facing similar problems, Congress eventually allocated more than $1 billion to fix and refurbish all the national parks.

As a result of this program, thousands of dollars were spent in

The Mission 66 construction program, a ten-year effort started in 1956, contained a myriad of projects to replace outdated facilities and prepare the Park for a busy future. (RMNPHC)

Rocky Mountain to improve the road system and rebuild or relocate entrance stations. A new eastern approach road was developed into Beaver Meadows, replacing an older entrance on a narrow roadway that edged the Big Thompson River. Widening highways, filling in "chuck-holes," fixing "dips and weaves," and enlarging parking areas and picnic spots along Trail Ridge Road all constituted projects within the "urgently needed" Mission 66 program.[6] Many other mundane but necessary elements were included, such as expanding campgrounds, reconstructing water and sewer systems, modernizing telephone and power systems, and building new housing for employees.

Quite a number of the Mission 66 projects enhanced the Park for the pleasure of the automobile-oriented visitor. The Park was envisioned as "an outdoor museum with unsurpassed accessibility." Linked to improved roadways were "visitor centers," where those entering the Park could receive a "general interpretation of the Park's resources."[7] One such structure was placed near the western entrance of the Park; another was developed at Fall River Pass; and a third was planned for Bear Lake. Not every facet of the Mission 66 plan was accomplished, but among the more noteworthy construction projects was the combination visitor center and Park headquarters building placed near the new eastern entrance. There, in a scenic meadow, the largest of the visitor centers was combined with administrative offices. Completed in 1967, the structure reflected the architectural style of Frank Lloyd

Purchasing property from inholders continued to be a lengthy and expensive process. Removing structures which some might term "historic"— like those of Stead's Ranch in Moraine Park—was not always popular with people who had a sense of nostalgia. Many cabin and resort sites were restored to their natural condition. (RMNPHC)

Wright. Described in contemporary accounts as "pure American" with its long, low profile, sheltering pines, stone walls and steel ornamentation, its natural colors made it blend into the surrounding landscape with Longs Peak dominating in the background. In that building alone, the Mission 66 program, with its desire to improve accessibility and also explain the Park to its mobile clientele, gained a fitting monument. The dozens of other Mission 66 accomplishments, from shelters to signs, from picnic tables to improved trails, were far less conspicuous even though they fostered a polished appearance for the Park. Considering all the projects undertaken, historian Lloyd Musselman critically concluded that "by making travel in the Park more attractive and comfortable," Mission 66 "detracted from the Park's scenic naturaliness." Campgrounds dominated where pioneer resorts once nestled and visitor centers could be judged too obtrusive in the context of a natural scene. "Roads wide and with gentle grades made Park travel easier," Musselman observed, "but not necessarily more meaningful."[8]

Nevertheless, restoring natural scenes within the Park had also been an important objective of Mission 66. The purchase of privately held land within Park boundaries was tied to that plan. Due to a long history of boundary adjustments, buying land from inholders could be traced back to 1923. By 1963, some 11,080 acres of land had been purchased at a cost of $3,235,000. The price of restoring the natural scene was high. Merely providing land for a new eastern approach road and entrance, for example, meant acquiring forty-three tracts of private land. Most of those land owners sold their property quite willingly; only a few contested the Park's plans or the purchase price.

This flurry of land buying included the purchase of most of the remaining old resorts. Rather than rehabilitate or modernize these pioneer structures, their removal became the order of the day. For example, Sprague's Lodge ceased its operations in 1958 and within a few years its main structure and outbuildings were totally removed. By 1960, the Brinwood Ranch-Hotel in Moraine Park, the Fall River Lodge in Horseshoe Park, and the Deer Ridge Chalet all faced a similar fate. Stead's Ranch, the Moraine Park remnant of Abner Sprague's 1870s homestead, was purchased in 1962. Bought for $750,000, the 600-acre ranch, with its accommodations for 185 guests, soon saw its barns, lodge, cabins, and its golf course disappear as its land was restored to a natural meadow. Not everyone applauded the destruction of these old hostelries, especially as they were replaced by new automobile campgrounds. "We can't quite understand why folks who desire lodge accommodations are to be denied the same privilege of 'living in the park,' " read the *Estes Park Trail*. "A hundred people living at a lodge create less confusion, less muss and fuss, than a hundred camping out."[9] Yet, in the view of Mission 66 advocates, "many of these lands are devoted to such uses as grazing, timber cutting, fencing, etc., which do not conform with the National Park theme of preserving the natural scene."[10]

What bothered some critics was the rapid destruction of resorts that might have had some historic value. A swift end came to decades of vacationing in those rustic, western-style lodges. Replacing those resorts were newer facilities nearby, such as Moraine Park and Glacier Basin campgrounds, along with new picnic areas and livery operations. To some nostalgic observers, campgrounds and liveries offered poor substitutes for the old resorts. "Change generally is a wonderful thing," pined the *Estes Park Trail*, "but sometimes its manifestations are difficult for the Old Cowpoke to swallow."[11] Nevertheless, efforts to acquire every acre of private property continued, playing a significant role in the march of

As soon as roads were cleared of snow and trails were passable, Rocky Mountain National Park received its annually increasing number of visitors. (RMNPHC)

progress and not stopping when Mission 66 ended. In 1974, for example, resort owner John Holzwarth, who was then aged seventy-one, made sure that his western slope dude ranch would become a part of the Park. Several times he "refused to be swayed by dollar signs" when developers offered him more than $1 million for 500 acres. Instead, he expressed concern about the aesthetic value of his property and its future use. "I can live with and die knowing that this valley will be for all and not a select few," Holzwarth commented. "It was a wonderful experience having the ranch, he reflected. "I am a part of it."[12] As private land owners such as Holzwarth were disappearing from the Park scene, many of them received compliments for their stewardship of the land. As one spokesman suggested: "It would be well for us who have enjoyed the park for two generations to thank those private people — inside the park and not on its fringes — for helping keep it beautiful and primitive."[13]

While the period of owning private land within the Park was almost at an end, increased use of the Park for recreation was beginning to boom. In 1956 alone, nearly 1.6 million visitors entered Rocky Mountain. Throughout the late 1950s and into the 1960s and 1970s that number increased annually, with visitation topping three million people in 1978 before finally slackening its bursting pace. Not only were more travelers coming to enjoy a drive across Trail Ridge Road, they were also venturing into the back-country in greater numbers. Nearly 2,000 people each year were climbing Longs Peak during the late 1950s and that number increased to nearly 10,000 by the late 1970s. Indicative of trends to come, on August 11, 1955, a single party containing 61 climbers stood on the summit of Longs Peak.

More mountain climbing and backcountry use meant a steadily increasing number of accidents. Hazards of the hills produced a greater toll as urbanites, flatlanders, and those with a reckless nature flooded into the Park. Rangers honed their rescue skills, always preparing for the unexpected. Dozens of searches and rescues began punctuating the rangers' record books. On May 30th, 1956, for example, while seasonal ranger Norm Nesbit was climbing on Hallett Peak, he learned that another climber, Patrick Dwyer, had taken a tumble nearby. Dwyer had fallen several hundred feet off a steep rock face. Fortunately, he had hit a slope of soft snow, which prevented his death, and then he slid another two hundred feet downward, eventually coming to rest on a rocky ledge. There he lay, badly injured with lacerations, head injuries, a dislocated shoulder, and overcome with shock. Ranger Nesbit quickly assessed Dwyer's condition and sent a companion dashing for help.

Hearing of the accident at Bear Lake, ranger Frank Betts immediately called two additional rescuers, Robert Frauson and Jerry Hammond. These three, like Nesbit, were "seasonal" rangers hired just for the summer, but all were strong mountaineers and skilled at their task. Jogging up the trail late that afternoon, the three men toted packs containing their personal climbing gear and ropes along with a lightweight litter upon which to haul the stricken Dwyer. Swiftly these men moved upward, climbing across fields of snow and ice until they reached the rocky ledges where Nesbit tended the fallen climber. Toward dusk that evening, the rangers loaded Dwyer into the litter and began the painstaking task of lowering him very cautiously down the steep snowfield onto Tyndall Glacier. Gingerly, they worked their way across the glacier's snow and ice, establishing frequent belay positions for extra safety. There, a single misstep sent ranger Betts slipping into a crevasse. He nearly disappeared from sight. Fortunately, each ranger had tied himself to the litter and Bob Frauson was belaying the litter itself. Disaster was averted. Betts was able to pull himself up out of the crevasse, allowing the men to continue hauling their semi-conscious victim toward medical help.

Night descended as the team worked its way down Tyndall Gorge. The men resorted to using headlamps to light their path.

Slowly they crossed Emerald Lake, its still frozen surface offering them an easy passage. With only four rangers and two companion climbers for help, carrying the loaded litter proved to be a gruelling task. But the men kept trudging with their burden, hoping that relief crews might arrive to assist them. When they reached Dream Lake, they discovered that the deep snow on the trail was too soft to support their weight. The ice on the lake had also disappeared. Their only choice was to wade in the icy water along the shoreline as a substitute for the covered trail. About a mile farther on, almost at midnight, a relief crew finally joined the rangers, carrying the litter the rest of the way to Bear Lake Ranger Station. Patrick Dwyer's life had been saved.

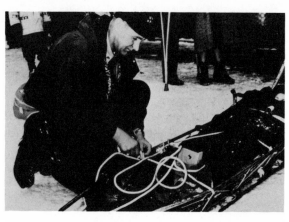

Rangers were faced with increasing numbers of accidents as urbanized Americans explored the mountains. Mountaineers such as ranger Bob Frauson found their skills always in great demand. (RMNPHC)

Rangers' efforts, like those of Bob Frauson, Frank Betts, Jerry Hammond, and Norm Nesbit, were seen simply as "part of the job." Though it was only a "seasonal" job, these men still risked their lives to protect Park visitors. They displayed a professional sense of dedication. At the same time, they also supplied their personal climbing equipment to effect the rescue, worked through the night without expecting "overtime" pay, and did not await relief crews or expect helicopters to land nearby. They were men who understood survival in the mountains. Never guessing that they would receive recognition for their efforts, those four seasonal rangers gained the rarely given National Park Service Valor Award in 1957 for the Hallett Peak rescue. No one was more surprised about that award than they were. They knew that many other rescues could have been considered far more dangerous, or "hairier" in their jargon. Rangers like themselves had helped many Park visitors without hearing even a word of thanks. And many rescues occurring in the years after the Hallett Peak affair would remain equally unrecognized. Yet on this rare occasion someone "higher up" had decided that their initiative, their courage, and their accomplishment deserved some recognition.

One problem rangers had to confront was the increased daring of a new breed of mountain climbers who were attempting to scale previously "unclimbable" rock faces, such as "The Diamond" high on the eastern face of Longs Peak. The Diamond consisted of eighteen acres of sheer granite, slightly slanting outward at its top, offering only a few fractures and ledges to aid a possible ascent. It remained one of the only unclimbed walls in the nation and that fact provided plenty of temptation for those seeking to challenge the "impossible." For years the National Park Service refused to allow climbers to attempt the face. Reasons given for placing the Diamond off limits included the obvious risks to rangers' lives if rescue became necessary. Park officials also claimed that they lacked sufficient ropes and other technical equipment to succeed in plucking a climber off the Diamond. Nevertheless, the revolution in big wall climbing techniques and the abilities of climbers, combined with their persistent requests, challenged the old prohibition against "stunt and trick climbing."[14]

In 1960 a new climbing policy went into effect, still demanding strict procedures and proper experience and equipment from the climbers, while finally allowing the Diamond to be attempted for the first time. Much to the dismay of several Colorado climbers, two Californians, David Rearick and Robert Kamps, both experts on the big walls of Yosemite, were first to apply for permission and meet all the necessary requirements. Their previous technical climbs, attention to safety, and agreement to help provide for a possible rescue all combined to give them first chance at the Diamond. Their climb began on August 1, 1960. After fifty-two hours on the face, of which twenty-eight and a half hours were spent climbing, Rearick and Kamps achieved the Longs Peak summit. One can only guess what was going through the minds of rangers Bob Frauson, William Colony, and John Clark as they watched the ascent. The presence of a twelve-hundred-foot coil of rescue rope placed at the summit in case of emergency must have offered the rangers little comfort. Any rappel off the over-hanging Diamond would have caused a rescuer to dangle some twenty feet away from the face itself. The walls that those adventuresome mountain climbers considered a challenge became an added responsibility to the Park rangers.

In the years following Kamps's and Rearick's feat, climbing the Diamond increased in popularity and numerous additional routes were pioneered. By the early 1980s rangers had to restrict the face

The 1960s marked a new era in mountain climbing in Rocky Mountain National Park. New techniques and equipment made many rock faces scalable for the first time. (RMNPHC)

Too many people attempting to climb Longs Peak at the same time diminished the wilderness flavor of that experience. At times, by the late 1960s, the cable route was virtually jammed with climbers. (RMNPHC)

to a single party climbing per day. Even then, no one would call climbing the Diamond commonplace. Aside from giving rangers more hazardous tasks, most of those daring mountain climbs are better classified as personal achievements rather than acts of historical significance. As the *Denver Post* editorialized about Kamps and Rearick: "They have pushed themselves to the outer limits of human capability . . . to find exhilaration and personal fulfillment through hardship, danger and challenge." The personal achievement of those climbers, the *Post* concluded, might also have served to challenge "a society grown soft and stale."[15]

For Americans "grown soft and stale" by the 1960s, Rocky Mountain National Park was offering more than just the Diamond. Activities of all sorts drew people into the out-of-doors. Ranger-naturalists at every visitor center encouraged travelers to investigate the Park more fully by parking their automobiles and walking away from the roadways. Naturalists helped reintroduce people to nature. In 1965, for example, ranger-naturalists offered the public a wide variety of free guided trips, tailored to many tastes and various levels of endurance. Listed among their engaging efforts were "Bird Walks," two-hour "Nature Walks," five-hour "Walks to the Lakes," "Half-Day Walks," "Three-Quarter-Day Hikes," "All-Day Hikes," and "Beaver Walks." Keeping a tradition from the 1920s alive, naturalists also provided nightly campfire talks. Many of those lectures were illustrated with slides and they continued to be educational, entertaining, and promotional as well as a means of meeting people and encouraging them to broaden their experiences in the Park. Just in case the naturalists failed to convert people into willing walkers, they carried their message to automobilists by offering "caravan" tours.

Car caravans, climbers, crowds, and the construction activities of Mission 66 all made preservationists wonder whether Rocky Mountain and other national parks were really being used properly. In one critic's view: "Mission 66 has done comparatively little for the plants and animals."[16] He inferred that a great deal had been done for the automobile-borne visitors. The "Parks are for People" motto of the era meant to some that the ideal of preservation was being sacrificed. By the late 1950s, demands came for greater protection of the wilderness within the national parks. David Brower of the Sierra Club simply stated: "The wilderness we have now is all that we will ever have."[17] So the question became whether national parks could really serve every recreational enthusiast equally — or whether the parks were intended to serve a special function. In 1965, Assistant Park Service Director Stanley Cain summarized the problem of the day: "The needs of our growing population, living in the immense and complex urban environment, having diverse and rapid means of transportation, with ever-rising personal income and tens of hundreds of thousands of hours of leisure time, require park and recreation programs of broadened and diversified dimensions."[18]

An old national park dilemma, the "dichotomy of preservation and pleasurable use," hit Rocky Mountain National Park hardest as it was welcoming "a continually exploding number of visitors."[19] People started to ask whether the Park could honestly be a wilderness preserve and also supply such things as automobile camping sites for every traveler who expected one. Observers wondered whether park planners had curried too much favor with concrete and Cadillacs. Was it possible for Rocky Mountain National Park ever to satisfy everyone? Seeing the continuous demands people placed upon their parks, one Park Service spokesman commented: "The problem of today is simply that the parks are being loved to death."[20]

Naturalist programs helped to reintroduce people to the wild environment of Rocky Mountain National Park. (RMNPHC)

A possible solution to all these demands was to define more carefully the purpose of the Park. That meant defining what sections should remain "wilderness" and establishing guidelines for acceptable activities that could occur within its confines to also insure preservation. Yet even in the most preserved sections of the Park, recreational pursuits would still occur. "Within our park concept there can be no question of locking up the wilderness," wrote Interior Secretary Stewart Udall in 1965. "The wilderness proper serves all park visitors. Those who penetrate it gain its fullest rewards. More often than not the undeveloped park wilderness beyond the roads furnishes the setting and the background that make each national park a unique and outstanding attraction."[21] And like many other national parks, Rocky Mountain still contained sections of wild land in a reasonably primitive condition. At the same time, it also had roads, campgrounds, visitor centers and other elements of civilization. What sections of the Park would remain "unimpaired for future generations" had to be decided.

Congress proposed to resolve the concern for wilderness. On September 3, 1964, the Wilderness Act became law, establishing the National Wilderness Preservation System. Wilderness was viewed

as a place "where man himself is a visitor who does not remain."
With an area containing at least five thousand contiguous acres,
a wilderness also had to retain "its primeval character and
influence, without permanent improvements or human habitation,
which is protected and managed so as to preserve its natural conditions."[22] Here the preservation aspect of national parks finally
received equal attention with recreational use. For decades the
"playground" idea was emphasized; now the "preserve" aspect
gained the spotlight.

Defining exactly what "wilderness" meant in Rocky Mountain
National Park proved to be a difficult task. Studies of possible
wilderness areas in the Park began in the mid-1960s and Park officials did not complete their work until a decade later. The Wilderness Act required that each roadless section of the Park be evaluated
to determine whether it was suitable for inclusion within the National Wilderness Preservation System. A decade of study and
debate resulted in the evolution of two documents intended to
direct Rocky Mountain's future: a "Master Plan" and a "Wilderness Recommendation." Through those years of discussion and
debate, many of the Park's problems came into sharper focus, from
crowded conditions in the corridors of development to the need
to create the proper balance of preservation and use. Not since the
years prior to the Park's establishment had people taken so much
time and trouble to concern themselves with the future of these
mountains.

When Park Service planners finally completed their "Wilderness
Recommendation" as a proposal, they had identified 91.5 percent
of the Park's 265,679 acres as worthy of wilderness status. Roadways would remain, but no more would be built; roadless areas
would be protected and restored to primitive conditions if possible. Historic pressures upon the Park as a pleasuring ground faced
compromise with preservation. Once all the details of the wilderness proposal were made public, those concerned about the Park's
future were invited to comment. Throughout late 1973 and early
1974 nearly a thousand individuals and organizations presented
their opinions about the Park's preservation. Testimony came at
several public hearings and letters poured in at National Park Service offices. The strong emotional attachment toward Rocky
Mountain National Park that people displayed gave evidence of the
significant role the Park played in their lives. Developing directions for the Park's future was not a matter people considered
trivial.

The majority of those who expressed their views strongly favored
the Park Service's "Wilderness Recommendation." Many wanted

Restoring elements of wilderness in the Park warranted a careful classification of appropriate facilities and activities. Businesses like the popular Deer Ridge Chalet were considered less desirable than in previous decades. (RMNPHC)

more wilderness than the Park Service plan provided. Development, in the preservationist view, had already usurped too much Park land. Expressing a typical viewpoint, one advocate of more wilderness wrote: "I am for eliminating all snack bars, curio shops, and facilities from the parks. These are incompatible with the beauty of the wilderness." Reminding officials of the Park's basic purpose, he added: "The reason for establishing a park is because there is something worth preserving. While compromises have to be made so that some can view the beauty of such an area, the compromise should never be such that the beauty is destroyed."[23]

Throughout those months of emotionally charged debate, very few spokesmen were willing to compromise their ideals or their vision of how the Park should be managed. Officials were urged by many to "decommercialize" and "de-urbanize" the Park and do everything to restore its natural condition.[24] "Car-oriented flatlanders," wrote one Boulder citizen, "require much education as to how to go about entertaining themselves in a wilderness."[25] Not only would a future containing "correct use" demand education for visitors, but officials were also asked to be more aggressive in eliminating private property ownership within the Park, removing Hidden Valley Ski Area, reducing traffic congestion on Park roadways, and insisting that diapers be used on horses.

The desire for a pristine environment within the Park came from many people who had recently encountered crowded or city-like conditions during one of their visits. Those voices of concern for wilder land carried a tone of urgency. "While looking for mushrooms in the park this last summer," one noteworthy letter read, "I witnessed 'hippies' cutting trees and sneaking them out to their campers, dogs and cats on the trails, and nearly had my motorcycle stolen. The park is so full of thieves that I really prefer to go into the Nat. Forest where I can carry a gun to protect myself if necessary."[26] Whether overly emotional or totally rational, those advocating wilderness presented an overwhelming mandate for protecting the Park in its wildest, most primitive condition.

Quite a number of other people, however, did not view roadways and other modern conveniences within the Park as harmful or detracting from the natural setting. "Placing these lands in wilderness status," according to one critic of the proposal, "has the effect of locking out a greater and greater segment of the public as people live longer and are less able to make arduous trips."[27] Another writer, similarly concerned that "those people who drive into and through the park would be discriminated against," stated: "I am objecting to the proposal that enjoyment of our National Park should be restricted to the rugged outdoorsman, a minority group!"[28] And another added: "Less than 5% of the park visitors are backpackers and trail-riders. It is ridiculous to assume that 95% of the visitors like to be jostled and bumped by other people so that the back country can be enjoyed by a few." He concluded "that we are getting an environmental fixation" and that history proved that Rocky Mountain National Park "cannot qualify as a wilderness by any stretch of the imagination."[29] Urging the Park Service to continue with greater "flexibility" in running the Park, some feared that wilderness classification would make the whole region "suffocate into stagnation."[30] Others worried that wilderness would threaten their nearby businesses: "If this act goes into effect the outcome to this community would be horrendous. We survive only by our summer tourist trade, and I am sure the government would not want an entire death of a community on their hands."[31] The very thought of eliminating a gift shop within the Park made one writer wax euphoric about "how much the tourists enjoy browsing in this unique shop in such a magnificent setting."[32] Like wilderness, curio shops and civilization also had many advocates among Park users.

With opinions so strongly expressed and expectations so vastly different, Park planners faced a perplexing task. Eventually their "Master Plan" and "Wilderness Recommendation" offered compromises, putting the Park's future somewhere between the desires of the factions. Preservationists had to accept some existing roads, campgrounds, and other elements of civilization. Those arguing for unrestricted use of the Park would have to accept a future that limited the use of automobiles, curbed development, and curtailed the construction of more roads and campgrounds.

Aside from creating some emotionally charged discussions, the effort to define the proper uses of the Park was an enlightening experience. More than ever, officials understood the necessity of striking a balance between preservation and use. In 1976, the "final" recommendation designated approximately 240,000 of the Park's 265,679 acres as wilderness. For administrative purposes that meant that the Park had to be divided into various categories: natural zones, in which the outstanding natural features of the Park were located; historical zones, which included such sites as Lulu City and the William Allen White cabins; and development zones, which contained campgrounds, roadways, Hidden Valley Ski Area, entrance stations, and other sites where "intensive use" predominated. Thus Park officials began managing Rocky Mountain National Park along the Wilderness and Master Plan guidelines.

But discussions and debates over wilderness also helped spotlight many older uses of the Park that continued to affect its aesthetic quality. Continuing demands for water, for example, meant that the reclamation projects developed earlier were to remain undisturbed regardless of any plans for wilderness. Projects such as the Colorado-Big Thompson Alva B. Adams tunnel symbolized the critical need for water in Colorado's arid climate, a need more urgent than either recreation or preservation. In 1981 Park officials identified five reservoirs and lakes with dams within Rocky Mountain National Park as well as seven pipeline facilities and seven ditches, all of which remained controlled by private interests. The hazards of some of those older projects became tragically apparent on July 15, 1982 when the seventy-nine-year-old dam at Lawn Lake failed. A deluge of escaping water swept down the Roaring and Fall rivers, swiftly flooding the streets of Estes Park. Sadly, the disaster resulted in the deaths of three people as the water rushed along its way.

As with privately owned lakes, reservoirs, and dams, the rights of private property owners within the Park remained protected by law. If people chose not to sell their land to the government, little could be done to alter that decision. Only if obtrusive structures were built or subdivisions planned would the National Park Service contemplate condemnation. Numerous boundary adjustments, especially along the Park's eastern side, made the private land issue more of a visible and aesthetic concern. By 1981 some 2,141 acres

Whether dealing with elk or adjacent private land or dozens of other issues, restoring natural conditions to Rocky Mountain National Park proved to be a challenging task. (RMNPHC)

of private land involving 80 parcels with 67 owners remained within the Park. Most sections of Rocky Mountain National Park, from Wild Basin to Moraine Park and from the Fall River to the Kawuneeche Valley, had inholdings of some kind. Allied with this problem was the adjacent 1,240-acre MacGregor Ranch along the Park boundary at the northern edge of Estes Park. During the 1970s and early 1980s the National Park Service attempted to obtain a "scenic or conservation" easement to maintain the undeveloped attributes of the property. The possibility that the ranch might sprout subdivisions or condominiums meant that another corridor for elk migration might be threatened. The aesthetic qualities of the site also mandated action toward preservation. With the Park increasingly surrounded by civilization, efforts to keep it "unimpaired for future generations" became ever more complex.

Even more than water rights and private land, the booming popularity of the Park challenged the pristine condition of its wilderness. Because so many wanted to enter and enjoy the Park, sophisticated methods for managing visits had to be developed. For an increasing number of people, enjoying the Park meant more than just driving across Trail Ridge Road. A recreational revolution in outdoor sports, especially in hiking and backpacking, had developed by the late 1960s, and the combination of this and the "environmental movement" propelled nature-lovers into the back country of the national parks. The increasing popularity of Longs Peak serves as a typical example of that era. Partially in response to the growing crowds climbing Longs Peak, Superintendent Roger Contor announced in 1973 that the cables at the 13,700-foot level, which had assisted climbers up a fifty-five degree slope since 1925, were being removed. Contor claimed that the "increase in the number of climbers" had created "traffic jams where large numbers of people are trying to ascend and descend at the same time." He added that if Longs Peak was to be considered wilderness it should be free of manmade facilities. In the early 1970s, climbers commonly waited up to an hour to use the busy cables. "As an example of the heavy use the mountain receives," Contor noted, "2,388 persons made it to the summit in a sixteen day period, August 11 to 26, 1971. That's 150 people per day!"[33]

Mountain climber and writer Bill Bueler found conditions just as busy in 1975. During his climb that August, Bueler spotted "at least two hundred climbers" attempting the summit just as he was, although "many of them were on the only mountaineering adventure of their lives." Bueler explained that he decided to climb this busy mountain because he saw it "whenever I look west from Loveland." He also admitted that "the challenge, the experience, the exercise, the scenery—were at least as important." Finally, he described his desire to enter wild country: "Another reason for climbing mountains, the love of wilderness, was put aside for this trip, for whatever else Longs Peak may offer, a wilderness experience it is not, at least by the regular-Keyhole-route."[34]

The activity Bueler found on Longs Peak would not abate during that decade. In 1980, backcountry ranger Bob Siebert claimed that hikers who expected to find solitude on the Longs Peak Trail "express disappointment at the heavy use they encounter." He concluded: "They're sort of astonished there are so many people. Some are disgusted. Others are just surprised." Gale Kehmeier of the Colorado Mountain Club offered a similar observation: "I walked it a couple of weeks ago and must have seen 300 people. You almost had to take a number and get in line." Ranger Larry Van Slyke attempted to put the problem in perspective as he commented: "Twenty years ago, rangers were doing more toward

THE LONG'S PEAK TRAIL

managing the environment. Today, we are people managers, managing people making an impact on the environment."[35]

What rangers and reporters observed was part of a national trend, a virtual stampede heading into the out-of-doors and toward the wilderness areas. Not only did Longs Peak receive more attention, nearly every niche in the Park saw increased use. The era when backpackers were reasonably rare, when they could camp anywhere, build campfires, and stay as long as they liked rapidly faded once greater numbers of people tried escaping to the wilderness. Soon, too many people were trying to use the same backcountry spots at the same time. "Many people need this wilderness," sympathized one local observer, "yet many people can love a wilderness to death."[36]

Increasing numbers in the Park made more restrictions and regulations inevitable. Former Chief Ranger James Randall recalled that during the summer of 1967 the Park Service studied every backcountry camping spot to determine its proper "use capacity." Soon after, all backpackers had to obtain permits that allowed them to camp at designated sites for limited amounts of time. Later, "cross-country" camping zones were also established that permitted more adventurous hikers to locate their own sites as long as they were away from roads or trails and a hundred feet from any water supply. Once this "Backcountry Management" idea went into effect, its regulations and restrictions reflected environmental concerns. Self-contained stoves, for example, became mandatory at many camping spots since forests were being ripped apart. The old, symbolic campfire cherished by Enos Mills had to be sacrificed as a new style of backcountry manners was introduced. Greater regulation appeared to be the only solution as the period from 1965 to 1975 displayed close to a 900 percent increase in Rocky Mountain's backcountry use. In 1965 only 7,000 "camper days" were reported in the backcountry and by 1977 that number had increased to 62,000 before finally tapering off.

Envisioning that visitation boom in 1965, one official noted: "A growing challenge for us is to entice the millions of users of the parks to join us in grasping the limitations and special pleasures which stewardship imposes on the use of the land."[37] Such words as "limitations" and "stewardship" were milestones on the path of managing use within the Park. Alternatives were few if maintaining an aesthetically pleasing experience for each visitor was considered a worthy goal. Crowded conditions, trampled campsites, denuded forests, and "wilderness experience deterioration" all made "people management" necessary. By 1972, a quota plan was instituted for Rocky Mountain's backcountry that put the carrying capacity concept into effect. Entering the wilderness to camp required a permit. If wilderness experiences fostered feelings of freedom, self-reliance, independence, and other allied traits, then some might argue that the chance to seek such values ended once the permit system began. But if traces of rugged individualism remained, most people admitted that entering wild country had become a somewhat civilized process.

The public generally accepted restrictions. They knew that their option was crowded and less solitary conditions. A study conducted by Dr. Richard Trahan of the University of Northern Colorado in 1977 indicated that "day-use limitations" were quite acceptable to most people if "justified on environmental grounds." The "day-hikers" Trahan interviewed were found to be "a well educated group concerned with protecting the park environment." Those Park users were willing to accept restrictions if "the quality of experience" and the "environmental impact" were honestly at stake. Limits upon freedom to explore were accepted if such action assisted the Park Service in "cushioning the impact of heavy visitor use." Dr. Trahan also investigated the level of aesthetic quality that hikers expected and experienced while walking the trails. When hikers encountered horseriders, for example, the aesthetic quality of the walkers' experience was diminished. Meeting fifteen to thirty horses on a trail when none were expected produced a "generally unfavorable impression of horse use on park trails." Among other horse-related elements hikers found obnoxious were the presence of manure on the trail, flies and insects caused by the droppings, the odor of horses, the dust they caused, and the "inconvenience of having to move off the trail."[38]

Studies such as those conducted by Dr. Trahan offered some insights into the opinions of Park users, what those visitors expected, what they encountered, and what they were willing to endure to sample wilderness. That people of the 1960s and 1970s were seeking temporary escapes from the confines of civilization, no one could deny. Of his contemporaries, conservationist Siguard Olson observed: "He lives in a jet age, the industrial age, the space age, an age of automation, growing technology, urbanization." The result, according to Olson, was "a hunger in people to escape for a little while and return to the natural, primitive scene" where they could "feast their souls on scenery and to catch this elusive something called 'primitive.' "[40]

Whether every Park visitor could discover Rocky Mountain's "natural, primitive scene" on a typically busy summer day in the 1970s sometimes seemed impossible, especially if solitude was one facet of a wilderness experience. In 1973, for example, one visitor

Defining appropriate uses for Rocky Mountain National Park meant asking some fundamental questions about long accepted, rather popular practices. (RMNPHC)

complained that after spending three days in the Park, "I saw very little of the wilderness." She was unable to obtain a permit. Instead, she found the campgrounds "a gravel haven for the ranks of the mobile set," "telephones and newspaper dispensers," "pre-planned entertainment every night of the week," and "black-topped roads at every turn." As a result, she questioned "the park's sincerity of concern for the wilderness."[41] Thus, while some were arguing that 91.5 percent of the Park was managed too strictly as wilderness, others, like this critic, complained that the remaining 8.5 percent contained far too much civilization.

A crisis of congestion also confronted officials within the developed areas of the Park. While Park roadways offered magnificent scenery, they also became a bit too popular. The Bear Lake Road paid the highest price of visitors' pressure. The travelers' tendency to stop along the way, to picnic and explore, led to a shortage of parking space. Illegal parking and continuous congestion became such problems, according to ranger James Wilson, that "you literally could not drive to Bear Lake."[42] On a typical summer day in 1974, 4,280 vehicles carrying an average of 3.4 passengers each traveled along the nine-mile route. The results of overcrowding made driving conditions hazardous if not impossible. Safety demanded that something be done.

In 1978 a free bus shuttle system was initiated along the Bear

Lake Road to entice visitors away from their automobiles. Encouraging Park visitors to "enjoy the area at a leisurely pace," this transportation technique was not unlike those instituted in Yosemite Valley and at the Grand Canyon in response to similar problems with automobile congestion. A few visitors, however, found the idea of buses in Rocky Mountain National Park far from their dreams of freedom of the open road. As one critic commented: "To be lined up, herded into buses, waiting in line, having to worry about missing the next bus could hardly be very satisfying."[43] But by inducing some people to leave their cars behind, the bus system quickly solved the Bear Lake congestion problem, almost ended the issue of illegal parking, and removed many hazards. In 1980, buses moved nearly 160,000 people along the Bear Lake Road. The main drawback of the system, however, was that it cost nearly $100,000 per season to operate.

Because the Bear Lake Road's transportation system ended congestion and made for a more pleasant visit to the Park, similar efforts were planned for the old Fall River Road and perhaps for Trail Ridge Road as well. Although some might grumble at the thought of leaving their cars or at the expense the Park Service — and taxpayers — incurred, the Bear Lake system proved that congested roadways could be managed without bringing inconvenience to visitors. Making travel through the Park "a pleasurable experience" was still possible in spite of the crowds.

Regulating a wilderness environment and running a transportation system merely serve as two examples of ways Park Service officials responded to the problems associated with too much popularity. But looking at the average Park visitor of this era only as a "problem" does not present an accurate picture of the average visitor. Just because millions of vacationers were entering the Park did not necessarily mean that all of them suffered a miserable, jostled experience. If discussions about wilderness in the early 1970s proved anything, it was that Rocky Mountain National Park was providing "a wide spectrum of opportunity in order to satisfy a great number of people."[44] Every person's expectations and experience in the Park were bound to be different. Not everyone would seek a trip into the remote wilderness; some would choose to stay in their automobiles. Still, about 20 percent of all visitors, meaning some six hundred thousand people, were taking the time to tramp the trails by the 1980s. While climbing Longs Peak in the busiest part of the summer could be considered a "mob experience," it was also a "park experience." The quality of an encounter with nature was tempered by Rocky Mountain National Park's small size, and proximity to urban areas when compared to other

Whether fighting forest fires destroys the wilderness ideal could be debated, for Rocky Mountain National Park represents an ongoing compromise between the concepts of use and preservation. (RMNPHC)

western parks. What people were discovering in Rocky Mountain was a "friendly wilderness," an area serving to educate and stimulate as well as provide recreation.

Changing times and travel habits meant the Park had to satisfy more people with a greater variety of interests. Park planners understood that methods of meeting visitors' needs, which appeared appropriate in the 1920s, no longer fit the realities of the 1970s and 1980s. Those masses of visitors the Park expected each season made it necessary to "channelize" people in order to avoid "resource damage." And regardless of preservation plans, some parts of the Park still deteriorated under the pressure of people. The tundra region through which Trail Ridge Road winds its way offered one example of such damage. As summertime sightseers sought snapshots and snowballs near snowbanks, their feet tramped the alpine tundra into oblivion. If the natural landscape was to predominate, constructing walkways and restoring damaged scenery was necessary. When Park visitors understood the aesthetic objectives Park ecologists had in mind, most of them willingly accepted constraints upon such impulses as meandering across meadows.

"An environmental ethic is developing," Edgar Menning, the Park Resource Management Specialist, offered. "And efforts to protect the park have made a difference."[45] People have stopped throwing litter hither and yon as they once did, Menning observed. They have also accepted a cultivated scene at Bear Lake, with its buck and rail fencing, its paved trails, its transportation system, and its obvious efforts to guide travelers' footsteps away from areas being restored to natural conditions. Since Bear Lake had become "the biggest destination point in the whole park," the area had to be managed much like any urban park. The reality of greater numbers of people visiting Rocky Mountain National Park forced Park officials to contemplate more research, more emphasis upon resource protection, and perhaps more restrictions.

Through such experiences as the 1956 Hallett Peak Rescue, the 1964 Wilderness Act, the 1978 Ouzel Fire, or the 1982 Lawn Lake Dam failure, idealism came in conflict with reality. Those seeking pleasure sometimes failed to find it, whether they sought solitude in the wilderness or merely a parking space at Bear Lake. The Ouzel Fire in particular tested idealistic notions about returning the wilderness to a natural, ecological cycle once the full potential of forest fire was realized. Park planners had to reconsider the concept of restoring every facet of wild lands. "Do we have to burn down a town to prove the folly of a policy?" asked a local critic.[46] "We have to put fire back in the natural ecosystem," replied one idealist.[47] Disagreements sharpened as issues grew more complex. Debates centering on whether forest fire was beneficial or destructive, whether the Park should be used or preserved, or what an ideal park experience should be for every park visitor all reflected a quest, a search for the Park's purpose. In reviewing the actions of the Ouzel Fire, a Park Service official might well have summarized the entire experience of Rocky Mountain National Park in its modern era when he observed: "A national park is not an island unto itself."[48]

EPILOG

"You have to understand why parks are here and what parks are.
They are different from other land areas. . . ."
Dwight Hamilton, Chief Park Naturalist, 1978[1]

ON A sunny June afternoon in 1982, Park Technician Dr. Ferrel
Atkins and I ambled around the site of Abner Sprague's old homestead in Moraine Park. Not much of the place remained for us to
see. In fact, if Dr. Atkins had not been able to point to places where
roads once ran, where buildings housed guests, and where a golf
course existed, most eyes would never have guessed that a homestead, a resort, and a restoration had all occupied that space over

Sitting vacant in Moraine Park, about to be removed, the ghost-like structures of the Sprague-Stead's ranch recalled a vacationing style of an earlier
era. Barely a trace of that old resort can be found today. (RMNPHC)

the course of a century. In a similar way, as our minds contemplate the current scenes of Rocky Mountain National Park, it is easy to overlook the many efforts and struggles those in the past encountered as they met these mountains.

As Dr. Atkins recounted the many details of Abner Sprague's life, one could almost envision how that hardy pioneer first saw this spot. There is no doubt that he saw the area change from its wildest state into a popular public park. Within his lifetime, Sprague saw people change the land and watched the land change them. Hunters in the wilderness became settlers; ranchers became resort operators; exploiters became conservationists; preservationists became park supporters; park officials became promoters; and park protectors became wilderness defenders. Only change was constant.

What Dr. Atkins could see in that old homestead site very few modern travelers could discern without benefit of an educated memory as a guide. For only by pondering the accounts of the past can we ever imagine what those pioneers first saw when their eyes met these mountains. Only by reading the letters of Isabella Bird to her sister can we really understand what it must have been like to climb Longs Peak in the absence of crowds waiting to attain the summit. Only by reviewing the many books of Enos Mills can we examine the birth of the conservation movement as it pertained to this section of the West. Only by paging through dozens of government documents can we sense the vision of Superintendent Roger Toll and other park officials as they planned for the future. What our memory's eye shows us in retrospect is a much grander vision than that enjoyed by Sprague, or Bird, or Mills, or Toll, but to them we owe gratitude for their concern for this small section of one of the planet's great mountain chains.

It is our fortune to be able to cast an eye toward the past and perhaps glean some nuggets of knowledge from the experience of those who have gone before us. They may help us put our present in perspective. Even more important, seeing how this land has been treated through time may help us determine how we prefer to see it in the future. For Rocky Mountain National Park's future, like its past, is now in our hands.

NOTES

Chapter One

1. Helen Sloan Daniels, ed., *The Ute Indians of Southwestern Colorado* (Durango: Durango Public Library Museum Project, 1941), 41–42.

2. Marie Wormington, *Prehistoric Hunters and Gatherers* (National Park Service: National Survey of Historic Sites and Buildings, 1960), 12.

3. Wilfred M. Husted, "Prehistoric Occupation of the Alpine Zone in the Rocky Mountains," in *Arctic and Alpine Environments*, ed. Jack D. Ives and Roger G. Barry (London: Methuen and Co., Ltd., 1974), 865.

4. Wilfred M. Husted, "A Proposed Archeological Chronology for Rocky Mountain National Park Based On Projectile Points and Pottery" (M.A. thesis, University of Colorado, 1962), 89.

5. Abner Sprague, "The Estes and Rocky Mountain Park National Parks," in *Estes Park Trail*, 21 April 1922, in Historical Data file, Rocky Mountain National Park Historical Collection (hereinafter cited as RMNPHC).

6. Wilson Rockwell, *The Utes: A Forgotten People* (Denver: Sage Books, 1956), 15.

7. Ibid., 15–16.

8. George C. Frison, *Prehistoric Hunters of the High Plains* (New York: Academic Press, 1978), 345.

9. Rockwell, *The Utes*, 17.

10. Virginia Cole Trenholm, *The Arapahoes, Our People* (Norman: University of Oklahoma Press, 1970), 3–32.

11. Ibid., 33.

12. Sprague, "The Estes and Rocky Mountain National Parks."

13. *Estes Park Trail*, 28 February 1930.

14. Alfred L. Kroeber, *The Arapaho* (New York: Bulletin of the Museum of Natural History, 1902), 22.

15. Oliver W. Toll, *Arapaho Names and Trails* (Privately printed: Oliver W. Toll, 1962), 41.

16. Robert C. Black III, *Island in the Rockies* (Boulder: Pruett Publishing Co., 1969), 116.

17. Colin B. Goodykoontz, "The Exploration and Settlement of Colorado," in *Colorado: Short Studies of its Past and Present* (Boulder: University of Colorado, 1927), 83.

18. *Denver Daily Times*, 12 September 1881.

19. E. J. Lamb, *Memories of the Past and Thoughts of the Future* (Press of the United Brethren Publishing House, 1906), 51.

20. Ibid., 49.

21. Louisa Ward Arps and Elinor Eppich Kingery, *High Country Names* (Estes Park: Rocky Mountain Nature Association, 1977), 8.

22. Lonnie E. Underhill and Daniel F. Littlefield, Jr., eds., *Hamlin Garland's Observations on the American Indian, 1895-1905* (Tucson: University of Arizona Press, 1976), 63.

Chapter Two

1. Milton Estes, "The Memoirs of Estes Park," *The Colorado Magazine*, 16 (July 1939): 5.
2. Jerome C. Smiley, *Semi-Centennial History of the State of Colorado* (Chicago: Lewis Publishing Co., 1913), 194-95.
3. Ibid.
4. H. E. Rensch, *Historical Background for Rocky Mountain National Park* (Berkeley: National Park Service, 1935), 9.
5. Harlin M. Fuller and LeRoy R. Hafen, *The Journal of Captain John R. Bell* (Glendale: Arthur H. Clark Co., 1973), 142.
6. Edwin James, *Account of an Expedition from Pittsburg to the Rocky Mountains* (Ann Arbor: University Microfilms, Inc., 1966), 63-64.
7. Ibid., 361, 376.
8. Hiram Martin Chittenden, *The American Fur Trade in the Far West* Vol. 1 (New York: The Press of the Pioneers, Inc., 1935), 59-60.
9. George F. Ruxton, *Life in the Far West* (Norman: University of Oklahoma Press, 1951), 11.
10. Francis Parkman, *The Oregon Trail* (New York: New American Library, 1950), 58.
11. Ibid., 226.
12. LeRoy R. Hafen and Anne W. Hafen, *Rufus B. Sage, His Letters and Papers, 1836-1847* Vol. 2 (Glendale: The Arthur H. Clark Company, 1956), 65.
13. Ibid., 276.
14. Ibid., 277.
15. Ibid., 278-79.
16. Ibid., 279.
17. Donald Jackson and Mary Lee Spence, eds., *The Expeditions of John Charles Fremont* Vol. 1 (Urbana: University of Illinois Press, 1970), 710-11.
18. William F. Drannan, *Thirty-One Years on the Plains and In the Mountains or, The Last Voice from the Plains* (Chicago: Rhodes & McClure Publishing Co., 1900), 72.
19. James F. Willard, "The Gold Rush and After," in *Colorado: Short Studies*, 103.
20. LeRoy Hafen, ed., *Colorado Gold Rush, Contemporary Letters and Reports, 1858-1859* (Philadelphia: Porcupine Press, 1974), 220-21.
21. Ovando J. Hollister, *The Mines of Colorado* (Springfield: Samuel Bowles and Co., 1867), 12.
22. Milton Estes, "The Memoirs," 5.
23. Ibid.
24. Ibid., 6.
25. Letter, D. Wright to Estes Park Chamber of Commerce, Historical Data, RMNPHC, p. 56.
26. Milton Estes, "The Memoirs," 6.
27. Ibid., 7.
28. Ibid., 9.
29. Ibid., 11.
30. William N. Byers, "Ascent of Longs Peak," in Historical Data, RMNPHC, p. 26.
31. Ibid.

32. Ibid., pp. 29–30.

33. Ibid.,p. 27.

34. Ibid., p. 30.

35. Milton Estes, "The Memoirs," 13.

36. Jules Verne, *From the Earth to the Moon and A Trip Around It (Round the Moon)* (Philadelphia: J. B. Lippincott Co., n.d.), 107.

Chapter Three

1. Earl of Dunraven, *Past Times and Pastimes* (London: Hodder and Stroughton, 1922), 142.

2. Isabella L. Bird, *A Lady's Life in the Rocky Mountains* (Norman: University of Oklahoma Press, 1979), 73.

3. Hollister, *The Mines of Colorado*, 41.

4. Bayard Taylor, *Colorado: A Summer Trip* (New York: G. P. Putnam and Son, 1867), 165–66.

5. Nell Pauly, *Ghosts of the Shootin'* (Grand Lake: Kaufman Press, 1961), 118.

6. Bird, *A Lady's Life*, 73.

7. Dale White, *John Wesley Powell, Geologist-Explorer* (New York: Julian Messener, Inc., 1958), 80–81.

8. William N. Byers, "First Ascent of Longs Peak," in Historical Data, RMNPHC, pp. 130 and 133.

9. Ibid., pp. 133–34.

10. L. W. Keplinger, "The First Ascent of Longs Peak," in Historical Data, RMNPHC, p. 143.

11. Byers, "First Ascent," p. 134.

12. Keplinger, "The First Ascent," p. 144.

13. Byers, "First Ascent," pp. 135–36.

14. Richard A. Bartlett, *Great Surveys of the American West* (Norman: University of Oklahoma Press, 1962), xiv.

15. Henry Adams, *The Education of Henry Adams* (New York: Houghton Mifflin Co., 1918), 309–12.

16. Anna E. Dickinson, *A Ragged Register (of People, Places and Opinions)* New York: Harper and Brothers, 1879), as cited in Historical Data, RMNPHC, p. 147.

17. Bird, *A Lady's Life*, 93.

18. *Rocky Mountain News*, 24 August 1868.

19. Dave Hicks, *Estes Park, From the Beginning* (Denver: A-T-P Publishing Co., 1976), 9.

20. Robert G. Athearn, *Westward the Briton* (New York: Charles Scribner's Sons, 1953), 49.

21. Earl of Dunraven, *Canadian Nights* (New York: Charles Scribner's Sons, 1914), 128.

22. Earl of Dunraven, *The Great Divide* (London: Chatto and Windus, 1876), 2.

23. Dunraven, *Canadian Nights*, 36.

24. Earl of Dunraven, "Lord Dunraven's Address," *Journal of the American Geographical Society*, 11(1879): 336.

25. Dunraven, *Past Times*, 142.

26. E. J. Lamb, *Miscellaneous Meditations* (Denver: Publishers' Press Room and Bindery Co., 1913?), 128–29.

27. Bird, *A Lady's Life*, 79.

28. Ibid., 113.

29. Lamb, *Miscellaneous*, 130.

30. Dunraven, *Past Times*, 140.

31. George Henry Kingsley and Mary H. Kingsley, *Notes on Sport and Travel* (London: Macmillian and Co., Ltd., 1900), 178–79.

32. Dunraven, *Past Times*, 149.

33. Dunraven, "Lord Dunraven's Address," 338.

34. Dunraven, *Canadian Nights*, 38–39.

35. Bird, *A Lady's Life*, 11.

36. Ibid., 116.

37. Pat Barr, *A Curious Life for a Lady* (New York: Ballantine Books, 1972), 1.

38. Bird, *A Lady's Life*, 89.

39. Ibid., 79.

40. Ibid., 125.

41. Ibid., 91.

42. Ibid., 94.

43. Ibid., 101.

44. Louisa Ward Arps, "Letters from Isabella Bird," *The Colorado Quarterly* 4 (Summer 1955) :37.

45. Bird, *A Lady's Life*, 248.

Chapter Four

1. F. V. Hayden, *The Great West: Its Attractions and Resources* (Bloomington: Charles R. Bordix, 1880), 97.

2. Abner E. Sprague, "My First Winter in Estes Park," *Colorado Magazine*, 16 (1940): 156.

3. *Estes Park Trail*, 5 May 1922.

4. *Estes Park Trail*, 2 June 1922.

5. *Estes Park Trail*, 16 June 1922.

6. Carrie Adell Strahorn, *Fifteen Thousand Miles by Stage* (New York: G. P. Putnam's Sons, 1911), 65.

7. Ibid., 68–69.

8. Ibid., 73.

9. J. S. Flory, *Thrilling Echoes From the Wild Frontier* (Chicago: Rhodes and McClure Publishing Co., 1893), 38.

10. Ibid., 41.

11. Ibid., 41–42.

12. Ibid., 46.

13. Ibid., 47–48.

14. Hayden, *The Great West*, 147.

15. Ibid., 164.

16. Joe Mills, *A Mountain Boyhood* (New York: J. H. Sears and Co., Inc., 1926), 223–24.

17. *Estes Park Trail*, 3 March 1922.

18. Georgetown *Colorado Miner*, 3 April 1880.

19. Goodykoontz, "The Exploration," 81.

20. Georgetown *Colorado Miner*, 31 July 1880.

21. Georgetown *Colorado Miner*, 18 September 1880.

22. Fort Collins *Express*, 21 July 1881.

23. Georgetown *Colorado Miner*, 17 December 1881.

24. Georgetown *Colorado Miner*, 12 February 1881.

25. Susan B. Baldwin, *Historic Resource Study, Dutchtown and Lulu City, Rocky Mountain National Park, Colorado* (Creative Land Use, 1980), 89.

26. Black, *Island in the Rockies*, 157.

27. Georgetown *Colorado Miner*, 14 July 1883.

28. Pauly, *Ghosts*, 175.

29. Georgetown *Colorado Miner*, 21 July 1883.

30. Pauly, *Ghosts*, 175.

31. *Estes Park Trail*, 24 November 1933.

32. *Estes Park Trail*, 1 December 1933.

Chapter Five

1. Enos A. Mills, *Your National Parks* (Boston: Houghton Mifflin, 1917), 333.

2. Hildegarde Hawthorne and Esther Burnell Mills, *Enos Mills of the Rockies* (New York: Houghton Mifflin Co., 1935), 24.

3. Frederick H. Chapin, *Mountaineering in Colorado* (Boston: Appalachian Mountain Club, 1889), 70.

4. Ibid., 23.

5. Carl Bode, ed., *The Portable Thoreau* (New York: Penguin Books, 1979), 598.

6. Lewis Mumford, ed., *Ralph Waldo Emerson: Essays and Journals* (Garden City: Doubleday and Co., 1968), 223.

7. Harold K. Steen, *The U.S. Forest Service: A History* (Seattle: University of Washington Press, 1976), 26–28.

8. G. Michael McCarthy, *Hour of Trial* (Norman: University of Oklahoma Press, 1977), 42.

9. Ibid., 62.

10. Hawthorne and Mills, *Enos Mills*, 77–78.

11. Lloyd K. Musselman, *Rocky Mountain National Park, Administrative History, 1915–1965* (Department of the Interior: National Park Service, 1971), 14.

12. William Allen White, *The Autobiography of William Allen White* (New York: The Macmillan Company, 1946), 446.

13. June E. Carothers, *Estes Park, Past and Present* (Denver: University of Denver, 1951), 80.

14. Florence Johnson Shoemaker, "The Story of Estes-Rocky Mountain National Park Region" (M. A. thesis, Colorado State College, Greeley, 1940), 49.

15. Enos A. Mills, *The Rocky Mountain Wonderland* (Boston: Houghton Mifflin, 1915), 321.

16. Hawthorne and Mills, *Enos Mills*, 128.

17. Mills, *Your National Parks*, 322–23.

18. *Estes Park Trail*, 28 April 1944.

19. Letter, H. J. M. Mattis to His Excellency Theodore Roosevelt, 28 August 1902, U.S.F.S. Historical File No. 11, Box 4, Federal Records Center, Denver.

20. Michael Frome, *Whose Woods These Are: The Story of the National Forests* (New York: Doubleday and Co., 1962), 60.

21. Letter, H. N. Wheeler to District Forester, 2 January 1923, U.S.F.S. Historical File, Federal Records Center, Denver.

22. Enos A. Mills, *The Story of Estes Park* (Estes Park: Robert H. and Enda Kiley, 1980), 97–98.

23. Letter, H. N. Wheeler to District Forester, p. 2.

24. Enos Mills, "National Forests vs. National Parks," in Enos Mills Collection, Western History Department, Denver Public Library, p. 2.

25. Ibid.

26. R. B. Marshall, "Report on an Examination of the Area of the Proposed Rocky Mountain (Estes) National Park, Colorado," 9 January 1913, Records of the Office of the Secretary of the Interior, R. G. 79, National Archives, p. 11.

27. Musselman, *Rocky Mountain*, 27.

28. *Denver Post*, 4 September 1915.

29. Enos A. Mills, *The Spell of the Rockies* (Boston: Houghton Mifflin, 1911), 116.

Chapter Six

1. *Denver Post*, 5 September 1915.

2. *Denver Post*, 6 August 1917.

3. William C. Everhart, *The National Park Service* (New York: Praeger Publishers, 1972), 21.

4. Roderick Nash, ed., *The American Environment* (Menlo Park, California: Addison Wesley, 1976), 19.

5. Ibid., 20.

6. Alfred Runte, *National Parks: The American Experience* (Lincoln: University of Nebraska Press, 1979), 29.

7. Aubrey L. Haines, *The Yellowstone Story* Vol. 1 (Yellowstone: Yellowstone Library and Museum Association, 1977), 218.

8. Mills, *Your National Parks*, 292.

9. Linnie Marsh Wolfe, *Son of the Wilderness: The Life of John Muir* (New York: Knopf, 1945), 186.

10. Mills, *Your National Parks*, xi–xii.

11. Bode, *The Portable Thoreau*, 613–14.

12. Mills, *Your National Parks*, 293–94.

13. *Denver Post*, 7 August 1917.

14. John Willy, "Five Days on Horseback in Rocky Mountain National Park," *Hotel Monthly*, 24 (October 1916): 53.

15. Ibid., 52.

16. *Denver Post*, 14 January 1915.

17. Letter, E. L. Baldwin to Superintendent, 26 July 1915, Box 399, R. G. 79, National Archives.

18. Department of the Interior, *Report of the Director of the National Park Service, 1917* (Washington, D.C.: Government Printing Office, 1917), 26.

19. Department of the Interior, *Report of the Director of the National Park Service, 1918* (Washington, D.C.: Government Printing Office, 1918), 181.

20. Enos A. Mills, "Exploring Our National Parks," *The New Republic*, 24 (10 November 1920): 272.

21. *Denver Post*, 9 August 1917.

22. Department of the Interior, *Report of the Director of the National Park Service, 1920* (Washington, D.C.: Government Printing Office, 1920), 137.

23. Department of the Interior, *Report of the Director of the National Park Service, 1921* (Washington, D.C.: Government Printing Office, 1921), 93.

24. *Report of the Director, 1918*, 180.

25. Report, Frederick M. Dille, File 1215, p. 1, Box 269, R. G. 79, National Archives.

26. *Report of the Director, 1921*, 93.

27. Report, "Department of National, State, and Provincial Parks," in RMNPHC, p. 46.

28. Department of the Interior, *Report of the Director of the National Park Service, 1926* (Washington, D.C.: Government Printing Office, 1926), 136.

29. Horace Albright, *Parks and Recreation* (November-December 1922), p. 86 in RMNPHC.

30. *Estes Park Trail*, 16 January 1925.

31. Roger W. Toll, *Mountaineering in the Rocky Mountain National Park* (Washington, D.C.: Government Printing Office, 1921), 10.

32. Musselman, *Rocky Mountain*, 195.

33. Ibid., 63.

34. *Denver Post*, 14 October 1928.

35. *Denver Post*, 13 August 1917.

36. *Denver Post*, 8 August 1917.

37. Letter, Way to Director, 18 August 1917, File 1215, Tray 473, R. G. 79, National Archives.

38. Letter, Albright to Way, 26 August 1917, File 1215, Tray 473, R. G. 79, National Archives.

39. Letter, Way to Director, 28 August 1917, File 1215, Tray 473, R. G. 79, National Archives.

40. Letter, Kennedy to Director, undated, File 1215, Tray 473, R. G. 79, National Archives.

41. Toll, *Mountaineering*, 42.

Chapter Seven

1. *Rocky Mountain News*, 20 June 1931.

2. Department of the Interior, *Report of the Director of the National Park Service, 1931* (Washington, D.C.: Government Printing Office, 1931), 69.

3. Clipping, *Denver Post*, 9 December 1930, File 630, Box 408, R. G. 79, National Archives.

4. Clipping, *Rocky Mountain News*, 5 June 1932, File 630, Box 408, R. G. 79, National Archives.

5. *Estes Park Trail*, 15 July 1932.

6. *Rocky Mountain News*, 5 June 1932.

7. Report, Charles W. Eliot, 3 July 1930, Central Files, 1907–32, R. G. 79, National Archives.

8. *Report of the Director, 1931*, 48.

9. *Estes Park Trail*, 15 July 1932.

10. Musselman, *Rocky Mountain*, 93.

11. *Superintendent's Annual Report, 1941*, RMNPHC, p. 15.

12. Letter, Director to Solinsky, 30 October 1931, File 600, Box 399, R. G. 79, National Archives.

13. *Estes Park Trail*, 16 September 1932.

14. *Report of the Director, 1931*, 6.

15. *Estes Park Trail*, 23 December 1932.

16. Dorr Yeager, *Bob Flame, Rocky Mountain Ranger* (New York: Dodd, Mead & Co., 1936), 237.

17. Jack C. Moomaw, *Recollections of a Rocky Mountain Ranger* (Longmont: Times-Call Publishing Co., 1963), 133–36.

18. *Estes Park Trail*, 25 November 1932.

19. Musselman, *Rocky Mountain*, 136.

20. *Estes Park Trail*, 25 November 1932.

21. Report, RMNP Superintendent's Monthly Report, 6 June 1933, p. 1.

22. Perry H. Merrill, *Roosevelt's Forest Army, A History of the Civilian Conservation Corps, 1933-1942* (Montpelier: Perry H. Merrill, 1981), 196–97.

23. Battell Loomis, "With the Green Guard," *Liberty* (April 29, 1934), 52–53.

24. Ibid.

25. Ibid., 53.

26. Battell Loomis, "The C.C.C. Digs In," *Liberty* (May 5, 1934), 47.

27. *Estes Park Trail*, 16 June 1944.

28. Musselman, *Rocky Mountain*, 124.

29. Ibid., 116.
30. *Superintendent's Annual Report, 1936*, RMNPHC, p. 17.
31. Musselman, *Rocky Mountain*, 124.
32. Ibid.
33. *Superintendent's Annual Report, 1943*, RMNPHC, p. 1.
34. *Superintendent's Annual Report, 1946*, RMNPHC, p. 1.
35. Ibid.
36. *Rocky Mountain News*, 5 February 1948.
37. Yeager, *Bob Flame*, 68.
38. *Report of the Director, 1924*, p. 1.
39. *Denver Post*, 11 September 1932.
40. *Estes Park Trail*, 26 June 1931.
41. Musselman, *Rocky Mountain*, 175–76.
42. *Superintendent's Annual Report, 1939*, RMNPHC, p. 12.
43. Musselman, *Rocky Mountain*, 181.
44. Yeager, *Bob Flame*, 278.

Chapter Eight

1. *Denver Post*, 17 August 1980.
2. Proceedings, *Park Management Conference, 1965*, File A-40, T-11796, R. G. 79, Federal Records Center, Denver, p. 65.
3. Report, Mission 66 for Rocky Mountain National Park, in RMNPHC, p. 2.
4. Everhart, *The National Park Service*, 35.
5. Report, Mission 66, p. 1.
6. Report, Urgently Needed Construction Projects, in RMNPHC, p. 9.
7. Report, Mission 66 Prospectus, in RMNPHC, p. 13.
8. Musselman, *Rocky Mountain*, 215.
9. *Estes Park Trail*, 18 October 1957.
10. Mission 66 Prospectus, p. 59.
11. *Estes Park Trail*, 4 September 1959.
12. *Denver Post*, 17 March 1974.
13. *Rocky Mountain News*, 25 March 1965.
14. Paul W. Nesbit, *Longs Peak* (Colorado Springs: Paul W. Nesbit, 1969), 29.
15. *Denver Post*, 4 August 1960.
16. F. Fraser Darling and Noel D. Eichhorn, *Man and Nature in the National Parks* (Washington, D.C.: The Conservation Foundation, 1967), 28.
17. David R. Brower, "Wilderness—Conflict and Conscience," *Sierra Club Bulletin* 42 (June 1957): 10.
18. Proceedings, Park Management Conference, p. 10.
19. Ibid., 20.
20. *Estes Park Trail*, 15 June 1956.
21. Stewart L. Udall, "The Ecology of Man and the Land Ethic," *Natural History* 74 (June-July 1965): 34.
22. Darling and Eichhorn, *Man and Nature*, 70.
23. Letter, Calvert to N.P.S. Regional Office, 20 January 1974, p. 1, in RMNPHC.
24. Letter, Millen to Park Superintendent, 18 January 1974, in RMNPHC.
25. Letter, Robertson (to Superintendent), 27 February 1974, pp. 1–2, in RMNPHC.
26. Letter, Sisler to Contor, 25 February 1974, p. 2, in RMNPHC.
27. Letter, More to Contor, 3 January 1973, p. 1, in RMNPHC.
28. Letter, Nock to Hearing Officer, 12 February 1974, in RMNPHC.
29. Letter, Price to Superintendent, 28 February 1974, in RMNPHC.
30. Letter, Murphy (to Superintendent), 30 January 1974, p. 2, in RMNPHC.

31. Letter, Mowery to Contor (1974), p. 1, in RMNPHC.

32. Letter, Rupel to Editor, 15 December 1973, p. 1, in RMNPHC.

33. Press Release, 16 July 1973, p. 2, in RMNPHC.

34. Loveland *Daily-Reporter Herald*, 21 August 1975.

35. *Denver Post*, 17 August 1980.

36. Transcript, National Park Service Wilderness Proposal Hearing, p. 66, in RMNPHC.

37. Proceedings, Park Management Conference, p. 20.

38. Report, Richard G. Trahan, *Day-Use Limitations in National Parks: Visitor and Park Personnel Attitudes Toward Day-Use Limitation Systems for Rocky Mountain National Park*, 1977, pp. 13−9-13.

39. Proceedings, Park Management Conference, p. 35.

40. Ibid.

41. Letter, Pettie to Fazio, 1 December 1973, pp. 1-2, in RMNPHC.

42. Interview, Mr. James Wilson, 12 December 1982.

43. Letter, Neuswanger to Contor, n.d. (1974), p. 1, in RMNPHC.

44. Interview, Mr. Chester Brooks and Mr. Edgar Menning, 16 December 1982.

45. Ibid.

46. *Estes Park Trail-Gazette*, 20 October 1978.

47. Transcript, Board of Review, The Ouzel Fire, 8 November 1978, p. 102, in RMNPHC.

48. Ibid., p. 93.

Epilog

1. Transcript, Board of Review, The Ouzel Fire, 9 November 1978, p. 118, in RMNPHC.

BIBLIOGRAPHICAL ESSAY

General Works

The history of Rocky Mountain National Park has always been linked to that of the adjacent communities of Estes Park and Grand Lake. One of the earliest histories of the region still available is Enos Mills's *The Story of Estes Park* (Privately printed, 1980). June E. Carothers's *Estes Park, Past and Present* (Denver, 1951) offers greater perspective. Edmin J. Foscue and Louis O. Quam's *Estes Park, Resort in the Rockies* (Dallas, 1949) is equally valuable. Brief historical introductions to the area include Ruth Stauffer's *This Was Estes Park: Historical Vignettes of the Early Days* (Estes Park, 1976) and Lloyd K. Musselman's *Rocky Mountain National Park, Its First Fifty Years, 1915–1965* (Estes Park, 1965). Caroline Bancroft's *Trail Ridge Country: The Romantic History of Estes Park and Grand Lake* (Boulder, 1968) and Dave Hicks's *Estes Park, From the Beginning* (Denver, 1976) note many historical highlights of the area. Offering personal insight are Harold Marion Dunning's *History of Estes Park* (Boulder, 1967), *Over Hill and Vale* (Boulder, 1956), and *The History of Trail Ridge Road* (Boulder, 1967). Especially valuable for its many details of early exploration and settlement as well as nomenclature is Louisa Ward Arps and Elinor Eppich Kingery's *Rocky Mountain National Park, High Country Names* (Boulder, 1972).

Mary Lyons Carins's *Grand Lake in the Olden Days* (Denver, 1971) and Nell Pauly's *Ghosts of the Shootin'* (Grand Lake, 1961) provide some pioneers' perspectives regarding events on the western slope. Of greater value is Robert C. Black III's *Island in the Rockies* (Boulder, 1969) with its definitive history of Grand County.

Equally important but less accessible are two National Park Service historic resource studies: F. Ross Holland, Jr.'s *Rocky Mountain National Park: Historical Background Data* (National Park Service, 1971) and Lloyd K. Musselman's *Rocky Mountain National Park, Administrative History, 1915–1965* (National Park Service, 1971). Older but still of value are H. E. Rensch's *Historical Background for Rocky Mountain National Park* (National Park Service, 1935) and Florence Johnson Shoemaker's *The Story of Estes-Rocky Mountain National Park Region* (Master's thesis, Colorado State College, Greeley, 1940).

Placing the national park idea into a national perspective are Alfred Runte's *National Parks: The American Experience* (Lincoln, 1972) and Joseph L. Sax's *Mountains Without Handrails: Reflections on the National Parks* (Ann Arbor, 1980). And for an overview of Colorado history see Carl Abbott, Stephen J. Leonard, and David McComb's *Colorado: A History of the Centennial State* (Boulder, 1982), Marshall Sprague's *Colorado, A Bicentennial History* (New York, 1976), or Robert Athearn's *The Coloradans* (Albuquerque, 1976).

Chapter One: *Tales, Trails, and Tribes*

Native Americans of the prehistoric era of course left no written records of their visits to Rocky Mountain National Park. Here archeology and ethnology dominate our study. Two introductory studies, Bruce Estes Rippeteau's *A Colorado Book of the Dead: The Prehistoric Era* (Denver, 1979) and J. Donald Hughes's *American Indians of Colorado* (Boulder, c. 1977), trace Colorado's natives through time. Offering a broader perspective are George C. Frison's *Prehistoric Hunters of the Great Plains* (New York, 1978), Jesse D. Jennings's *Prehistory of North America* (New York, 1974), and H. M. Wormington's *Ancient Man in North America* (Denver, 1957). Also useful is Edwin N. Wilmsen's *Lindenmeier: A Pliestocene Hunting Society* (New York, 1974).

Two valuable studies center on archeology within the Park. An older work, Mary Elizabeth Yelm's *Archeological Survey of Rocky Mountain National Park — Eastern Foothill District* (Master's thesis, University of Denver, 1935) gave archeology a boost in the region. Wilfred Marsten Husted's *A Proposed Archeological Chronology for Rocky Mountain National Park Based on Projectile Points and Pottery* (Master's thesis, University of Colorado, 1962) has become essential for understanding the Park's prehistory. Equally important are James B. Benedict's *The Fourth of July Valley: Glacial Geology and Archeology of the Timberline Ecotone* (Ward, 1981) and (with Byron L. Olson) *The Mount Albion Complex: A Study of Prehistoric Man and the Altithermal* (Ward, 1978). Older speculative studies, such as Betty Yelm's and Ralph L. Beals's *Indians of the Park Region* (Estes Park, 1934) are being replaced by numerous valuable articles such as Wilfred M. Husted's "Early Occupation of the Colorado Front Range," *American Antiquity*, 30–4 (April 1965): 494–98, and David A. Breternitz's "An Early Burial from Gordon Creek, Colorado," *American Antiquity*, 36–2 (April 1971): 170–82.

Indians associated with the Park region may be examined in broader scope in Virginia Cole Trenholm's *The Arapahoes, Our People* (Norman, 1970), Alfred L. Kroeber's *The Arapaho* (New York, 1902), and Wilson Rockwell's *The Utes: A Forgotten People* (Denver, 1956). Among the more recent scholarly studies, Anne M. Smith's *Ethnography of the Northern Utes* (Santa Fe, 1974) offers unique analysis of Ute lifeways. An early effort to connect Rocky Mountain National Park with its Native American heritage led to a 1914 expedition through the region with elderly Indians as detailed in Oliver W. Toll's *Arapaho Names and Trails* (Privately printed, 1962).

Chapter Two: *Into the Domains of Silence and Loneliness*

The exploration of Rocky Mountain National Park has to be considered in the context of Colorado history. Regarding the expedition of Stephen Harriman Long, see Dr. Edwin James's *Account of an Expedition from Pittsburg to the Rocky Mountains* (Ann Arbor, 1966) or Harlan M. Fuller and LeRoy R. Hafen's *The Journal of Captain John R. Bell* (Glendale, 1973). For an overview of the American fur trade, Hiram M. Chittenden's *The American Fur Trade of the Far West* (New York, 1902) is only one of numerous studies. Essential to the Park's earliest link with frontiersmen is LeRoy R. Hafen and Anne W. Hafen's *Rufus B. Sage, His Letters and Papers, 1836–1847* (Glendale, 1956). For other visitors in the region see Donald Jackson and Mary Lee Spence's *The Expeditions of John Charles Fremont* (Urbana, 1970) and Francis Parkman's classic tale *The Oregon Trail* (New York, 1950). Jack Roberts's *The Amazing Adventures of Lord Gore* (Silverton, 1977) offers some insights into the way the Rockies were viewed by the 1850s.

Because gold brought such people as Joel Estes to Colorado, the search for mineral wealth ultimately affected Rocky Mountain National Park. For an overview of that era see George F. Willison's *Here They Dug the Gold* (New York, 1931) or LeRoy R. Hafen's *Colorado Gold Rush, Contemporary Letters and Reports, 1858–1859* (Philadelphia, 1974). The experience of Joel Estes has been treated in almost every general history of Rocky Mountain National Park. The most reliable source of information regarding Joel Estes remains Milton Estes's "The Memoirs of Estes Park," *The Colorado Magazine*, 16(July 1939): 121–32. Longs Peak entered the realm of fiction for the first time in Jules Verne's *From the Earth to the Moon and A Trip Around It* (Philadelphia, c. 1865).

Chapter Three: Searching for the Song of the Winds

Isabella Bird's travels continue to keep readers entertained. Two works put her Colorado visit in perspective: Robert G. Athearn's *Westward the Briton* (New York, 1953) and Marshall Sprague's *A Gallery of Dudes* (Boston, 1966). Dorothy Middleton's *Victorian Lady Travellers* (New York, 1965) describes the European context from which Bird came. Isabella Bird's own *A Lady's Life in the Rocky Mountains* (Norman, 1979) has become a minor classic in the history of the Rocky Mountain National Park.

Concerning the Earl of Dunraven, his own works offer a fine introduction. His *Canadian Nights* (New York, 1914), *Past Times and Pastimes* (London, 1922), and *The Great Divide* (London, 1876) are worth searching for, as is George Henry Kingsley and Mary H. Kingsley's *Notes on Sport and Travel* (London, 1900), since they shed light on some controversial aspects of the Earl's tenure in Estes Park. For an early settler's view of the Earl see E. J. Lamb's *Memories of the Past and Thoughts of the Future* (Denver ?, 1901) and *Miscellaneous Meditations* (Denver ?, c. 1913).

For the era of geological and geographical exploration, William H. Goetzmann's *Exploration and Empire* (New York, 1966) is the best place to start and Richard A. Bartlett's *Great Surveys of the American West* (Norman, 1962) will also prove helpful. The Longs Peak climb of John Wesley Powell and his many other adventures may be found in Dale White's *John Wesley Powell, Geologist-Explorer* (New York, 1958) or William Culp Darrah's *Powell of the Colorado* (Princeton, 1951). Worth searching for are William N. Byers's 1868 articles in the *Rocky Mountain News* detailing his climb with Powell that August. William N. Byers's "First Ascent of Longs Peak," in *The Trail* (October 1914) and L. W. Keplinger's "The First Ascent of Longs Peak," in *The Trail* (June 1919) afford interesting views of that event.

Numerous individuals and issues within this era have received attention. Albert Bierstadt's role has been elaborated in Gordon Hendricks's *Albert Bierstadt, Painter of the American West* (New York, 1974). Geological surveys brought hangers-on and for examples see Henry Adams's *The Education of Henry Adams* (New York, 1918) or Anna E. Dickinson's *A Ragged Register (of People, Places and Opinions)* (New York, 1879). Whether Isabella Bird was really in love with Mountain Jim has been explored in Louisa Ward Arps "Letters from Isabella Bird," *The Colorado Quarterly*, 4(Summer 1955): 26–41, and Pat Barr's *A Curious Life for a Lady* (New York, 1972).

Chapter Four: Dreams with Silver Lining

Much of the information on the life of Abner Sprague can be gleaned from the numerous articles he contributed to the *Estes Park Trail*. Other details concerning that era of ranching may be found in Florence Johnson Shoemaker's *The Story of Estes-Rocky Mountain National Park Region* (Master's thesis, Colorado State College, Greeley, 1940) and Louisa Ward Arps and Elinor Eppich Kingery's *High Country Names* (Estes Park, 1977). Western slope settlement is best discussed in Robert C. Black III's *Island in the Rockies* (Boulder, 1969).

For an overview of mining during this era see Duane Smith's *Rocky Mountain Mining Camps* (Bloomington, 1967) or an older examination, J. S. Perky's *Homes in and Near the Rocky Mountains* (Fort Collins, 1880). A definitive examination of Rocky Mountain National Park's mining era is Susan B. Baldwin's *Historic Resource Study, Dutchtown and Lulu City, Rocky Mountain National Park, Colorado* (Creative Land Use, 1980). Numerous articles appearing in the Georgetown *Colorado Miner*, the Fort Collins *Express*, and the *Rocky Mountain News* help reconstruct the rise and fall of mining along the North Fork. An interesting mix of geological exploration and promotion can be seen in F. V. Hayden's *The Great West: Its Attractions and Resources* (Bloomington, 1880). End results of such booms are described in Robert L. Brown's *Ghost Towns in the Colorado Rockies* (Caldwell, 1969).

The view of ranches becoming resorts is evident in E. J. Lamb's *Miscellaneous Meditations* (Denver ?, 1913 ?) and in Mary Lyons Carins's *Grand Lake in the Olden Days* (Denver, 1971). Joe Mills, brother of Enos Mills, offered *A Mountain Boyhood* (New York, 1926) which also provides details of that era. Travelers left their impressions and one of the most noteworthy is Carrie Adell Strahorn's *Fifteen Thousand Miles by Stage* (New York, 1911). J. S. Flory's *Thrilling Echoes From the Wild Frontier* (Chicago, 1893) offers an interesting contrast.

The shooting at Grand Lake received definitive treatment in Robert C. Black III's *Island in the Rockies* (Boulder, 1969). Nell Pauly also described the event in *Ghosts of the Shootin'* (Grand Lake, 1961). It is still worthwhile to read the newspaper accounts detailing that incident, especially from the Georgetown *Colorado Miner* during July of 1883.

Chapter Five: For the Benefit and Enjoyment of the People

Of those involved in the creation of Rocky Mountain National Park, none have exceeded the attention given Enos Mills. A sympathetic biography, Hildegarde Hawthorne and Esther Burnell Mills's *Enos Mills of the Rockies* (New York, 1935), still should be examined. Confronting the hero-naturalist image of Mills is Carl Abbott's "The Active Force: Enos A. Mills and the National Park Movement," *The Colorado Magazine*, 56 (Winter/Spring 1979): 56–73 and " 'To Arouse Interest in the Outdoors': The Literary Career of Enos Mills," *Montana: The Magazine of Western History*, 31 (April 1981): 2–15. Putting Mills into perspective within the movement to create Rocky Mountain National Park was the task of Patricia M. Fazio in *Cragged Crusade: The Fight for Rocky Mountain National Park, 1909–15* (Master's thesis, University of Wyoming, Laramie, 1982). Enos Mills's own works still attract readers, with *The Adventures of a Nature Guide* (New York, 1923), *The Grizzly* (Sausalito, 1976), *The Rocky Mountain National Park* (New York, 1924), *The Rocky Mountain Wonderland* (Boston, 1915), *Wild Life on the Rockies* (Boston, 1909), and *The Spell of the Rockies* (Boston, 1911) offering a sample of the books that made him popular.

The conservation movement preceded Mills and it is always helpful to explore some of its philosophic roots in Carl Bode's *The Portable Thoreau* (New York, 1979) or Lewis Mumford's *Ralph Waldo Emerson: Essays and Journals* (Garden City, 1968). The establishment of national forests may be seen in Arthur H. Carhart's *The National Forests* (New York, 1959), Michael Frome's *Whose Woods These Are: The*

Story of the National Forests (New York, 1962), and Harold K. Steen's *The U.S. Forest Service: A History* (Seattle, 1976). National forests in Colorado received attention in Michael McCarthy's *Hour of Trial* (Norman, 1977) and Len Shoemaker's *Saga of a Forest Ranger* (Boulder, 1958). Rangers became romantic figures in Zane Grey's *The Young Forester* (New York, 1910) and Hamlin Garland's *Cavanagh, Forest Ranger* (New York, 1910).

Appreciating the mountains took many forms. Frederick H. Chapin's *Mountaineering in Colorado* (Boston, 1889) promoted mountain climbing. William Allen White's *The Autobiography of William Allen White* (New York, 1946) presents Moraine Park as a perfect resort. Peter Wild's *Pioneer Conservationists of Western America* (Missoula, 1979) described the varied avenues conservation could take.

Chapter Six: Paradise Founded

The story of Agnes Lowe, the Eve of Estes, was detailed in *The Denver Post* over the first two weeks of August, 1917. Several other documents relating to that event are in Rocky Mountain National Park files in the National Archives. Other highlights of the Park's early administration are described in the *Annual Reports of the Director of the National Park Service* and the *Superintendent's Monthly Reports.* Lloyd K. Musselman's *Rocky Mountain National Park, Administrative History, 1915–1965* (National Park Service, 1971) offers the most comprehensive discussion of this era.

The origins of national park policy and philosophy are best found in Hans Huth's *Nature and the American* (Berkeley, 1957), Roderick Nash's *Wilderness and the American Mind* (New Haven, 1967), and Alfred Runte's *National Parks: The American Experience* (Lincoln, 1972). Robert Shankland's *Steve Mather of the National Parks* (New York, 1951) provides insight into the beginnings of the National Park Service as does William C. Everhart's *The National Park Service* (New York, 1972). A broader view of all the parks is given in John Ise's *Our National Park Policy* (Baltimore, 1961). A review of the national parks of the period is submitted in Robert Sterling Yard's *The Book of the National Parks* (New York, 1920) and Enos Mills's *Your National Parks* (Boston, 1917). Some insights into the administration of national parks during that period may be gained from Horace M. Albright and Frank J. Taylor's *Oh, Ranger!* (Stanford, 1928).

Superintendent Roger Toll wrote numerous letters, reports, newspaper and magazine articles, and memoranda that are scattered throughout Park files and archives. His *Mountaineering in the Rocky Mountain National Park* (Washington, 1921) affords a glance at his promotional efforts. Numerous issues of the *Estes Park Trail* display events and individuals significant to the Park. For a point of view from a Park visitor see John Willy's "A Motor Ride from St. Joseph, Mo., to Estes Park," *Hotel Monthly*, 24 (September 1916): 48–56 and "Five Days on Horseback in Rocky Mountain National Park," *Hotel Monthly*, 24 (October 1916): 40–53. William Sherman Bell explored the complexities of the Park's jurisdictional dispute in "The Legal Phases of Cession of Rocky Mountain National Park," *Rocky Mountain Law Review*, 1 (1928): 35–46. The death of Agnes Vaille was described in Carl Blaurock's "Tragedy on Longs Peak," *The Denver Westerners Roundup*, 37 (September-October 1981): 3–12.

Chapter Seven: Publicity Pays Off

Promotion of the Park continued during the early 1930s and Chief Naturalist Dorr Yeager's *Bob Flame, Rocky Mountain Ranger* (New York, 1963) affords a unique example of such efforts. Later, his *Your Western National Parks* (New York, 1947) broadened the scope and discarded the fiction. Somewhat more rustic and realistic was Jack C. Moomaw's *Recollections of a Rocky Mountain Ranger* (Longmont, 1963).

Aside from dozens of government reports on the subject, road building in Rocky Mountain National Park is best described in Glen Kaye's *Trail Ridge* (Estes Park, 1982) and Lloyd K. Musselman's *Rocky Mountain National Park, Administrative History, 1915-1965* (National Park Service, 1971).

Origins of the Civilian Conservation Corps may be found in Paul Conkin's *The New Deal* (New York, 1967), David C. Coyle's *Conservation* (New Brunswick, 1957), and Edgar B. Nixon's *Franklin D. Roosevelt and Conservation, 1911-1945* (Washington, 1957). A general overview of the CCC is provided in Perry H. Merrill's *Roosevelt's Forest Army, A History of the Civilian Conservation Corps, 1933-1942* (Montpelier, 1981). Insight into the life of a CCC enrollee is provided by Battell Loomis's "With the Green Guard," *Liberty* (April 29, 1934): 52-53 and "The C.C.C. Digs In," *Liberty* (May 5, 1934): 46-47.

Building the Colorado-Big Thompson Project is best described in contemporary articles appearing in the *Estes Park Trail*. Edmin J. Foscue and Louis O. Quam offer a chapter on the subject in *Estes Park, Resort in the Rockies* (Dallas, 1949).

Chapter Eight: The Price of Popularity

Events of the most recent historical period, like the 1978 Ouzel Fire, are best described in numerous newspaper articles, especially in the *Estes Park Trail-Gazette*. Kent and Donna Dannen's brochure *Fire!* (Estes Park, c. 1980) describes the event within its ecological context. Official documents, such as the Board of Review Transcript of November 8, 1978, are most useful. Oral interviews with principal eyewitnesses, such as Superintendent Chester Brooks, Edgar Menning, and James Olson, helped reconstruct that event.

Numerous government documents provide details of the popularity of Rocky Mountain National Park and the need for Mission 66. William C. Everhart's *The National Park Service* (New York, 1972) put that program in its national context. Casting a critical eye upon such efforts is F. Fraser Darling and Noel D. Eichhorn's *Man and Nature in the National Parks* (Washington, 1967).

Details of rescues must be reconstructed from sketchy newspaper accounts or from files of the Chief Ranger. The Hallett Peak rescue was described through oral interviews with Jerry Hammond and Frank Betts and from related documents supplied by Mr. Betts. Adventures on Longs Peak are described in Paul W. Nesbit's *Longs Peak* (Colorado Springs, 1969) and Glenn Randall's *Longs Peak Tales* (Denver, 1981). An oral interview with William Colony provided insight into the Rearick-Kamps climb.

Discussions regarding wilderness preservation within the Park are best found in National Park Service Wilderness Hearing transcripts from 1974. Hundreds of letters on the issue may also be found in the Park archives. Helping create the mood for that discussion were Stewart L. Udall's *The Quiet Crisis* (New York, 1967), Roderick Nash's *Wilderness and the American Mind* (New Haven, 1967), and Raymond Frederick Dasmann's *A Different Kind of Country* (New York, 1968). More recent explorations of similar issues may be found in Joseph L. Sax's *Mountains without Handrails: Reflections on the National Parks* (Ann Arbor, 1980) and Eugenia Horstman Connally's *National Parks in Crisis* (Washington, 1982).

Numerous National Park Service reports and studies deal with administration of the Park. Ken R. White Company's *Rocky Mountain National Park, Transportation Study, Phase I Final Report* (1975) and Richard G. Trahan's *Day-Use Limitation in National Parks: Visitor and Park Personnel Attitudes Toward Day-Use Limitation Systems for Rocky Mountain National Park* (1977) are two of many such documents.

INDEX

C.W. Buchholtz is the executive director of the Rocky Mountain Nature Association and the Rocky Mountain National Park Associates in Estes Park, Colorado. He is the author of two books, *Man in Glacier* (1976) and *Rocky Mountain National Park: A History* (1983) and co-author of four others, *Yosemite National Park: A Photographic and Comprehensive Guide* (1989), *Mesa Verde, Canyon de Chelly and Hovenweep* (1987), *Rocky Mountain National Park* (1986) for National Parkways, and *Littleton, Colorado: Settlement to Centennial* (1990). In addition, he has published several dozen articles, chapters, and academic reviews and for the past decade and has been a regular book reviewer for Denver's *Rocky Mountain News*.